Oxford
in the History of the Nation

A.L. ROWSE

OXFORD
IN THE HISTORY OF
THE NATION

WEIDENFELD AND NICOLSON
London

Designed by Sheila Sherwen
for George Weidenfeld & Nicolson Ltd

Filmset by Keyspools Ltd, Golborne, Lancs
Printed by Tinlings (1973) Ltd, Prescot, Merseyside
(A member of the Oxley Printing Group)

ISBN 0 297 76939 1

Contents

Acknowledgments

Photographs and illustrations were supplied or are reproduced by kind permission of the following. The pictures on pages 65 and 136 (right) are reproduced by kind permission of the Warden and Fellows of Christ Church, Oxford; on page 160 (left) by kind permission of the Warden and Fellows of All Souls College, Oxford; on page 173 by kind permission of the Warden and Fellows of Keble College, Oxford; on pages *116*, 146, *189*, *218–19* by kind permission of the authorities of the Ashmolean Museum, Oxford. Bodleian Library 8, 18, 21, 25, 43, 66, 81, *99*; Frick Collection 54; Thomas Photos 12 (left), 36, 37, 40, 62, 78, 84, 136 (left), 138, 169 (left), *220*; The Mansell Collection 15 (right), 27, 49 (left); National Monuments Records 49 (right), 50, 165; National Portrait Gallery 96, 112, 128, 130, 153, 160 (right), 169 (right), 227 (left), 195 (right), 202, 205, 208; John Peacock 180 (top and bottom), 182, 187, 207; G. Wren Howard 146 (left), 149; Radio Times Hulton Picture Library 30, 222, 227 (right), 243, 250 (right), 251; Woodmansterne *73*, *74*, *113*; British Museum (photographs by John Freeman) 15 (left), 89, 92, 108, 111, 145, *192*; University Picture Press 250 (left); Oxford University Press 233; Hill Harris, Oxford 119; Fitzwilliam Museum, Cambridge 77; Annette Brown *100*, *190–1*; Weidenfeld and Nicolson archives and the Victoria and Albert Museum 46, 71; Weidenfeld and Nicolson archives and the British Museum *114–15*; Private Collection 201; Weidenfeld and Nicolson archives 11, 12 (right), 61, 139, 140 (top and bottom), 143, 177, 185, *217*.

Numbers in italics indicate colour illustrations.
Picture research by Annette Brown.

To John Sparrow
in return for many kindnesses over the years

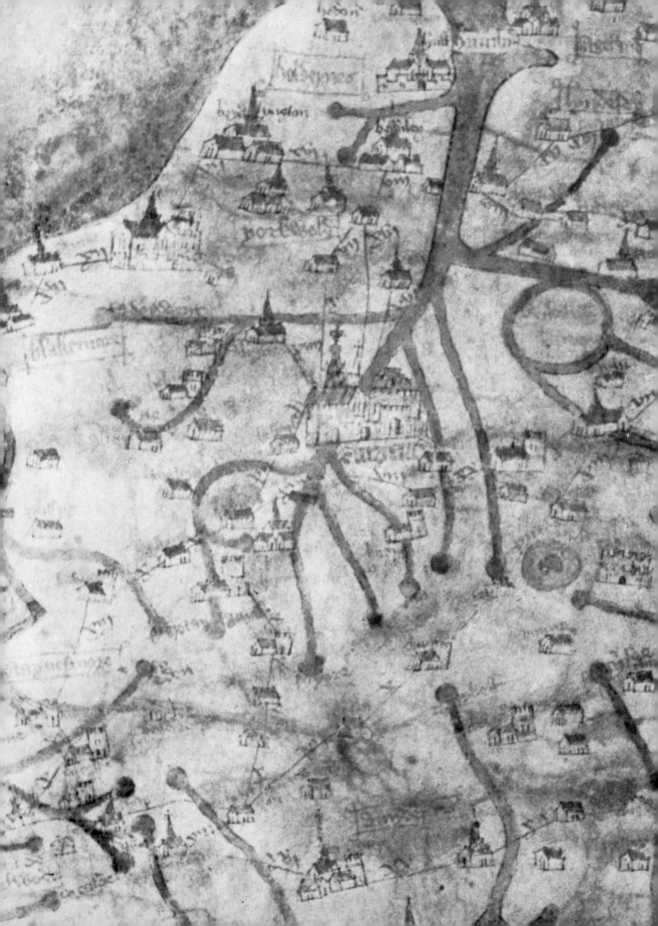

I
Early Oxford

THE town of Oxford is much older than the university and it had a long history of considerable significance behind it for centuries before a university came into being. It was in its origin a frontier town, deliberately created by the Anglo-Saxon kings, round about the year 900, as a bastion against the Danes, making their incursions southwards from what became the Danelaw. We may regard the town as an artificial creation, from its rectangular formation within its walls, the four ways converging upon Carfax (Quatrevoies) from the beginning as now. And we shall see evidences of its close royal associations, with some privileges in consequence.

For defence, it was an obvious choice; again we shall see that aspect coming to the fore in later centuries, in the Barons' Wars against Henry III and King John, up to the Civil War of the seventeenth century, in which it was the royalist capital.

The site is striking for anyone with an eye to see. First of all, the ford from which it takes its name: this is at Hinksey, on the western side of the old town, now within the city boundaries. Prehistoric travellers by the Icknield way, from south west to north east, kept to the high ground along the ridges from (modern) Swindon and Faringdon to Appleton, where there was no river to cross except the Thames at Hinksey, where the ford has a firm bed of gravel. This was the only serviceable route into Berkshire until after the Norman Conquest, when Robert d'Oilly made Grandpont, the arched causeway across Folly Bridge that carries across the marshes which protected the town on the south.

There was a settlement here in British and Roman times – numerous coins testify to that; but no town, or villa, so far as is known. The gravelly spit of land which provided the site for the Anglo-Saxon fortified 'burh' was admirably protected by the Thames on the west, the Cherwell on the east, marshes on the south, while a moat was dug out along the narrow northern neck, beyond the North Gate. Set among so many waters, with the upper tributaries of the Thames converging upon it, the country round was subject to flooding right up to our time – Alphonse Daudet, looking out over Christ Church Meadow, said, 'C'est le rheumatisme vert': still, all the more defensible.

Its position on the Thames was not so favourable to traffic as might be sup-

9

posed; for the river ran swift down to Dorchester, and barges came up-river usually no farther than Henley. But Oxford was well placed as to medieval roads and routes – the Roman road that passed from Dorchester to Bicester northwards on the east; the important north-south route from Northampton to Winchester that ran not far to the west. If we think of Anglo-Saxon England as that half of the country to the south of Watling Street, Oxford was fairly in the centre of it, and could draw supplies equally from London, Bristol or Southampton.

Nothing is known of St Frideswide, except that – unlike St George – she existed; for her saintly bones were venerated in an Oxford church. She probably belonged to the main age of Saxon saints, 650 to 750. But a dedication of an old parish church to the Celtic St Budoc reminds us that Oxford stood on another frontier than that between Saxon and Dane: it leans towards the west, the Welsh Border and the Celtic fringe. Oxford became the university town of the west, as Cambridge that of the east, especially of East Anglia. Welsh, Irish and Cornish students flocked to Oxford through the ages, and we shall shortly observe some significant Celtic associations, fertilizing in their effects. Oxford was very much at the crossroads of cultures.

The *Anglo-Saxon Chronicle* tells us that in 911–12 King Edward occupied London and Oxford and the lands belonging to them, which must mean the shires of which they formed the base. They were held against the Danes of the midlands. At Oxford the king laid out his 'burh' with a stone wall – fifteen furlongs of it, with a number of houses held from him with the obligation to keep ward and the wall in repair. In the fearful chaos to which the Danish invasions reduced Anglo-Saxon England there was a slaughter of Danes at Oxford in 1002. It is said that some of them – there was a Danish element in the population – fled for refuge into the tower of St Frideswide, which was burned to smoke them out. In these agreeable – and characteristically human – exchanges the Danes burned the wooden town in 1010. Before Swein's massive invasion of 1013 Oxford and Winchester surrendered at once. Five years later a distracted country accepted the rule of the formidable Cnut. In 1018 a national assembly met at Oxford, convenient for both Wessex and Danelaw; here the leading English from all over the country agreed with Cnut's following upon the basis of an Anglo-Danish state, while all parties swore an oath to observe King Edgar's, i.e. English, laws.

This agreeable consummation did not last beyond Cnut's life. On his death a council at Oxford in 1036 accepted his weakling son, an illegitimate Harold, as regent for the legitimate Harthacnut, a hardly less dim figure. Both shortly died, when the English selected from their old royal line Edward, to be celebrated as the Confessor. These events illustrate the town's importance in this early period, one of the leading Anglo-Saxon 'burhs', with a large population of some 3,500 and seven moneyers to provide coinage for the area. In the last year of the Confessor's

Right: A fourteenth-century stained glass window from Christ Church Cathedral, showing St Frideswide.

Left: The Norman Tower of the castle begun in 1071 by Robert d'Oilly.
Right: The south door of St Peter's-in-the-East.

reign, when his power was exerted by Harold Godwinsson, Northumbria revolted against his brother Tostig and marched an army to Northampton. Harold conducted negotiations from Oxford, on behalf of the king, but had to accept his brother's deposition from the earldom and the substitution of Morcar. This weakened his position when he succeeded Edward, on the eve of the Norman Conquest.

This revolution, a disaster to the English, aimed heavy blows at the country's well-being in its early stages: resistance entailed suffering and destruction, trade languished, thousands of houses all over the country were razed to build the castles by which the military rule of the Normans held it down. Oxford reflects this: before the Conquest it had some 950 houses, when Cambridge had under 400. Twenty years later Domesday Book records more than a third of these houses as unoccupied, ruinate or damaged. Some portion of this was owing to the characteristic building of the castle, at the western key to the town, looking to the ford at Hinksey and the approach through the marshes.

The Norman master, Robert d'Oilly, began building the castle as early as 1071, five years after the epoch-making battle of Hastings; three years later he began the chapel of St George's within the castle, and set about restoring the damaged town in his grip. From this early Norman period we still have considerable remains, relics which the perceptive eye can discern amid the devastation and indignities – the Woolworths, Marks and Spencers, Tescos and Littlewoods – of our own progressive time. Among the earliest must be the tower of St Michael, still standing sturdily at the end of Cornmarket where the north gate used to be: from its look it would seem to have been built by Anglo-Saxon workmen, with long-short coigns and window-openings that rustically echo the Roman. More mature Norman work is to be seen in the chancel arch at Holywell, the doorway at St Ebbe's, the beak-head door, crypt and chancel of St Peter-in-the-East with its fine corbel-table of expressive animal and human heads; in the grand portals and interior of St Frideswide's monastery (now Christ Church cathedral). Also in the splendid tower of Robert d'Oilly's castle, still looking down upon sounding waters, and in the crypt of his chapel.

Once the Normans were in a position to organize the country in their strong grip, progress was registered in stone. In 1121 St Frideswide's priory was begun, and shortly after St Bartholomew's hospital founded on the eastern road out of the town. In 1129 Robert's son founded Osney priory amid the western meadows and waters; it became an abbey, of which considerable remains – including a fine tower – subsisted into the eighteenth century. A few years later Godstow nunnery was founded, up the Thames at the end of the town's magnificent Port Meadow of 440 acres, open pasture for the cattle of the freemen (these still have a corporate existence with certain rights). We can see the shell of the nunnery chapel, and the wall of the precinct within which came to rest the body of Henry II's love, Fair Rosamund. She died at Woodstock in 1176 – her well still exists in the Park – and 'for love of her the King conferred many benefits on the convent'.

Oxford benefited from its proximity to Woodstock, the favourite hunting-lodge of these early kings. Henry I built Beaumont palace in the town in 1130; Henry II's queen, Eleanor of Aquitaine, frequently resided here and gave birth to Richard Coeur-de-Lion in 1157, while John was born at Woodstock in 1166. This drew more closely again the town's ties with the crown – reflected in the privilege it enjoyed, with London, of assisting the Chief Butler at the coronation feast, while Winchester assisted the Chief Cook. Oxford's traditional claim was allowed, in the persons of the mayor and two aldermen, at the restoration of Charles II: they received a gift of three maple cups, and the city a gilt cup with cover, which remains among its plate.

The town's importance is reflected markedly in national events. In the growing anarchy of Stephen's reign – owing to the disputed succession between him,

Henry I's nephew and Henry's daughter, the Empress Matilda – her half-brother, Earl Robert, came from Gloucester to Oxford to render homage to Stephen, but shortly went over to take the leadership of his sister's party. In 1141 Stephen had to storm Oxford, which had become her headquarters, and drive the empress into the castle. Here she held out for ten weeks, until food supplies failed and she was forced to make her romantic escape. On a midwinter night, a sentinel having been bribed, the empress, clad in white, escaped over the snow and frozen rivers to Abingdon and thence to the castle at Wallingford. I often think of that apparition as I pass the castle mound on the way to the railway station.

Convenient as Oxford was for the Welsh borders, the Welsh princes came here to do homage to the empress's son, Henry II, in 1177. A council considered Henry's new scheme for the administration of Ireland, as a dominion under the nominal lordship of his young son John. After Richard I's coronation the Welsh prince, Rhys, came to Oxford to meet him; since he would not recognize Richard's overlordship, the latter would not receive him – Rhys returned to Wales and successful resistance.

In 1197 there was a heated dispute at a council over Richard I's claim upon his knights to serve abroad; this gallant and selfish crusader cared nothing for the well-being of his country, so long as he could give himself up to the pleasures of fighting (and of his fighting companions). His neglect of the country – as well as his failure to produce an heir – led to the troubles under his treacherous brother, King John.

Here in 1205 the baronial opposition offered their obedience to John only on condition of his maintaining the rights of the kingdom. His loss of Normandy exacerbated the conflict, which grew to the height of civil war. In 1213 he summoned the barons and knights on their loyalty to Oxford: they did not turn up. Two years later, after agreeing to Magna Carta at Windsor, a conference to mediate between king and magnates was arranged by those doves, four bishops: now John declined to listen, he said that he had received nothing but ill-treatment since those June days in the meadow at Runnymede, the memory of which was so cherished in the breasts of Parliamentarians – though all parties were somewhat confused as to what it signified.

Here we may pause to look at the town.

When Maitland came over to Oxford to lecture on the fields of his Cambridge ('After all, what fields has not Oxford made her own?'), he showed that Cambridge was essentially an agricultural community, with its town-fields, whereas Oxford was a town of tradesmen. In 1155 the favourably inclined Henry II gave Oxford its basic charter, confirming to it all the customs, laws and liberties as those enjoyed by London. In turn Oxford became the model for the constitution

Left: The ruins of Osney Abbey, founded in 1129 by Robert d'Oilly's son 'amid the western meadows and waters'. *Above:* The seal of Oxford University, *c.* 1360.

of towns as widely apart as King's Lynn and Plymouth, as well as Burford, Bedford, Portsmouth, Yarmouth. A common seal was the visible sign of the emancipation of the borough; Oxford enjoys the earliest, 1191, along with York.

Within the town the merchant guild regulated all trade, with specified exceptions; while the cloth industry enjoyed an unqualified ascendancy. There were several wool-markets about the town; there were numerous weavers; and on the eve of St John the Baptist at midsummer the tailors caroused, paraded about with musical instruments and lifted up their voices in song. To this we may add the gabble of bells, for in 1200 Oxford had twenty churches, large and small. The ascendancy of the clothiers aroused everybody's envy, and gradually they were pressed out; with the introduction of the fulling mill, perhaps they were glad to go, out into the country beside its streams. Whereas, in the reign of King John, there had been sixty weavers in the town, a century later there was not one.

By this time the university had come into being to take their place, and more: in about 1300, when the number of students was at its height – before the Black

Death – there were perhaps 1,200.

There was an important Jewish quarter, running from the Blue Boar and Peckwater down to the main gate of Christ Church. The cemetery was outside the east gate – in accordance with Christian superstition; the later botanic garden occupies its site, fertilized by their bones. In addition to their useful services as bankers – Oxford banks are still not far away, around Carfax – the Jews contributed a modicum of Hebrew learning, from which students could profit, and to the early cultivation of medicine.

We must look at the factors which drew students here and, operating together and eventually fusing, made a *studium generale*, i.e. a university.

We have seen what a very convenient meeting-place Oxford was; but what made it a propitious place for students to come to was probably the presence of those favouring institutions, the priory of St Frideswide, the college of canons of St George within the castle, where Archdeacon Walter (d. 1151) was provost – and possibly a remarkable succession of archdeacons with their close association with the bishops of Lincoln, into which diocese Oxford fell. We shall find the association with these bishops, significant in itself, closely connected with the development of the university.

By the second half of the twelfth century there was already a Norman scholar, who called himself master of Oxford, lecturing away; other eminent teachers followed, such as Alexander of Neckham, and a leading legal scholar, Vacarius, to instruct in Roman law. Henry II's recall of English students from Paris in 1167 probably gave the final impulse to a *studium generale* here, made it almost a necessity. But already Robert Pullen was lecturing on theology by 1133, and that was a graduate subject. In 1141 a famous scholar became prior of St Frideswide's: this was Robert of Cricklade, who had travelled in Italy and Sicily, whence came the recovery of Greek learning. Robert wrote numerous theological works and, more original of him, an abridgement of Pliny; the importance of this was that it contained virtually a summary of ancient knowledge of science.

Meanwhile there was the literary activity coming out of St George's, the importance of which has not been appreciated as a creative factor in what was to come; indeed, it is impossible to overestimate it. Archdeacon Walter was a gifted orator, learned in foreign history, the patron and friend of Geoffrey ap Arthur – better known as Geoffrey of Monmouth. Walter and Geoffrey both witnessed the foundation charter of Osney, and Walter left lands to Godstow. The best thing he ever did was to encourage Geoffrey to write his *History of the Kings of Britain*. To this end the archdeacon lent him an ancient book containing the deeds of the British kings. Alexander, Bishop of Lincoln, desired Geoffrey to translate the prophecies of Merlin from the Welsh; and he dedicated his poem, *Vita Merlini*, to the subsequent Bishop Chesney. We see taking shape before our eyes the 'matter of Britain', which was to have such a prodigious future in European art, painting, music, sculpture, but above all in literature.

In the medieval mind there was no such discouraging division between fact and fancy as with modern people – as we can see with their prime subject of theology, 'queen of the sciences'. Geoffrey's book was a reduction of ancient British legend and lore to form credible, if also credulous, medieval history. No book except the Bible has exerted such a creative influence. Its stories of King Arthur and his knights, of Merlin and Guinevere, the place-names cited – Caerleon, whose Roman amphitheatre must have excited his imagination (his uncle was bishop of nearby Llandaff), Tintagel, that romantic headland where a Norman castle overlies a Celtic monastery within a prehistoric encampment – were naturalized in France, Germany and Italy. Within half a century there were romances of the Grail, of Lancelot and Tristan, Perceval and the Round Table in French and German. These subjects inspired frescoes in Italy as well as sculptures on Romanesque portals abroad.

In Britain Geoffrey's book was abridged, then translated into Anglo-Norman by Wace; next into English with Layamon. It entered into the chroniclers as history right up to Holinshed, for even the Elizabethans did not distinguish clearly between history and the legendary pre-history of Britain. Thus it had its creative influence on Shakespeare, in *Cymbeline* and *King Lear*, and on Spenser's *Faerie Queen*. Far greater was its influence with Malory, the greatest prose writer of the Middle Ages; and through him came the belated flowering of Arthurian writing with Tennyson, Swinburne, Matthew Arnold and Thomas Hardy.

It is thought that Geoffrey's seminal work had some practical influence, too, in welding together the diverse elements in Anglo-Norman society, to fuse the practical aggressive Norman mind with the remote imaginative Celtic past – as well as the present, for Bretons had taken part in the Norman Conquest of the English: a kind of revenge. Then, also, there were the Roman relics to connect up, so much more in evidence and more striking then.

Altogether it is astonishing what that single work coming out from the shadow of the tower of Oxford Castle achieved – I often think of it as I pass by.

There were other Celtic affiliations to underline the western character of Oxford, and show how open it lay to inspiration from Wales and the west. The next archdeacon of Oxford was another Walter, called 'of Coutances' – he ended as Archbishop of Rouen; he is thought to have been of Cornish birth, and his personality certainly had some Celtic overtones. We cannot go into the career of this excessively busy, political prelate in whom Richard I reposed confidence. Gerald of Wales speaks of his generosity and his curious influence over animals; his diocese described him as 'Magnificus'.

INCIPIVNT·GESTA·REGVM·BRI
TONVM·QVALITER·COMPOSITA·SVNT

Um meru multa et de multis
sepius anmo reuoluens in hi
storiam regum britannie ma
dorem nimium contuli q mi
mentarum qn de eis Gildas et
Beda loculento tractatu fecerut
Nichil de regibus qui ante in
carnatonem xpi inhabitauerant
michil etia de Arturo cteris q̄
qm pluribs qui post incarnatonem
successerunt repissem cum et gesta eorum digna eternitatis laude constarent
et a multis populis quasi inscripta iocunde et memoriter predicarent. Talia
michi et de talibus multotiens cogitanti obtulit Walterus exceftordensis
archidianus uir in oratoria arte atq in exoticis hystoriis eruditus quidam
britanni sermonis librum uetustissimum qui a bruto pmo rege britonum usq
ad cadwalladrum filium Cadwallonis actus omm continue et ex ordine puilc
orationibus proponebat Rogatu itaq illius ductus et si infra alienos ortulos
falerata msi collegerim. agresti tn stiloppisq calamis contentus codicem
illum in latinum sermone transferre curaui. nam si ampullosis dictionibus pa
ginam illi sem dum legentibus ingererem. dum magis in exponendis
uerbis qm in historia intelligenda ipos moraria opteret. Opusculo igi
tur meo robto dux claudiocestrie faueas. ut sic de dexteo et de monitore
tuo corrigat q non exhaustis morementensis fonticulo censeat exortu. Sed
sale minerue tue conditum illius dicat editio. que illustris henricus rex
anglorum generauit. que philosophia liberalibs artibus erudiit. que inna
probitat in militia militibs prefecit Unde britannia tibi nunc tporibus nostris
ac si alterum henricum adepta matuo gratulat affectu. INCIP·LIB·pmus

Ritannia insularum optima in occidentali occeano inter
Galliam et hiberniam sita octingenta miliaria in longum
ducenta uo in latum continens. quicquid mortaliu usus exigit
indeficienti feralitate ministrat. Omni et gne metalli fe
cunda campos late pansos ht. Colles qi prepollenti cul
ture aptos in quibus frugum diuersitates ubtates glebe tporibus suis
proueniunt ht nemora uniuersis ferarum gnibus repleta quorum in saltibs
et altnandis aialium pastbs gramia coueniunt. et aduolantibs apibus
flores diuersorum colorum mella distribuit ht cum prata subaerimotibus

Walter Map, archdeacon at the turn of the century, *c.* 1197–1208, came from the Welsh borders and was a friend of Gerald of Wales, who describes him as a notable wit; in consequence many poems are attributed to him. He was much at court, and composed the book by which he is still known, *De Nugis Curialium* ('Court Trifles'), by snatches at various times. We are not concerned by that so much as by his share in translating the great prose romance of Lancelot, at Henry II's request, and in the spread of Arthurianism. Out of this came the German Lancelot romance (and so, on to Wagner!).

The Norman Earl of Gloucester was a patron of Geoffrey of Monmouth; we see how these Celtic influences enclose Oxford in their embrace so fruitfully. In 1187 the prolific Gerald of Wales was here, giving a three-day reading of his new *Topography of Ireland* to an audience of scholars: to much applause, he says – a recognizable Celtic touch. Afterwards he generously entertained the doctors of the faculties – and this is no less so. So things were shaping up. At St Frideswide's the sub-prior Bothewald was writing his Latin poems. The nucleus, for students dispersed about the town – as in a modern university – was the church of St Mary's, with a stone-built school in its churchyard, and attendant Catte Street, upon which I look as I write. Here were the parchment makers, the illuminators and bookbinders of an incipient university. John of Tilbury invented a system of shorthand for scholars to take notes in. The scholars themselves formed a kind of guild to protect themselves against profiteering townsmen, as study became the chief industry of the town. Indeed bachelors and masters of arts were comparable to apprentices and master craftsmen in their guilds, town and university were for some time much on a par, the university far more democratic in constitution, the town an oligarchy.

Naturally there were rows, riots and affrays. A serious one in 1209, in which a townswoman was killed, led to an exodus of some students to Cambridge, though they were not organized there until twenty years later. So the sister university may be more properly called the daughter university.

Left: The manuscript of Geoffrey of Monmouth's *History of the Kings of Britain*, presented to the Bodleian Library by Archbishop Laud.

2

The Medieval University

UNIVERSITIES are one of the most obvious and important legacies of the Middle Ages to the modern world. We must keep in mind that medieval universities were like modern ones, with students milling about the town, lodging in private houses, halls and hostels, unkempt, fractious and undisciplined. The government – if that is the word for it – of the university was rather democratic: at Oxford the majority of the young masters of arts in congregation elected the chancellor and proctors. Hence endless rows and waste of time on conflicts of jurisdiction, the usual human palaver about 'rights', and so on.

The increased efficiency of sixteenth-century society after the Reformation put a stop to much of that: students, who were mere boys, were brought into the colleges at Oxford and Cambridge, which were expanded to receive them, and organized to teach and discipline them properly within their walls. The ascendancy of the colleges within the two English universities dates from that time. In the Middle Ages the colleges were small institutions, not very important, except for Merton and the new model of New College. Just as a qualified master rented premises for a school in which to lecture, so a hall was a boarding-house established by a graduate for a number of scholars, of whom he was the principal. So the title of principal became that of heads of halls, like St Edmund Hall (and of some colleges constituted out of several halls, e.g. Brasenose, Jesus, Hertford), as against the more regular collegiate title of warden.

There were many such halls; though they had no endowments, some of them had a long-continued existence. Only St Edmund Hall exists today, but that is because in effect it has become a college, though sticking proudly to its old name. Early students lodged where and how they could. Chaucer's Oxford scholar lodged with a carpenter who worked for the abbot of Osney:

> A chamber had he in that hostelry
> Alone, withouten any company,
> Full fetishly ydight with herbès sweet.

That is an idealized picture, for all the realistic filth of the story that follows;

Right: The warden, scholars and choristers of New College, against a background of the college buildings.

medieval students were essentially poor and beggarly, and lived in dirt and squalor. Today's students are somewhat cleaner, if no better.

It is not now thought, as used to be, that Oxford originated in an emigration from the university of Paris: it had its own independent origins. But relations were very close between the premier university of western Christendom and its junior, and there was much coming to and fro between them in that cosmopolitan world. The prime figure in the development of Oxford as a university, Robert Grosseteste (1175–1253), its first chancellor, had studied at Paris.

Grosseteste's name tells us that he had a noticeably large head, and he was an indubitably great man: on two counts, both intellectually and for his immense influence in practical affairs, his contribution to the life of his time, the thirteenth-century flowering of culture, which we can still observe in the cathedrals and churches of that age. He was a poor boy, born of humble Suffolk parents. At Paris he was one of the first Englishmen to be in touch with the most exciting new current of thought – the rediscovery of Aristotle's scientific works, of Greek natural science and logic, mediated through the scholars of Moslem Spain. He took a fruitful part in translating the new knowledge and carrying it to Oxford.

The reception of Aristotle, and the synthesis adumbrated by Aquinas, led to an intellectual storm in Paris; naturally enough, for Aristotle *pur sang* created grave difficulties for theology, and theology was the queen of medieval sciences. Aristotle's cosmology, with the universe posited as resting upon an unmoved mover, was contrary to the Christian doctrine of Providence; while the concept of the universe as eternal went against the Christian notion of Creation. The new texts of Aristotle reached Oxford hardly later than Paris; but the storm – ecclesiastical censures, episcopal condemnations and what not – was nothing like so severe in England, for Oxford philosophy was never dominated by Aquinas as at Paris. The Platonic strain mediated through St Augustine remained important: to flower in the characteristically ambivalent and 'elusive' thought of young Duns Scotus.

Theology was the main concern of medieval intellects, into which the chief energy of their minds went, for want of more exact information. The required study in the schools at Oxford was the *Sentences* of Peter Lombard, a popular summary of theology. Perhaps logic came second, for men hoped to acquire further knowledge by deducing consequences from accepted propositions, building up a conceptual structure merely by argument, getting further and further away from sense-data, to be explored usefully only by scientific methods of investigation, experiment, etc. (It seems that the inward-looking exploration of mere words, the mesmerized concern with words and logic, largely logomachy – so beloved by the later Middle Ages – has returned to modern Oxford.) We cannot do justice to this side of the medieval mind here – we may remind ourselves that every one of these energetic intellects, Grosseteste, Thomas of York,

Roger Bacon, Duns Scotus, devoted a whole department of their thought to the fruitful problems of angelology – as to the no less questions

> Of providence, foreknowledge, will and fate,
> Fixed fate, free will, foreknowledge absolute;

it is not surprising that they 'found no end, in wandering mazes lost'. Nor that 'ever out they came as in they went'. The more realistic humanist, Scaliger, commented when a guide showed him the schools at the Sorbonne, where the theologians had disputed for three hundred years: 'And what, pray, have they settled?'

We confine ourselves more modestly to Grosseteste's sympathy for natural science, and his appreciation of the necessity for mathematics in its study. It was something in that credulous age that he declared for the sphericity of the earth, and understood the principle behind the discovery of magnifying lenses. He was no less interested in music and architecture. We may give him credit for something of the glory of his cathedral at Lincoln, the English Chartres – even more soaring when it acquired its three spires, high up on that ridge above the huddle of mean medieval houses, pointing upward to the heaven of man's creation.

We cannot go into Grosseteste's influence in the political and practical life of the time, except to say that it prefigures the enormous part played in church and state by prelates and administrators who received their training at Oxford, and were able to make a more effective contribution because they shared a common intellectual background. The words that Powicke wrote of St Edmund of Abingdon, who taught at Oxford before the university had taken shape, may be applied to Grosseteste and numerous others who followed in his wake: 'The impression made by St Edmund, first in his lifetime but still more after his death, reminds us of a quality which is too easily overlooked in the political and social life of the Middle Ages, the influence of men of outstanding character in sustaining the purpose and firing the imagination of men of action.'

At Oxford Grosseteste had taught and directed studies, but subsequently as bishop of Lincoln, in which diocese Oxford lay, he was in a position to foster its growth. Everybody (except the canons of his own cathedral) appreciated him for the great man he was; even Roger Bacon, who expressed admiration for few others.

A further impulse was provided by the arrival of the friars, the Dominicans (Blackfriars) in 1221, the Franciscans (Greyfriars) in 1224, who located themselves down between ancient St Ebbe's and the river. Only a few grey walls remained up to our time to shroud their memory, and Paradise Square to remind us of their paradise or garden – all now buried under a huge shopping centre, to serve the uncontrolled population explosion of our time. The Dominicans had more of an upper-class appeal, though in time leading members of the order made their contributions to thought. The Franciscans, however, included the intellectual leaders who won European fame for Oxford – Roger Bacon, Duns Scotus, William of Ockham – and in the next century put it ahead of Paris. Hastings Rashdall (1858–1924) tells us that 'in the generation which intervened between Scotus and Wyclif Oxford was the scene of immense intellectual activity', and also had close contacts with the political and religious life of the country. The popular appreciation of the situation may well have been expressed in the saying, 'Oxford for schools, Cambridge for eels.' It is no exaggeration to say that medieval English philosophy was Oxford philosophy, while Oxford scholasticism had a character of its own with a leaning to mathematics and natural science.

It is striking, when one considers the far greater achievement of Cambridge in modern mathematics, that medieval mathematics meant Oxford, especially in the thirteenth century. John Holywood, better known as Sacrobosco, taught algorism here, i.e. the new Arabic arithmetic, that was to displace the Roman system based on Boethius. His work on arithmetic was for many years a standard authority. Far more widespread in its influence was Sacrobosco's work on the sphere: it became the textbook used throughout western Europe, and held its place right through the sixteenth century up to the reception of the Copernican system.

Sacrobosco was followed by the spectacular and controversial, almost legendary, figure of Roger Bacon (he appears as Friar Bacon in Elizabethan drama). A Somerset man, he was long-lived (1214–92), very prolific and, having an original, unorthodox mind, was regarded with suspicion by inferior brains, of whom he was more than usually contemptuous. He 'took no part in the outward affairs of the university' and was highly critical of contemporary education. The scholastic tradition represented by Grosseteste, Adam Marsh and Thomas of York had already established the claims of natural science; Bacon, a somewhat solitary worker, was able to carry these much further.

We may, we must, ignore his metaphysics and his angelology alike. With his passion for knowledge he was an addict of Aristotle and Arab science. He advocated the revision of the calendar in accordance with planetary observations, he observed the phenomena of meteorology and the propagation of force. 'Perhaps the outstanding manifestation of his scientific bent lies in that extraordinary foresight which led him to see the magnifying properties of convex lenses, the inherent power in gunpowder, and the possibility of flying machines and of mechanically propelled boats.' Rouse Ball says that 'he explained the phenomena of shooting stars, and stated that the Ptolemaic system was unscientific in so far as it rested on the assumption that circular motion was the natural motion of a planet, while the complexity of the explanations required made it improbable

The 'spectacular and controversial, almost legendary figure of Roger Bacon'. From an illuminated manuscript in the Bodleian Library.

that the theory was true'. This was to question Aristotle's cosmology, and pointed the way to Copernicus and Kepler, who realized that planetary motion was not circular, but elliptical. 'In optics he enunciated the laws of reflection and in a general way of refraction of light, and used them to give a rough explanation of the rainbow.' No wonder ordinary persons suspected this man of genius, and denied him the credit of his work.

In addition he took a close interest in philology, the study of languages, the power in words. He thought there was some 'truth' in magic – one might instance not only the power of words but the fascination of the human voice (compare the response of animals, the possibilities of hypnosis and mesmerism). Hence the public rewarded him with the character of a magician and his thought exerted less impact than it might have done. It seems, however, that an undercurrent of his influence crackled along under the surface; even the similarity of name may have stood for something with his successor, Francis Bacon.

These great Franciscan thinkers – we need not deny their greatness because we are unsympathetic to their thought – were but the crests of waves of speculative activity. There were several other notable figures: John Pecham, a Sussex man who became Archbishop of Canterbury; Thomas Bradwardine, another Franciscan archbishop, is more to be remembered for his eminence as a mathematician. He wrote voluminously on arithmetic and geometry, on proportions and squaring the circle. These became the textbooks both at Oxford and Paris, where they were subsequently printed. Duns Scotus is more than a generation later than Bacon, having been born in 1266 and dying in 1308, at not much more than forty. His writings are hardly less voluminous and have been even more disputed. Since they are almost wholly concerned with metaphysics, we may take leave to question the authoritative statement that Scotus was 'the greatest thinker that ever wore the Franciscan habit'; though he may have been recognized as such 'even in his own day', for contemporaries can hardly ever tell. We may accept the fact that his system of thought was found stimulating on the continent: there was much in it to appeal to Germans. He died in Cologne.

His thought seems to have been so radically confused as to be described, in our time, as 'elusive'. In epistemology he took up a middle-of-the-road position, by which he sought to bridge the chasm between the knowing mind and the external universe of objects, by refining upon the dominant Oxford realism. Scholastic realism meant that universals, or the general ideas abstracted from the mass of diverse phenomena of common experience, have an objective existence, are 'real', or the only real element in what we know. The opposing doctrine of nominalism insisted that all objects are singular and there are no other real objects; universals or abstract ideas are mere names, and realism therefore due to a confusion of words with things. Scotus tried to combine these two opposing positions. 'He attempted to combine into one system the demands of faith, the Augustinian view of necessary truths, and the exigencies of Aristotelian logic ... Thus Scotus constructs a bridge between the extreme realists and the nominalists, between the Thomists and the Augustinians.' It sounds a tall order for so brief a life. Scotus is described, by a Frenchman (Carré), as having an 'English' trust in the natural understanding – perhaps we should say 'British', since he was a Scot. Anyway, the movement of thought at Oxford in his time was towards a more extreme form of realism, which was perhaps why the bridge collapsed, or did not hold. 'This movement away from a preoccupation with universal entities towards a concern with individual items marks a turning-point in the history of Western thought.' This was of importance for the future of religious belief, for it opened wider the breach between philosophy and theology and emphasized the fact that Christian revelation could not be rationally demonstrated. We may ignore Duns Scotus' angelology.

The early fourteenth century produced an outstanding intellectual figure in William of Ockham (d. 1349), as the later part of the century did in John Wyclif

(d. 1384). Both exerted a widespread influence not only in England but in Europe, the effects of which were registered in actual, as well as in intellectual, history. Realism at Oxford, with its emphasis on abstractions, was associated with mathematics. Perhaps it would not be fanciful to say that the new nominalism, with its insistence that individual objects are the constituents of the external universe, tended to be a solvent of abstractions shown to be composite (e.g. God, transubstantiation), to subvert the Thomistic rational case for religion and impel men towards the realities of society and politics. Oxford nominalism made a fundamental distinction between the world of things and the mental representation of them, the concepts being merely signs, not even copies. Many 'problems' of philosophy were therefore spurious. (Here we meet the characteristic position of Oxford philosophy today – the wheel has come full circle.)

Ockham is still a name with the phrase 'Ockham's razor', which entered into popular usage: it meant that entities should not be multiplied beyond necessity,

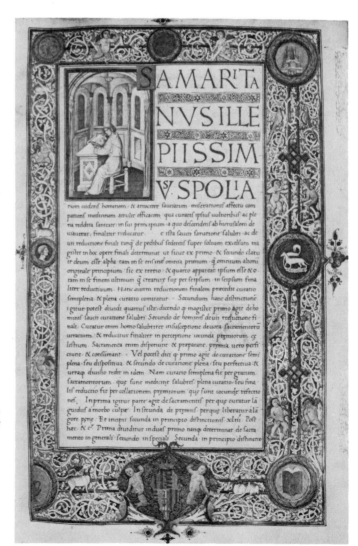

Duns Scotus, the great theologian and philosopher, who lived a generation after Roger Bacon.

i.e. reduction to simplicity was the path to knowledge, not needless complication. It is significant that the most subtle of Oxford logicians was the one who saw most acutely the limitations of the method and how little was to be learned from it. Ockham, six hundred years ago, depreciated abstract thought – himself the cleverest of them – denied rational 'proofs' of religion and had little use for metaphysics. He was above all a logician; but he saw that logic did not deal with things, nor even thoughts: the terms used were arbitrarily imposed for the sake of convenience, and did not prove anything as to the relation of those terms to our thoughts or to existing realities. Argument is only true *ex supposito*, on the basis of what we assume. (It reminds one of Collingwood, the most brilliant – and solitary – mind in the Oxford of my time, who arrived at the position that all we know is simply answers to the questions we put – a perhaps excessively sceptical view, in complete contrast with what he began with in *Speculum Mentis*.)

The sceptical consequences of Ockham's views are obvious: belief in God cannot be rationally demonstrated, hence a complete divorce between the realm of reason and that of faith. Ockham himself did not go so far as to say that 'the concept of God is a composite concept formed by uniting many ethical and physical notions separately found in the natural order and among men', i.e. a human construct. But he evidently thought that speculation on the nature and attributes of God was futile, as it is; that there was no point in theology, as there is not. Since this pursuit had been the main concern of philosophical thought, it was condemned by the chancellor at Oxford as heretical, i.e. original.

Ockham did not achieve the prodigious feat, for his time, of ceasing to believe in God: he fell back upon the sovereign notion of God's omnipotent, but inscrutable, will. (Karl Barth, so fashionable six hundred years later, has got no farther.) We see how this in Ockham points onward to Luther and Protestantism. But far more valuable and original than that (a retrograde movement compared with humanism) is this: 'The tendency towards empiricism in theory and in the study of nature that characterises the mind of the Renaissance had its sources in the work of Ockham.' He has been described as 'one of the most decisive thinkers in the history of western ideas'. In him we see the break-up of the unity and universality of the medieval mind; with him we reach the parting of the ways, a portent of the modern world.

Like Locke, centuries later, he had to leave Oxford: he went to Paris, taking the force of his nominalism with him. 'It was at Oxford that the novel theories of philosophical and religious truth were first developed, and from Oxford they were carried to Paris and to the other centres of reflection in Catholic Europe', notably Germany. We may regard the personality and thought of Ockham as a catalyst in this development: from this time continental schools divided along these lines. At Paris Ockham exerted a notable influence upon Marsiglio of

Padua, who proceeded to develop a completely secular view of the state – another radical departure from the unitary cast of medieval thought, and again completely modern.

We need not concern ourselves with Ockham's embroilment with the Papacy over the issue of apostolic poverty. As a Franciscan he was bound to come down on the side of poverty – at least, for Christ and his apostles; as Pope, enjoying the cultivated refinements of life at Avignon, John XXII could hardly accept this 'leftist' heresy, subversive of society and its necessary arrangements. Imprisoned for a time at Avignon, Ockham escaped to take refuge with the Holy Roman Emperor, locked in a dispute for power with the Papacy. Ockham employed his powerful pen in the secular cause of empire against papacy – another portent; it must have given satisfaction when this particular pope, John XXII, was found guilty of the heresy of the beatific vision.

We need follow the most modern of medieval thinkers no further. Ockham's practical influence upon political thinking, underwriting secular claims, was immense in Germany. His intellectual accomplishment as a logician stands; condemned by the orthodox, Ockham had the satisfaction of seeing his system of thought eventually adopted: 'by the end of the century it had become the generally accepted system in the leading school of Europe'. In the same way Locke's philosophy, particularly his political philosophy, came to dominate the century after James II's expulsion of him from Christ Church. We may regard Ockham as 'the Oxford medieval thinker of the most profound originality and revolutionary significance' – far more so than Wyclif – leaving 'the way to knowledge open to the layman and scientist's free inquiry untramelled, into the world of the senses and of human experience'.

John Wyclif's intellectual significance is far less than Ockham's, his practical influence even greater, not only in England but in Bohemia, and thus ultimately upon the German Reformation. A generation younger than Ockham, he was born just before 1330 and died in 1384. An abrasive Yorkshireman, he had a gift for leadership and had a minority appeal at Oxford among the rough and rude northerners, of the two 'nations' into which students were divided. (The northern nation meant those from north of the Trent, including Scots; the southern included Welsh, Irish, Cornish along with the English south of the Trent.) A tiresome and tireless disputant, Wyclif was as conceited as a don can be – only he had something to be conceited about.

He was the foremost logic-chopper of his time, enjoying his prestige, before he became notorious as a reformer and the catspaw of the political interests of John of Gaunt (who manipulated him as a newspaper magnate might manipulate a notorious don in our day). Philosophically he was conservative, nothing original

John Wyclif, precursor of the
Reformation. From an engraving
by Hondius the Elder.

about him, while his passionate interest in theology was retrograde. McFarlane,
his biographer in our time, says crisply,

Had his death occurred in 1374 Wyclif would be remembered only by specialist historians as one of the lesser ornaments of medieval Oxford. They would know him as the
author of a number of philosophical works of no particular brilliance, several of which,
despite his enormous reputation, have not yet been found worthy of print.

McFarlane then qualifies this unkind reflection by allowing that 'even if his
intellectual weapons were not his own they were wielded with uncommon
skill ... Was Wyclif a great thinker? We can only guess, though with the knowledge that those better placed than we, even when they abhorred his influence,
were willing to concede that he was.' From these slightly inconsistent statements
we may deduce that Wyclif was an acute disputant, before he went on to more
important things.

Wyclif's works are very voluminous – to us unreadable – and are based mostly
on his lectures in the schools, where he was engaged in incessant dispute, in the
scholastic manner – until two of his works, one on spiritual dominion, the other
on civil dominion, chimed with the clamorous demands for reform in church and

state in the 1370s, just as Cranmer's views on Henry VIII's divorce made him a fit instrument to be taken up by the king, or Luther's views on Rome suited the interests of the German princes. At the same time the long delay in recognizing Wyclif's eminence by suitable preferment sharpened his nose for clerical abuses: he began to attack the higher clergy and was taken up by John of Gaunt for his own purposes.

This led him to the conclusion that if ecclesiastics – especially the higher ones – abuse their privileges, the secular power might deprive them; that, in these circumstances, lay-patronage was to be preferred. This was music to laymen's ears. Wyclif, encouraged, was led on to the view that popes might err and be deprived. This was referred to Rome. He now wrote a treatise on that inflammatory work, the Bible; his remarkable sense of history, for his time, led him to see that there was no historical justification for quite recent developments in Catholic doctrine, transubstantiation for example, or indeed papal claims to supreme power in Christendom. He was becoming a heretic: this was opening the door to revolution.

There was all too much tinder about already, and in 1381 the Peasants' Revolt gave the upper classes a severe shock: they closed ranks, no more use for Wyclif. The aristocratic Archbishop Courtenay summoned a synod in London in 1382 at which Wyclif's heresies were condemned, divine displeasure at them being expressed by an earthquake during the proceedings. Fortified by this, the archbishop carried the campaign to Oxford, where there was much excitement and some minority support for Wyclif. A convocation was summoned to St Frideswide's, where the remaining Wyclifite leaders were made to recant. Wyclif himself had withdrawn to Lutterworth where he shortly – fortunately for himself – died, of high blood-pressure.

There remained Wyclifite sympathizers in the university; they might even be dignified by the name of a faction, for the next archbishop – another aristocrat, Arundel – was no less harassed by the problem of Lollardy. In 1408 he summoned a provincial council in Oxford to formulate constitutions against the sect by which they might be judged and condemned to the flames, according to the new statute introduced for the burning of heretics. But truth could not be burnt out, and the dispersal of the Lollards from Oxford spread them about the countryside, whence they could never be extinguished. One of the most memorable was William Taylor, principal of St Edmund Hall, who had a strong influence upon the Lollard leader, Sir John Oldcastle, before being burned alive as a lapsed heretic in 1423. Unlicensed preachers spread the gospel from Oxford, as Methodism did centuries later, with John Wesley and his lay preachers.

Moreover, the Lollards had an irresistible means of propaganda in the English translation of the Bible which Wyclif inspired and his followers accomplished.

Carried out in the next generation, with the help of his Oxford disciples, 'it remained the best English version until the time of Tyndale and Coverdale'. It is impossible to overestimate the importance this must have had – appealing as it did far beyond the ranks of the Lollards themselves – in preparing the ground for the reception of the Reformation, when it broke upon the country.

McFarlane sums up Wyclif thus:

His catastrophic incompetence as a practical reformer [what power had he to carry out the reforms he desired?] does not, however, in the least embarrass his modern admirers. Doctrinaires, for all the adversity and disillusionment that they suffer in their lives, have one consolation: they may enjoy long after death apotheosis at the hands of equally doctrinaire historians. It is not surprising that with this naive approach to history they are also grossly unfair to the men on whom fell the duty of persecution. It is more important to understand than to side instinctively with the underdog.

This is surprising, coming from a man of McFarlane's liberal sympathies – though the less so when one knows that he had a cautionary figure for his Wyclif under his eyes, in his own college, in writing the book. Of course, it is perfectly true (a) that it was the duty of the archbishops to keep order in the nursery; (b) Wyclif was just like an academic liberal in believing, all too ineffectually, that men can be guided by the light of reason, 'little though his experience justified this belief: it is a delusion common among academic orators'.

On the other hand, wasn't Wyclif *right*? Wasn't he correct in saying that transubstantiation was a recent addition to Catholic doctrine, and in itself nonsense? And what about the future? Wyclif's appeal to commonsense and reason, on these and other matters, was ultimately to win through. In a world where few know the difference between accuracy and inaccuracy, a good egg or a bad egg intellectually – they *never* can tell – this is important.

McFarlane was unwilling to allow Wyclif any influence on the Reformation. This is without imagination and historically inaccurate. It is true that the English Reformation came into being as an act of state, agreed upon by Henry VIII and Parliament. All the same, Lollardy prepared the ground for Protestant propaganda; it was one of the elements in the combustion: right up to the threshold of the Reformation Lollard heretics were being persecuted. They were there.

Similarly with Wyclif's influence overseas. His philosophical works reached Bohemia in the 1390s; his inflammatory theological works in the next decade. A couple of Czech scholars came to Oxford to copy his two works on spiritual and civil dominion. Wyclif's follower, Peter Payne, principal of St Edmund Hall, attached the university seal to a declaration that Oxford and England agreed with John Hus's revolt against papal dominion. When the Wyclifites were dispersed, Payne went to Bohemia and became an official, in charge of foreign relations, for many years in the Czech revolutionary state. When Luther set going the German

Reformation, one of the first works to be printed was Wyclif's *Trialogus*, at Basel, in 1525.

These are all significant pointers to the indubitable influence of Wyclif overseas, radiated from Oxford, for no one was more wholly an Oxford man.

It was these exceptional men who made the reputation of Oxford in the world, not the average student; as a later Oxford historian, H. A. L. Fisher, used to say of the latter, 'they recur'. There were many other gifted men who made their mark in the realm of the mind or in public affairs – some in both, like Thomas Bradwardine, a leading mathematician who became Archbishop of Canterbury. This reminds us that the leadership of the Church in England in the later Middle Ages was almost wholly in the hands of Oxford men, right up to the Reformation. (It was the Reformation that made the fortune of Cambridge.)

Practically every Archbishop of Canterbury had received his early training at Oxford. Courtenay himself, who personally conducted the campaign against Wyclif, was well acquainted with the internal affairs of the university, having been chancellor in 1367, when he successfully resisted the claim of the Bishop of Lincoln to control his election. Henceforth the university was independent; this displeased the friars, upon whom he enforced obedience to its rules. For more than a century before Courtenay his predecessors on the throne of St Augustine had been Oxford men, beginning with St Edmund of Abingdon. Others who followed were Kilwardby, Pecham, Winchelsey. In the fourteenth century came Simon Mepham, John Stratford, Bradwardine; then Simon Islip and William Whittlesey, who studied at Oxford though he hailed from Cambridgeshire.

In the fifteenth century all the archbishops after Arundel are Oxford men in succession: Chichele, Stafford, Cardinal Kemp, Cardinal Bourchier, Cardinal Morton, Deane, Warham. After that come Cranmer and the Protestants, all Cambridge men: Parker, Grindal, Whitgift, Bancroft, when Oxford resumes the lead with the Stuarts. The one exception that proves the rule – and points to something of significance – is that with the Catholic rule of Mary, Cardinal Pole was archbishop, after Cranmer's burning. We are reminded, too, that all the cardinals seem to have been Oxford men – was there ever a Cambridge cardinal, except Fisher whose 'head was off before his hat was on'?

Other ecclesiastics besides archbishops played leading parts in the life of the nation, as we have seen with Grosseteste – as administrators of their sees or even of the country, as formative figures in its institutions or as saintly persons setting good standards for society. We cannot traverse the medieval episcopate here, merely cite an example or two from each class. St Thomas of Cantilupe, Bishop of Hereford, had been chancellor of the university. Walter Stapledon, Bishop of Exeter, was Lord Treasurer and responsible minister in the evil days of Edward II;

he paid for it with his life at the hands of the mob in Cheapside. It may have been a salutary execution; but Stapledon was a loyal Oxford man who at least devoted his money to a good purpose, the foundation of Exeter College. More familiar names are those of the princely Cardinal Beaufort, who largely ran the country during the long minority of Henry VI, Bishop Foxe, Henry VII's minister, and Cardinal Wolsey, who governed the country until Henry VIII took over for himself – and therewith the Reformation.

We must return to the university and its affairs within. After the excitements and the scandal of Wyclifism, undoubtedly a decline set in. But we must not impute this to its suppression; other factors are responsible – the long-drawn-out strain of the French war, the drain upon the nation's energy in trying to hold Henry V's conquests in France, their loss and the internal conflicts culminating in the Wars of the Roses. Archbishop Arundel had no ill will towards the university in ordering that none of Wyclif's books should be used unless approved by a committee of twelve in *each* university, though there may have been a sting in the tail of this, for Cambridge was indubitably more orthodox. (It is amusing to come upon a Cambridge friar copying out passages from Wyclif with approbation, which in the reaction he subsequently erased.) There remained people with Wyclifite sympathies at Oxford, and the university had not operated the archbishop's order. When Archbishop Arundel arrived in 1411 to carry out a visitation, he came up against strong opposition in the name of the university's liberties. He found the university church locked against him; St Mary's was placed under an interdict and, after an appeal, the pope revoked the university's exemption from visitation.

Whatever such extraneous entertainments, discussion continued within the walls, some of it fruitful and some of it even resulted in useful inventions. For his treatise on the astrolabe Chaucer used the calendar of latitude and longitude based on Oxford, compiled there at the request of John of Gaunt. 'Oxford owed her reputation as a kind of medieval Greenwich to scholars like John Maudit, who compiled a famous astronomical table, *mirabiliter inventus in civitate Oxon.* MCCCCX.' In Merton College there was a group of mathematicians, while in founding New College William of Wykeham ordained that two of the Fellows should be students of astronomy.

Of far greater practical importance was the part Oxford played in spreading instruction in the English language. It seems that, where Latin sermons were the thing in St Mary's, English sermons were preached to the university at St Peter's-in-the-East. John Trevisa, himself a Cornishman, tells us that from mid-fourteenth century two Oxford grammar masters, John Cornwall and Richard Pencrich, had initiated the habit of construing Latin directly into English, instead of French. Two of these three, if not the third also, would have started life speaking Cornish, and would so have had some special linguistic sensibility. Trevisa, by precept and practice, became a leading proponent of the use of English for prose works and a formative influence in the development of English prose. We cannot go into his voluminous works here, mainly translation – there is a growing international interest in them, with a project for their publication. Trevisa may have had Wyclifite sympathies, for, leaving Oxford for the shelter of Berkeley Castle, he contributed to the translation of the Bible.

Another Celt, Bishop Reynold Pecock from Wales, carried discussion of matters of faith a far stage forward in English. A Fellow of Oriel, he was a contentious person, an ingrained publicist. He began by being orthodox enough, writing books against the Lollards. But he was a rationalist, irrational enough to think that people could be convinced by reason. An original mind, he argued himself into dangerous territory. He could not see that the antiquated and credulous minds of the early Christian centuries – St Jerome, St Augustine and others of the Fathers nigh a thousand years before – should be any authority to the enlightened fifteenth century.

This aroused the enmity of another Oriel man, Gascoigne, the chancellor who, being well off, was very influential in Oxford, in the reaction against Wyclif. The return to the early Fathers was becoming popular, as against the extravagances and complexities of the schoolmen – a pointer in its way to the intellectual reaction of the Reformation. Pecock urged that the writings of the Doctors, and even the Fathers, of the Church should be judged by the light of reason, and – with exceptional historical sense – that they must not be regarded as inspired, but viewed critically in accordance with the time when they were written. This heretical notion was condemned, and Pecock's critical work, the *Just Apprising of Doctors*, was not suffered to survive. But when he went on to apply reason to the Creed and reduce it to more credible propositions, and to supply 'a better and more comprehensive collection of virtues' than the Ten Commandments of a barbarous people two thousand years before, he was lucky to survive himself. The kindly consideration of Mother Church condemned him of heresy, and made him recant, i.e. withdraw what he knew to be true.

Since Pecock was a Lancastrian, and the Yorkists were in power, it was rendered easy to deal with him, though he was a bishop. As part of his penance he was relegated to the damps of Fenny Thorney in 1459, where he was to be confined to 'a secret close chamber within the abbey, where he may have sight to some altar to hear mass', but he was not to 'pass the said chamber'. There, in secrecy, he shortly died. Both Bale and Foxe suggest that he was 'privily made away'. We do not have to believe that: they believed, like most people, what they wanted to believe. It is sufficient that the most original Oxford mind of the century was snuffed out like a candle.

The vaulting of the Divinity School, a building planned by the university from the 1420s on a scale 'quite disproportionate to its resources'. It took two generations to complete.

Towards the middle of the fifteenth century the university as such was declining, the numbers of students falling off and halls closing down, until by the time of the Reformation only a dozen remained. But we must remember that colleges were being founded throughout this time, and they, with their buildings, endowments and specific corporate life, were to grow stronger as the university as such shrank. The university itself undertook building and received benefactions. In the 1420s it planned the Divinity School on a splendid scale – quite disproportionate to its resources. It took two generations to complete it, which it did in about 1480, and the university was forced to beg and dun all possible benefactors – one sees

Duke Humphrey's library at the Bodleian. The books he gave to the university were lost at the Reformation.

their initials in the decorative stonework of that magnificent vaulting, the masterpiece of Richard Winchcombe. Some of them occur again and again and are easily recognizable – T.K., for example, Thomas Kemp, Cardinal Kemp's nephew, Bishop of London. There it is, as it was praised for its beauty by Erasmus, the finest monument of the medieval university.

Duke Humphrey of Gloucester proceeded to give his magnificent library, probably the finest of the time in the country. It was fascinating in character, for it had not only the schoolmen – plenty of those in Oxford libraries – but also a modern inflexion, new texts of the classics, Italian translations, manuscripts of

Dante, Petrarch and Boccaccio, scientific works on astronomy and medicine. Further books with a Renaissance flavour were given by the scholarly and Italianate Tiptoft, Earl of Worcester, a ruthless Oriel man who came to a sticky end in 1470 as a Yorkist. To house all the books and manuscripts the university was forced to build a library over the Divinity School – today affectionately referred to by its denizens as 'Duke Humphrey'. In the event it proved a mistake to have given the books to the university; for in the disarray and initial predatoriness of the Reformation they were lost and scattered. If they had been given to a college they would have survived – and thereby hangs a moral.

In spite of discouragements, and the distractions of the Wars of the Roses, the university plodded on with the rebuilding of St Mary's; but that was not completed until the country settled down, after Bosworth, under the rule of Henry VII. Already by this time a printing press was established, and turned out nearly a score of books during its existence, 1478–86 – portent of a new world. By this time the buildings of the colleges were rising all round the town to dwarf the university, except for St Mary's and the Divinity School. The colleges at Cambridge were no less spectacular, Henry VI's chapel of King's most of all. When one considers the altogether greater munificence of the Lancastrian and Tudor monarchs to Cambridge – with such foundations as King's, St John's, Christ's and Trinity – one cannot resist a certain conclusion. They gave very little to Oxford. By the early fifteenth century Cambridge was beginning to come up and to provide eminent servants to church and state, though not yet to provide the leadership at Lambeth. The Lancastrian monarchs made a point of their orthodoxy and represented a reaction from the lax court and society of Richard II. Oxford was undeniably tinged by Wyclifism; Cambridge was undoubtedly more orthodox. One cannot but think that this stood for something in the over-pious minds of Henry VI, founder of King's, and the Lady Margaret, mother of Henry VII, foundress of St John's and Christ's; while even Henry VIII, who founded Trinity, prided himself on his theological orthodoxy.

Left: St Mary's Church, completed during the reign of Henry VII.

3
The Rise of the Colleges

OXFORD and Cambridge are distinguished from other universities by the dominance of the colleges within them. The earliest Oxford colleges – Merton, Balliol, University – go back to the second half of the thirteenth century, from about 1260; the first Cambridge college is Peterhouse, 1284, founded after the model of Merton. As yet they were far from dominating the landscape, though by the end of the century the noble, cathedral-like chapel of Merton had arisen to perpetuate the memory of Walter de Merton as the real founder of the English collegiate system and an indication of what was to come. In time the ancient town would be transformed by the new colleges.

The town's importance, or its convenience as a meeting place, continued to be reflected in national events. In 1222 Archbishop Langton held a provincial council at Osney Abbey. In 1258 Oxford became the focus of the developing crisis between Henry III and his barons led by Simon de Montfort, and the scene of the famous Parliament from which emerged the 'Provisions of Oxford'. These constituted the baronial programme for the government of the country, which was breaking down from the extravagance and incompetence of Henry III as a ruler. Magnificent as an aesthete, to whom we owe Westminster Abbey, he was not much good as a politician. (However, wouldn't we prefer the creator of Westminster Abbey to the best politician going?)

Simon de Montfort – whom the Victorians venerated as the creator of Parliament (they should see that institution today!) – led the attack on royal government at Oxford. There emerged from the confrontation the celebrated Provisions, which the hapless king was forced to accept. The antiquated office of Justiciar was to be revived, government placed in the hands of a council of fifteen, elected by four out of the joint body of twelve of the King's Council and twelve magnates; three Parliaments were to be held each year, with a legislative commission of twelve. The idea was joint government of king and barons. It was unworkable, of course; the king protested that it would not work – but then he should have been more conscientious at his job. (We must remember that these people running the country, king and magnates alike, were Frenchmen.)

The fact that the Provisions of Oxford were unworkable did not prevent their

Left: The interior of the library of Merton College, founded by Walter de Merton in the thirteenth century, which laid the basis of the collegiate system.

being reissued once and again in the conflict between Henry and his Poitevins on one side, and the 'great' Simon and his supporters on the other; they were made statute law. The conflict for power was what mattered, and this was very evident at Oxford, where the barons made a clean sweep of the royal sheriffs in the counties, and associated the knights of the shires in an inquiry into nationwide complaints against government. This has been held to be very significant in the precious evolution of Parliament, but the conflicts that raged in and around Oxford were ultimately settled on the battlefield.

In the spring of 1264 King Henry made Oxford his headquarters, to which he summoned his host. He took up residence with the Dominicans; the masters and scholars were sent out of the way, for more real disputes. Four bishops descended on the town, like angels, to negotiate peace, but in vain. The king paid a propitiatory visit to the shrine of St Frideswide – also in vain; he went on to defeat at the battle of Lewes. For some months de Montfort ruled the country, summoning the Marcher lords to meet him at Oxford at the end of November. Next August he encountered defeat, and death, at Evesham – so perhaps Henry's visit to St Frideswide had not been in vain after all.

It was just at this time, and against this background of disturbance, that colleges began to come into existence. Merton is the first and most influential model in the creation of colleges during the next century, though it is interesting to observe the diversity and differing characteristics of the various colleges. Both University College and Balliol were already beginning to take shape, but note how different each was from the real thing which Walter de Merton created. University College originated in a bequest from Durham in 1249 to maintain scholars at Oxford; the peculiarity of this college is that it came into existence by the initiative of the university – hence its name. The scheme was for a tiny community to live in a hall together with any others willing to board with them; further endowments from Durham and the north country enabled it to grow. This draws our attention to an interesting theme – the prevalence of local patriotism when the county, or diocese, was a community in itself, and the frequent affiliations of colleges to those of their founders and the source of their wealth. We shall note the local attachments of colleges as one of the more interesting things about them.

Balliol originated in penance, the penance of John de Balliol, who was scourged for his sins at the door of Durham cathedral in 1255, and fined a sum for the maintenance of scholars at Oxford. The little community was in being before Balliol's death in 1269, when it was put on its feet by his more pious wife, Dervorguilla. It was simply a hall of students, not a real college, i.e. a landholding corporation. From the first it was closely connected with the Franciscans, with their ideal of poverty; so perhaps the old Balliol idea of 'plain living and

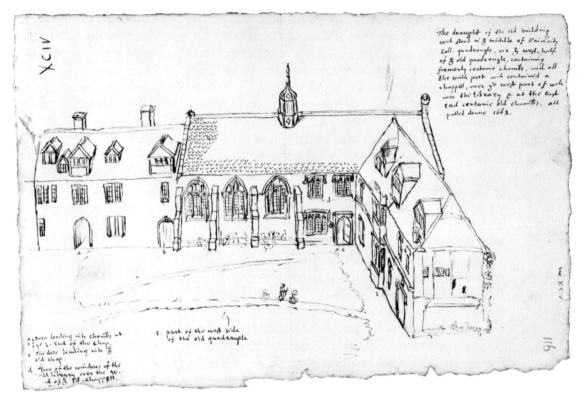

The chapel and buildings of University College, which 'came into existence by the initiative of the university – hence its name'.

high thinking' stands for something in the tradition. The doctrinaire Wyclif was master from 1360 to 1367: he had no interest in the arts, unlike a Grosseteste, merely a certain response to nature, such as even Puritans sometimes exhibit. From the first Balliol was an undergraduate society, some sixteen scholars, with the funds administered for them, unlike a college proper. We see that it too had a north country start, and this was strengthened at the Restoration by the benefactions of Snell, with his Glasgow connections. Hence the infusion of Scotch in Balliol, the notable recruitment of poor ambitious scholars that was to give the college its colouring in the past century.

Also in the 1260s Walter de Merton was planning something grander and different: 'His scholars were no mere pensioners but a corporate fraternity, with a common life, common property, a common Head.' His scholars, aged about nineteen, were already graduates; the aim was to enable them to become masters and teach in the schools, or to advance to the study of theology. Eight of the original scholars were nephews of the founder, and the number could be increased among his kin, with a preference for the diocese of Winchester. Nothing wrong in this: a medieval ecclesiastic was expected to provide for his family, and these kinsmen were being maintained on a more equal basis as clerics than by the secular custom of primogeniture. A certain number of Fellows might study canon and civil law; this was the best equipment for service to church and state, and its study grew in consequence. We find a number of archbishops who came up this way: Islip, Stratford, Chichele, the first two of whom were Merton men. So were Bradwardine, the two Kemps and a number of leading mathematicians. Merton enjoyed a notable primacy during the first century of its existence; and this not only from the generous scale of the foundation but from the careful provisions of its statutes, which became a model for other colleges, at Cambridge as well as at Oxford.

The founder even bought an estate at Cambridge, providently, in case of need for emigration – perhaps because of plague or social disturbance. Hence Merton Hall at Cambridge, an early thirteenth-century building which Walter de Merton bought in 1271, now 'one of the few domestic buildings of so early a period surviving'. This provident founder also started the custom of appropriating advowsons, i.e. nominations to livings, to provide for his Fellows when they went out into the world to serve the Church. He is thus 'the founder of that system of college livings which was almost unknown out of England'. This was destined to play a large part in the far future in elevating parish life in the country by the residence of scholarly clergymen, many of whom made contributions to knowledge, apart from anything else. (Think of such an excellent example as Gilbert White, Fellow of Oriel, spending most of his life at Selborne, and what he made of it!)

Before the end of the century the greater monasteries began to make some provision for likely monks to study at Oxford. In 1280 Edmund of Cornwall, Henry III's brother, rich with spoil from Cornish tin, founded Rewley Abbey, near the present railway station. This was a regular Cistercian house, not a college; but it was intended to serve the convenience of students from other houses. Durham College was started for the benefit of Durham monks, and the bibliophile Bishop Richard de Bury intended to bequeath his splendid library to it; but he had spent so much money on the books that they probably went to pay his debts. The Augustinian canons had a house on the site of Frewin Hall, in which Albert Edward, the future Edward VII, was placed, somewhat optimistically, for his Oxford education. A more endearing memory is that of Erasmus, who resided there; the gateway he would have used remains on New Inn Hall Street. Even more eloquent relics are the row of monastic houses on the south side of Worcester quad, with their sculpted rebuses over the doorways: these are the separate *camerae* of individual Benedictine monasteries. With the Reformation such institutions, already pretty feeble, came to an end, their buildings gradually made use of for more vigorous secular colleges.

The next college, Exeter, 1314, was markedly regional in character, for its Fellows were to come from Exeter diocese, eight from Devon, four from Cornwall. Walter Stapledon had given lavishly for the building of his cathedral, for providing grammar schools at Exeter and Ashburton and for maintaining poor scholars at Oxford, before he was killed by a London mob; they sacked his library for good measure, since ordinary human beings dislike culture (it brings home to them their inferiority). Wyclif had some support among the Fellows here – notably Rigg, the chancellor, who was made to recant. Exeter produced an exceptionally large number of distinguished persons from among its west countrymen. Sir Robert Tresillian, Richard II's Chief Justice, hanged by the 'Good' Parliament of 1388 for his support of the royal prerogative. Michael Tregury was made rector of Henry V's new university of Caen, and ended as Archbishop of Dublin, where one sees the slab that Dean Swift erected over him in St Patrick's. Sir John Fortescue, another Chief Justice, was the author of a famous book, *The Governance of England*, and other constitutional works. It is pleasant to think that Palmer's Tower, the original entrance on the north, continues the memory of a Launceston schoolboy out of the Middle Ages.

The Elizabethan age produced a considerable group of Catholic exiles among the Fellows of Exeter – second only to those of St John's and New College – as also a second founder in Sir William Petre, another Catholic. He made a fortune out of monastic lands, upon which he was able to establish his undeviatingly Catholic family. Himself a Devonian, he was very generous to Exeter, doubling its revenues and providing eight Fellowships open to the several counties where he possessed estates. John Ford, the dramatist, was another Devonshireman, from a farm near Bagtor on the southern slopes of Dartmoor. Among Caroline figures we find Attorney-General Noy, who thought up ship money for Charles I, and Sir John Eliot, his intolerable opponent. Sir Bevil Grenville, among the many good men who died for the king, confessed that he found himself wanting in more serious knowledge, since at Oxford he 'fell upon the sweet delights of reading poetry and history'. He was a charming man, infinitely more so than those addicted to the weightier pursuits of theological and political disputation, like Eliot. Numerous Exeter west countrymen made names for themselves in that disputatious age – 'John for the king', gallant old John Arundell of Trerice who held out in Pendennis Castle to the end; Sidney Godolphin, the Cavalier poet, killed at Chagford; the brilliant and reptilian Shaftesbury, the humourless Clifford of the Cabal, who killed himself out of popery and devotion to stupid James II. A more sympathetic figure is the sceptical (and credulous) Joseph Glanvill, whose

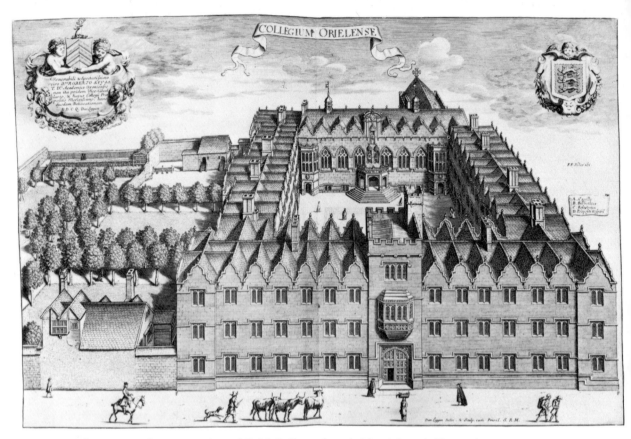

A seventeenth-century view of Oriel College, founded by Adam de Brome in 1324, a Fellowship at which, in the early nineteenth century, became 'the blue ribbon of academic life'.

Vanity of Dogmatising set off the most Oxonian of poems, Arnold's 'Scholar Gipsy'.

Matthew Arnold, like his father the Doctor, was a Fellow of Oriel, the next college to be founded, in 1324, by Adam de Brome, Almoner to the unfortunate Edward II. This college was different again in that the Fellows enjoyed complete autonomy, and they could come from any part of England. This provision may have had something to do with a long-term effect: in the unreformed period before the Commission of 1853, when New College and All Souls slumbered peacefully under the incubus of their founders' kin, an Oriel Fellowship became the blue ribbon of academic life, and many were the Fellows of Oriel to win fame.

This could hardly have been foreseen when Adam de Brome created his modest foundation for a provost and ten graduates. The college gained a name outside the walls of the university as the life-long residence of Thomas Gascoigne (1403–58), chancellor during several years, the well-born and outspoken critic of Wyclifism, of Bishop Pecock, of abuses in the Church, indeed of anything that departed from the narrow path of orthodox rectitude. Not a very attractive man, he was at any rate a personality, could express it and has come down to us in consequence as such.

In the Elizabethan age Oriel produced a not particularly distinguished but notorious cardinal, William Allen, founder of Douai college for Catholic exiles abroad; still, since he was one of Oxford's cardinals, his figure graces Cecil Rhodes's front on the High. After Allen had left young Walter Ralegh came up as an undergraduate in 1572: a personality so strong left stories of himself even in his student days. In the next century followed two egregious Puritans: Sir Robert Harley, chairman of Parliament's iconoclastic commission to destroy images, crucifixes, paintings, stained glass, etc., in the churches; and the odious William Prynne, who hated the theatre and pursued poor Archbishop Laud to the death.

Queen's College was founded in 1341 by Queen Philippa's chaplain, Robert Eglesfield. He had large ideas, and evidently hoped for generous benefactions from the queen, under whose patronage he placed his infant institution; these, however, were not forthcoming. He had to content himself with a provost and twelve masters; but there were several chaplains and twelve poor boys to serve. The tone of the college was different again; it was very religious, the Fellows were to sit round only three sides of 'high table', as in representations of the Last Supper, and they were to wear blood-red in memory of the Passion of our Lord.

More permanent has been its north country complexion. The founder had come from the diocese of Carlisle, and so gave preference to natives of Cumberland and Westmorland; to these further scholarships were added for Yorkshire youths later. Since Eglesfield himself graduated from the rude Lake District to court, his court manners received curious expression in the provision that his Fellows *might* talk French, as well as Latin – as if they did! Interesting characters emerged from this background: Wyclif himself lodged there for a time, though not a Fellow. More amusing would, or could, have been the provost who was confessor to naughty, but kind-hearted Jane Shore, mistress of Edward IV, then taken on by the handsome Dorset, but made to do penance by the moralistic murderer, Richard III. (Bosworth was his penance.) Queen's also had its cardinal, Christopher Bainbridge, a Westmorland scholar, who, becoming a cardinal, was poisoned by a rival at Rome in 1514. Many north country men of distinction emerged from those portals to make their mark in the world.

In 1361 Archbishop Islip founded Canterbury College: its peculiarity was that it attempted to bring together regulars, i.e. monks, and seculars. Here again we cross the path of Wyclif, who became warden in 1365 for a short time. Towards the end of its existence the young Thomas More was briefly here. The little institution was absorbed into the omnivorous body of Wolsey's great foundation, its name remembered now only in Canterbury Quadrangle and Gate of that college.

And so we come to New College, 1379, the grandest of Oxford colleges until Wolsey's, the model for the later medieval period as Merton was for the earlier. Once again the statutes were modelled on Merton, but in greater detail and with the accumulated experience of the century that had passed. William of Wykeham's foundation was on a far bigger scale, for no less than seventy scholars over the age of fifteen, already on the way to becoming bachelors; after two years' probation they became full Fellows. The founder's striking new departure was to found the first of English public schools, Winchester College, to feed his foundation at Oxford. This plan was followed by Henry VI in founding King's at Cambridge, with Eton to feed it. And this was intended by Wolsey with his college and a school at his native Ipswich, which would have given Oxford a firm foothold in East Anglia. This was frustrated by his fall, and East Anglia became a largely Cambridge preserve.

William of Wykeham was no scholar, but a practical administrator and a builder – he had been in charge of Edward III's programme of buildings at Windsor. This is the point of Wyclif's jealous comment in 'Why Poor Priests have no Benefices'. 'And yet they will not present a clerk able of cunning [knowledge] ... but a kitchen clerk, or a pen clerk, or wise of building of castles or worldly doings, though he cannot read well his psalter.' Here we see why Wyclif appealed to an academic proletariat. It is true that the practical Wykeham nobbled an immense number of benefices for himself – but out of them came the magnificence of New College. Distributed equally around the inferior, there would have been nothing to remember them by, no signal achievement, merely the trivial lives of people consuming the substance without anything to show for it.

William of Wykeham took a close personal interest in the building of New College; hence the regular integrated plan imposed, the quadrangular model which was henceforward followed in Oxford and elsewhere. The religious side of the foundation was strongly emphasized – Wykeham's reply to Wyclif; the whole complex of buildings was dominated by the most splendid chapel yet built here. It has been sadly mutilated by the Reformation, of course, with which Wyclif's reforming ideas eventually triumphed.

Lincoln College, 1427, was founded by Oxford's diocesan specifically to combat heresy, an oath against which was exacted from its Fellows. These were few in number: it took the benefaction of another bishop of Lincoln to make them up to twelve. (It is still one of those described by Lord David Cecil in the 1930s as 'the little bicycling colleges in the Turl'.) The Fellows were, however, to be graduates; three parish churches were impropriated to support them: St Michael's, St Mildred's and All Saints – of which the last is, as I write, being absorbed into the college as its library. In the early Elizabethan age the rector, John Bridgewater, remained a Catholic and was deprived; he brought up under his wing William Gifford, who rose to occupy the first see in France, as Archbishop of Rheims, 1622–9. This was, perhaps, going a bit far.

Meanwhile Cambridge was catching up in collegiate foundations in the fourteenth century. In the thirteenth century there had been only Peterhouse, 1284, to follow in the wake of Merton, University and Balliol. But in the next century there followed in rapid succession King's Hall and Michaelhouse, out of which Trinity was refounded in the sixteenth century to become the grandest of all English colleges. Next came Clare Hall, 1347; Gonville, 1349, to become better known as Caius; Trinity Hall, 1350; Corpus Christi, 1352. And so onwards into the fifteenth century, with Godshouse, 1439, to become Christ's; King's, 1441, with the most splendid of all college chapels; Queen's, 1448; St Catharine's, 1475;

Left: William of Wykeham – 'no scholar, but a practical administrator and builder' – the founder of Winchester College and New College; from his tomb in Winchester Cathedral.
Right: All Souls College, founded partly for the growing study of canon and civil law, and also to pray for the souls of the faithful departed.

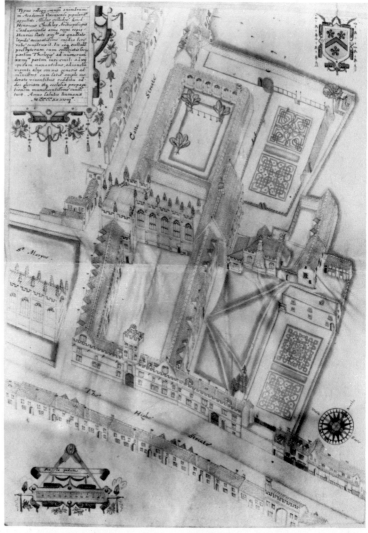

Jesus, 1497. Cambridge was indeed catching up; it may be that the superior wealth and resources of eastern England were beginning to tell, along with the marked Lancastrian patronage. But even after the Reformation Oxford remained the larger in number of students.

The next two foundations, All Souls, 1438, and Magdalen, 1448, reflected the ideas of the great – or, perhaps we should say simply the rich – William of Wykeham: these colleges were in a sense daughters of New College. The founder of All Souls, Archbishop Chichele, had been a Fellow there; Wykeham had made marked provision for the growing study of canon and civil law, so necessary in administration. Chichele was an ecclesiastical lawyer, and he distinguished his foundation by a large legal element, no less than sixteen jurists out of forty Fellows. This came to have a dominating influence upon the character of All Souls: since lawyers were not tied to the academic or clerical life, they were freed for government service. It may be partly due to this that All Souls did not recruit undergraduates during the sixteenth century, and thus exemplified into the twentieth century the original character of a medieval college. It is not, as popularly supposed, that All Souls was peculiar in this; it was the other colleges that changed in character.

But All Souls did have a peculiarity in its foundation: its secondary purpose was as a chantry to pray for the souls of the faithful departed (to some of us they mean more than the living), especially those killed in the Hundred Years' War (we may add those killed in the worse holocaust of the two wars inflicted by the Germans upon our time). The chantry element disappeared at the Reformation, i.e. the masses, though the prayers continue. The element of public service was to the fore from the first, as the founder intended: Sir William Petre and Sir John Mason were secretaries of state – Mason the son of a cowherd of Abingdon – Weston was Lord Chancellor of Ireland. Robert Recorde (a Welsh Rickard) was the leading mathematician of the early sixteenth century, the first to write his books in English; Linacre, greatest of medical scholars. This medical line came up again in the middle of the seventeenth century with Sydenham, the leading clinician of the age, and John Mayow, whose researches on respiration were of great originality and promise: his early death held up the development of physiology, it has been said, by two centuries. The young Christopher Wren came on from Wadham to All Souls as a Fellow from 1654 to 1657, where he accomplished some of his early mathematical work.

It was the legal and public-service aspect of All Souls that mainly gave it its character. We need not cite such public servants as Sir Leoline Jenkins and Sir William Turnbull, Secretaries of State; a more curious pointer is this: the Welsh, having little interest in English common law, became prominent in the study of

Right: The famous tower of Magdalen College, founded in 1448; its choir has been a distinguishing feature from the first.

civil law. So it is that the first five out of six of the principals of Jesus, the Welsh college, were civil lawyers from All Souls.

Magdalen was another daughter of New College, founded by William of Waynflete, another Bishop of Winchester. Waynflete's surname was Patten and he provided a tomb for his father in the chapel he built. We see the mitred son holding the pillow at his father's head and again as a tubby little prelate sculpted above the chapel porch. Waynflete had been a master at Winchester and head-master of Eton, and is underestimated as an educational innovator. His college was for forty Fellows and thirty scholars; the chapel was made very important in the scheme, with four chaplains, eight clerks, i.e. choirmen, and sixteen choris-ters. So the choirs of New College and Magdalen have been distinguishing fea-tures from the first. Apparently from early on Magdalen could board independent students, who paid for themselves; here we have 'commoners', a great pointer to the future. These were to become the most numerous element in the Elizabethan age, and this meant the end of the medieval halls: 'once the colleges admitted fee-paying undergraduates the halls were doomed' – they had no endowments, nor had they the same tutorial advantages. Oxford (and Cambridge) would take on their modern character in which the colleges were dominant.

The Fellows were to be graduates, with a preference for natives of Lincolnshire, Waynflete's county of birth, or Oxfordshire, or those born in the dioceses of Winchester or Norwich. The statutes, modelled on New College, were carefully considered, everything thought out in meticulous detail, down to the condemna-tion (contemporaries might note) of 'inordinate hair'. From early on Magdalen was tinged by royal affiliations, not all of them beneficial. Edward IV, popular as always, paid an agreeable visit; Richard III, of the unpopular personality, fol-lowed shortly upon usurping the throne from his brother's son, and shortly after ordering the murder of the two princes who were never seen again after that August. James II tried to force a Catholic president upon the college and his eventual defeat is still celebrated with a Gaudy. The Edwardian president, Sir Herbert Warren, a notable royal snob, secured the (later) Duke of Windsor for the college. When Mrs Annie Besant tried to recommend her protégé, Krishna-murthi, to Warden Spooner (of New College and spoonerisms), as 'an incarna-tion of our Lord Jesus Christ', that very fly old gentleman did not think that New College could support such a prodigy, and advised her to send him to the president of Magdalen.

Magdalen, however, produced two cardinals, in Wolsey and Pole. The Refor-mation did its usual damage to the chapel, knocking down images, defacing the reredos, dispersing treasures and vestments, as at All Souls and elsewhere, indeed everywhere. Magdalen suckled a believer in this sort of thing in John Foxe, the martyrologist. An equally characteristic specimen of the new deal was the

Elizabethan president, Laurence Humfrey, a leader in advanced Protestant views. He was the first married president: a pew in chapel was allotted to his obstreperous wife; I do not know if his twelve obstreperous children were similarly provided.

Meanwhile, in the later Middle Ages, the town of Oxford was becoming less important than it had been in the earlier period. London was becoming all in all – its wealth and greatness expressed in the dominating grandeur of Old St Paul's, a bigger building than Wren's with a spire much taller than his dome: one of the grandest churches of Christendom. Within Oxford there was naturally a relative decline of the town compared with the growing university, and this was visibly expressed in the buildings, with the rise of the colleges and halls amid the little two-storey tenements of the townsfolk.

Earlier town and university had been on a par; but the influx of students created unprecedented problems, with regard to housing, prices and order. Students were beggarly, townsfolk were poor and tried to make what they could out of them. Hence constant rows, riots, conflicts. Most of the town records perished in the destructive Civil War, but it is clear that the town was ruled by an oligarchy of the better-to-do, while the university was more democratic, and therefore more disorderly. As early as 1252 there had been a bloody affray between northern students and Irish, after which the university tried to impose the regulation that students were to reside in a hall. Medieval students were mercurial and migratory, and in 1334–5 there was a migration to Stamford, which might have led to the development of a third university. There are relics of this episode in a gateway at Stamford, where Brasenose Hall was, and the brazen knocker carried thither, which the college bought back as recently as 1890; while, up to the year 1827, Masters of Arts had to take an oath not to lecture there.

The Black Death, even apart from its horror, had an unsettling effect upon medieval society. In Oxford conflicts between town and gown reached their height with the riots of 10 February 1355, St Scholastica's day, when the whole town was given over to armed uproar – an anything but scholastic occasion. Some eleven persons lost their lives; this made a great impression on civilized Victorians who set store by human life. The town was placed under interdict by the Church, to which the university's interests were dearer. The consequences were important: the university emerged with increased privileges, and gained a final ascendancy over the town which was to endure right up to the last century.

4
Humanism and Reformation

BY 1500 Oxford, like England in general, was recovering from the turmoils and insecurity of the Wars of the Roses, with the settled and politic government of Henry VII. There had been an odd episode at Oxford when, after the decision at Bosworth, a handsome youth in the town, one Lambert Simnel, was taken up by an ambitious priest to impersonate first one of the princes whom Richard III had disposed of in the Tower, and afterwards the son of Clarence, whom his kind brother Edward IV had previously disposed of in the Tower. Henry VII was able to produce Clarence's son and show him publicly – though people's foolery in the matter was not ended (particularly in Ireland, bent on taking whatever opposite line came to hand) until lives were lost on the battlefield of Stoke in 1487. The humane Henry did not execute the priest but had him imprisoned, pardoned the youth and gave him a good job in the royal household. The king bore no grudges and, on his visit to Oxford the year after Stoke, made a gift of forty oaks from the forest of Shotover for the roof of the university church – it is pleasant to think that it comes from those familiar and endearing slopes.

Immeasurably more important was the new impulse coming from Italy, which we recognize under various names, the new learning, the revival of letters, humanism, the Renaissance, to give renewed inspiration to the university, a fresh direction to the intellectual life of the country. (An unlearned Duke of Norfolk thought, however, that England was never merry since the new learning came up.) We may distinguish two phases in this fertilizing movement. The first flowered in Oxford with the fascinating group of scholars and reformers, who wanted reform in church and state without breaking the integuments of society and without altogether departing from tradition. This group formed a circle around two men of genius, Erasmus and More, and included such gifted men as Linacre and Colet, with others who made signal contributions to the life and scholarship of the time.

In the next generation this vital impulse was carried to Cambridge where, with younger men, it became Protestant. There was such a thing as Protestant humanism, and again Erasmus was a link; he spent more time at Cambridge,

Left: Sir Thomas More: the famous portrait by Holbein. The conflict in More's mind between serving God and serving the State was 'much at the heart of humanism'.

though he was not happy there. William Tyndale, who had such a decisive influence with his translation of the Bible – as prose, a work of genius – migrated to Cambridge, more fertile soil for one of his opinions. The exacerbation of opinion, still more the struggle for power, led to the crisis of the Reformation. During the ulcerated middle decades, with chops and changes, hangings and burnings, the hopes of humanism, of rational and moderate reform, became submerged – until the settlement of Elizabeth's reign and the long internal peace enabled them to bloom again, with the utmost creativity in drama and literature. Elizabeth herself, her tastes and those of her circle, may be regarded as exemplifying Protestant humanism, as did the English Church on the whole. But there was another strain in Protestantism, stronger because much less cultivated, and therefore more popular: nasty Puritanism, aggressive, philistine, determined to have its way – which it had, with the Civil War.

Both these strains were strong at Cambridge, whose fortune was made by the Reformation, and it took the lead in both. As an American scholar concludes, 'Cambridge became, what it had not been in the past, a university of the first rank.' We shall observe the divergent characteristics and the consequences for society at large, as well as within the university. It is of significance that the Elizabethan age was a resumption of the Edwardian course; the leading Elizabethans were Edwardians. Elizabeth, like Edward vi, had been taught by Cambridge tutors; the governing circle, Cecils, Bacons, Walsingham, were Cambridge men; so were all the Protestant archbishops of Canterbury. It lights up the point for us that those Cambridge bishops, Cranmer, Latimer and Ridley, should have been burned at Oxford.

Queen Mary's tutor had been an Oxford humanist, Vives, and Cardinal Pole had belonged to the circle of Catholic reformers, until the sharpening of opinion and the struggle for power led men, as usual, to kill each other. Oxford was undoubtedly damaged by it, and lost some notable men with the Catholic exiles under Elizabeth – another cardinal with Allen, the famous Jesuit Robert Parsons, a brilliant scholar with Edmund Campion, all of whom might have been stars in the Elizabethan firmament. When the Catholic Church reformed itself with the Counter-Reformation – it would be better to call it the Catholic revival – it was Oxford disputants abroad, Parsons, Bristow, Sanders, Gregory Martin, who took on Cambridge opponents like Cartwright, Fulke and Whitaker. It was of no importance which side had the better of the argument – such disputes settle nothing; power is what matters, and in Reformation England power was with the Cambridge men.

All was not lost, however, if the cause was. Allen founded at Douai a centre of Catholic education which continued through the centuries, until it was repatriated with the French Revolution. At Louvain the Oxford contingent, several of them Wykehamists, made a formidable group in scholarship and controversy – even if some of their effects were deleterious and drove good men to useless martyrdom: John Donne, who knew all about it from the inside and had been deeply influenced by their writings when young, regarded it as no better than suicide. It was, to say the least, highly unecumenical. The translation and production of the Douai Bible – largely the work of Gregory Martin, Campion's companion at St John's – was a more constructive effort and exerted its influence, even on the translators of the Authorised Version. (Scholarship sometimes transcends nonsense-opinions; we may compare Martin's work with that of another Oxford convert today, Father Knox's one-man translation.)

Within Oxford, too, Protestantism ruled; Catholics were but a small minority. There were even advanced Protestants, like Laurence Humfrey and John Reynolds, whom Elizabeth herself 'schooled for his obstinate preciseness'. Reynolds' elder brother William, a New College Wykehamist, became an exile at Douai and Rheims, controverted Whitaker, and helped to revise the Douai New Testament. Harding, another Wykehamist exile, challenged Bishop Jewel's very reasonable apology for the Church of England. Jewel was an Oxford man; his defence of the moderate reform accomplished by the English Church while retaining the essentials of Catholic order and belief remained the classic statement of the case, until a nobler and more philosophic spirit transcended it with Richard Hooker's *Laws of Ecclesiastical Polity*.

It is clear that, as things settled down, Oxford maintained a more moderate and conservative course, less disputatious and excited – possibly less interesting – than Cambridge. Aristotle retained his place, Ramus was regarded in proper perspective, even the Schoolmen were not wholly neglected. When the reformed English Church proved itself, it found its ethos, its abiding character, with Hooker; and Catholic hierarchical order once more sprouted Catholic doctrine. So one sees the Anglican Church of the seventeenth century coming back for its leadership to Oxford; its succession of archbishops is resumed with Abbot, Laud, Juxon, Sheldon, with whom the restoration of church and king was accomplished, after the interruption of a Cambridge Puritan with Oliver Cromwell.

These differences of inflexion are historically significant; we shall observe their consequences later in the diverging paths of Oxford and Cambridge.

In the high Middle Ages, the thirteenth and fourteenth centuries, the connexion between Oxford and Paris was close and contacts were frequent; less so with the loss of Normandy at the end of the Hundred Years' War. The cultural ascendancy of France had been very marked; what was new about Renaissance humanism was that the inspiration came from Italy, where the revival of classical antiquity in all forms was in progress. Thither, by the second half of the fifteenth century,

Oxford scholars began to flock to imbibe the new ideas, with such early figures as John Free and Tiptoft. The stream grew steadily larger for the next century and a half. Free's patron who sent him to Italy was William Grey, subsequently a bishop: he had resided in Balliol and left this smallest and poorest of colleges his library – hence it is that Balliol now has the finest private medieval library to survive in England.

William Grocyn may be taken to represent the tradition, for he was a complete Wykehamist – of both Winchester and New College – who went to Florence to imbibe the new knowledge and came back to lecture on Greek from the new perspective. His friend and executor, Thomas Linacre of All Souls, is much more important; for he spent many years in Italy, in close association with the Aldine Press in Venice, translating the whole of Galen into Latin, thus making Greek medical knowledge available for modern Europe. When he returned to England he founded the Royal College of Physicians, an indispensable move in bringing the backward country up to date.

Hardly less important was John Colet, though no Greek scholar. He was an inspired moralist, whose new approach to the scriptures was to get back behind mountains of medieval commentary to the meaning of the text and its simple interpretation. It was probably Colet's influence that led Erasmus to undertake his edition of the New Testament, with its reverberating effect in stimulating the urge towards Reformation. At the same time both Colet and Erasmus despised the veneration of images and relics. On both counts one sees what encouragement this gave to the reformers – though that, to civilized persons, is no reason for the wholesale destruction of medieval sculpture, simply because fools worshipped the works of men's hands under a misapprehension. To appreciate, not to worship, would have been the right idea, but fanatics were unable to content themselves with this rational position. Colet's chief practical contribution was the foundation – for he was a rich man – of St Paul's School, to educate the citizenry of London for their place in society: the school was twice the size of medieval Winchester and Eton.

By 1520 there was already extensive use at Oxford of Erasmus' edition of a Latin grammar; while, under his influence, Colet insisted on the study of Greek at school at St Paul's. Now for school use William Lily, who had travelled widely in the Levant, compiled a Latin grammar, which became standard throughout the country for the next century and was a powerful instrument in forming a common background of discourse for the leading elements in Tudor society. William Latimer of All Souls, a good Greek scholar, studied in Italy and came back to help Lily and Grocyn in their work. These men formed a group of friends, to whom others like the antiquary Leland were recruited. The young Thomas More came to Canterbury College briefly, but he remained in contact with the university and its affairs, becoming its steward, helping to save Wolsey's college on his fall, and intervening against the reactionaries who were obstructing the new movement for Greek and Erasmus' new educational curriculum.

A portent of a quite different character appears with the coming of William Tyndale, who was here for five years, 1510–15; after taking his degree he moved to the more propitious soil, for the Reformation, of Cambridge – more open to the easterly winds coming from Germany. Tyndale had come under the influence of Colet's teaching about the need for the soul to take scripture neat, and he set out on his life's work translating it, beginning with Erasmus' New Testament. For this purpose, and for the dubious benefit of print, he crossed to Germany, the fountain-source of inspiration. When the testaments arrived in England, the generous-minded Wolsey made a plea for toleration; but the bishops were adamant, and an Oxford man was arrested as agent for the distribution.

Tyndale's original works proclaimed the whole programme of the English Reformation: the supreme authority of scripture in the Church, the supreme authority of the monarch in the State; in doctrine, the Protestant doctrine of justification by faith. More, licensed by the bishops to read Tyndale's noxious works, took him on; residence in Germany eroded Tyndale's belief in transubstantiation – the eucharist was but a commemoration. This was shocking; and St Thomas More replied to it in very unsanctified language in his *Dialogue*, one of the most important of his works. Tyndale answered in no less unchristian terms; further works from both protagonists left them, surprisingly, of the same opinion as they were before. It is a fact of historic importance that 'the classic controversy of the English Reformation' should have taken shape between these Oxford men.

More was the greater scholar, with the more original genius; Tyndale had the gift for English prose and for speaking directly to the heart of a ploughboy, as he had wished, and with detonating effect. Tyndale's name became a household word with the triumph of the English Reformation, of which he may be regarded as a founding father, along with Wyclif. His influence through his translation of the Bible was prodigious, not only on successive versions, all of which were indebted to him, but also on the development of English prose, for he wrote in the glad morning of the language.

The Victorian age, penetrated by Protestant prejudice, made a saint of Tyndale as Catholics have done of More. What the Victorians did not realize was that Protestant fanaticism meant a deflection from the hopes of humanists for rational and ordered reform. And in the conflict that arose from too much faith on each side both protagonists perished for their absurd, and mutually exclusive, convictions: More executed on the scaffold, Tyndale strangled then burnt at the stake. Ironical and pathetic – but this is what happens when men are so devoted to their illusions.

The crucial dilemma in More's mind, the conflict between the absolute claims of religion and his sense of duty to serve the State, was much at the heart of humanism. For the humanists stressed the necessity of an educated laity to meet the expanding needs of government; this appears in all their books and, where the Middle Ages had relied largely on clerics for administration, we shall observe an increasing number of university-educated laymen take their place, gradually confining clerics to the Church. From this point of view Wolsey is the last great medieval, playing a dominant role in both church and state. With his crash, and the consequent Reformation, the crown exerted a unified control – no longer did the universities owe any allegiance to the pope: a visible change from the Middle Ages.

Leading ministers, all laymen, became chancellors, with over-riding powers of supervision, jurisdiction and patronage. They became the final court of appeal – William Cecil for Cambridge, Sir John Mason, then Leicester, for Oxford. Within the university, as schools-instruction became less important and the halls petered out, the colleges came to dominate the university and their heads to be the leading figures in its government. All this made stronger links and bonds in a more efficient society than the more demotic ways of medieval life had provided.

In short, the transition effected in the sixteenth century made for a most stimulating and varied period and, we may add, of crucial importance for the contribution of the university to the life of the nation.

We may now observe these developments at work in the foundation of new colleges. Brasenose Hall had existed since the thirteenth century; in about 1512 it became a college, though evidence of its former status remains in the title of principal for its head. It was refounded by an ecclesiastic and a layman together: Bishop Smyth of Lincoln paid for the building, and Sir Richard Sutton for the site – four neighbouring halls were absorbed into it. There were to be twelve Fellows. After the usual straitened beginnings, by mid-century the number of undergraduates had notably increased. This reflects the fact that colleges were now taking in commoners, i.e. fee-paying undergraduates. Their resources were thereby increased: it became worthwhile for Fellows to make careers as tutors; the tutorial system developed – a number of men exerted widespread influence upon generations of pupils, winning a more than local name. Archbishop Sandys, a Cambridge man, sent his clever boy Edwin to Corpus at Oxford specially to be under the tuition of the judicious Hooker. By a decree of 1576 all undergraduates were supposed to be under a Fellow of a college as their tutor. Brasenose continued to increase in number and to prosper. This attracted substantial benefactions, especially from Alexander Nowell, Dean of St Paul's, a celebrated Lancashireman. Further bequests strengthened the affiliations with Lancashire,

The thirteenth-century knocker, 'Brasen Nose', of Brasenose Hall.

until the Hulme Bequest later produced so much money, with the increase of land values, that the revenues were scaled down and the college shorn by the intervention of the courts. The Lancashire connection is witnessed by the career of the eminent Elizabethan lawyer, Egerton, Lord Chancellor Ellesmere, and his love of books by his splendid collection now in the Huntington Library in California.

Corpus Christi was founded in 1517 by two ecclesiastics, and was well endowed from the first, for twenty Fellows and twenty scholars. Bishop Fox of Winchester had intended a monastic college, but Bishop Oldham of Exeter persuaded him to make it secular with a handsome contribution. Fox's aim was 'to provide a complete course of training for the national service in a single institution'. To this intent one half of the members were undergraduates. There usually were some

The Norman door and
chapter house of St
Frideswide's priory,
Christ Church.

boys in the colleges in a preparatory category; Fox subjected them to a rigorous
process of weeding out: if they were no good they went. They were to be chosen
from the country areas where the college's estates were, on the view that a charitable endowment arising from a certain district should be applied to its natives: the
likely sons of tenants were given a chance in the world. Fox did not want his
Fellows to hang on in college, but to go out into the world and serve. Distinctive
was the endowment of three professorships in Latin, Greek and theology, to give
public lectures to the university – and here we see a college trenching upon what
had been the monopoly of the schools.

From the first Corpus attracted gifted men, the most brilliant being Nicholas
Udall who, besides his Lutheran proclivities, had others that were gayer. The
author of the first of English comedies, *Ralph Roister Doister*, and a lost biblical
play, *Ezekias*, performed at Cambridge, Udall was one of the founding fathers
of the Elizabethan drama. The most brilliant schoolmaster of his time, he was not
only a beater of his boys: an awkward *contretemps* at Eton made no permanent
setback to his career: he was a favourite with both Edward VI and Queen Mary,
Tudor people being more tolerant of such peccadilloes. Bishop Gardiner made

him schoolmaster to young Edward Courtenay in the Tower, and gave him the charge of the schoolboys in his household. Udall may be said to have been interested in his subject, and therefore good at it: he ended as headmaster of Westminster. Beside him other Corpus men of the century, Bishop Jewel, the precision Reynolds (though, as a youth, he had acted in plays, and in female costume!), even good Richard Hooker, seem somewhat dull.

The founding of what became Christ Church by Cardinal Wolsey in 1525 was on an outsize scale, like everything about him. For the purpose he got papal licence to suppress ancient St Frideswide's priory and no less than twenty monasteries to endow it. There were to be a dean, sixty senior students and forty juniors; with the chapel and choristers an establishment of 180 persons. The great man's time was drawing to an end, and the buildings were hurried forward. Thomas Cromwell engaged in the business of suppression – a useful apprenticeship for what was to come on a national scale. It is astonishing how much the cardinal accomplished before his crash: three sides of his big quadrangle, with the largest hall and kitchen in Oxford, on the fourth the foundations of a chapel that was to have been larger than King's at Cambridge long remained. Fine as the spectacle is when we enter at Tom Gate today, imagine how much more splendid it would have been as Wolsey intended it, with a vast chapel on the north side to balance the hall, with a connecting cloister all round like that at Magdalen. He was bursar there when the tower was built; he left the foundations for an even larger one at the end of the hall at Christ Church. The best royal masons, who had been trained at Hampton Court and Greenwich, were employed; Wolsey sent rich gifts of vestments and missals – both shortly to disappear in the hurricane of the Reformation. A glutton for work, as for everything else, he made minute provisions for his college (he had intended as chancellor to re-cast and codify statutes for the university) supervising everything from a distance, caught as he was in the inextricable tangle of a hopeless foreign policy and an immovable royal will.

To make his college the grandest in the country – and a memorial of his undoubted greatness – he brought in the best scholars he could find, some of them from Cambridge already infected with Lutheranism. Some of these were delated for heresy, so was the brilliant composer who had been recruited for the chapel, John Taverner. The tolerant Cardinal – far more so than More, who was a persecutor – let Taverner off as being 'but a musician'. He went on to repent of his musical compositions and to become an agent of Cromwell in suppressing monasteries in the eastern counties. Fancy anyone repenting of such glorious works as his 'O western wind' Mass – he was the finest of early Tudor composers – for such an occupation!

Wolsey's magnificent work was not complete when he fell from power, though vastly more fell with him, ultimately the medieval Church and papal jurisdiction in England. In the ruin of all his hopes Wolsey's concern for his 'poor college' at Oxford was very touching. Actually he had made it by far the richest in the university, endowed with £2000 a year. But there was some doubt whether Henry VIII would allow it to survive; the school Wolsey was founding at Ipswich to serve his college was swept into the royal maw. In the end, in the last year of Henry's life – when he bethought him of what he would bequeath to posterity – he decided to reconstitute the college as a second founder.

Osney Abbey had been spared at the dissolution to be the cathedral of a new diocese of Oxford – a very proper provision, separating it from over-large Lincoln. Osney with its fine central tower and ample monastic buildings would have served well for a cathedral establishment, and made a fine western approach to Oxford, where now is an unimpressive railway station. But the folly of Henry VIII's last French war was so costly that it halved the number of monastic churches that were to be saved for cathedrals and, alas, Osney was one to be sacrificed. In 1546 its lands were appropriated to re-endow Cardinal College as Christ Church, Wolsey's endowments having been dispersed, and ancient St Frideswide's was turned into the cathedral of the new diocese. It was an economic measure. At the same time Henry did something for Cambridge to outdo Wolsey at Oxford: he made himself the founder of Trinity College there on an even grander scale.

It is usual to notice the ecclesiastics and theologians, with their dreary disputes; notably Peter Martyr, an Italian Protestant brought in, complete with wife – another new feature for collegiate life – to bolster up the new doctrines. Even before the Catholic, if schismatic, Henry died the shrine of St Frideswide had been destroyed and her bones thrown out. (In our time this admirable work of sculpture has been in part re-assembled, or what was left of it. The watching chamber of wood, from which to keep an eye on the precious relics – so valuable to the medieval mind – survived.) When Peter Martyr's wife died, she was buried in St Frideswide's available grave: the Marians dug her body up and threw it out. In the process the remains of both ladies got mixed: no-one can tell which or what, if anything, is below the restored shrine today.

Far more valuable to our minds is the notable contribution made by Christ Church dramatists to the developing English drama. Cambridge, especially St John's, was going in more for comedy and topical satire. Oxford went in for tragedy and spectacular productions, especially in Christ Church hall. A distinguished group had come up from Westminster school, with which Elizabeth I knitted a connection for the college, where Latin plays were performed by the boys. William Gager was the leading figure, whose work has been overlooked because it is all in Latin. His play *Meleager*, performed before Leicester and Sidney, was a success; he followed this with a comedy, and a *Dido* complete with hunts-

THOMAS WOLSEY, CARDINAL ARCHBISHOP OF YORK.
1526.

Cardinal Wolsey, founder of Christ Church, who intended the college to be the grandest in the
country – 'a memorial of his undoubted greatness'.

Tom Quad from Neale's *Visitation*, 1566, showing Tom Gate, the hall, and intended cloisters.

men and hounds, and 'a tempest wherein it hailed small confects, rained rosewater, and snew an artificial kind of snow'.★

When Elizabeth, James or visiting grandees came to Oxford they were entertained with plays at Christ Church. Richard Edwards left to become Master of the Children of the Chapel, but came back to produce his play *Palamon and Arcite*, much appreciated at the queen's first visit in 1566. He is still remembered for his charming poem, 'In going to my naked bed', with its refrain,

> The falling out of faithful friends
>   the renewing is of love.

In the next generation we find more decisive contributions by better-known dramatists. George Peele was at Christ Church for ten years, 1571–81, before he

★ Cf my *The Elizabethan Renaissance: The Cultural Achievement*, chap. 1.

left for London and the theatre. John Lyly, grandson of the humanist William Lily, was at Magdalen for four years, 1571–5, before he went to London to write his celebrated comedies for performance at court. With these men we observe the comparable contribution of Oxford to the drama, against that of Cambridge with Greene, Nash, and Marlowe. While with Philip Sidney, from Christ Church, we have one of the veritable creators of Elizabethan literature, not only with the work he accomplished and the standards he set in poetry and prose, but with the patronage he exerted, as a leader in society, for other writers. He meant to see a literature in English come into being which could hold up its head to Italian, and before he died – at thirty-two! – he had set it on its way.

We may say of Sidney and Spenser that they were the noblest exemplars of Protestant humanism, the one from Oxford, the other from Cambridge.

At the same time as Cromwell set on foot his investigation of the monasteries, in 1536, the universities were visited. Cromwell was a highly intelligent administrator, in touch with humanist thought and able to direct it to the purposes of reform. Of the two Visitors he sent to Oxford the more active, Dr Layton, was a Cambridge man. It was he who reported that they had 'set Dunce in Bocardo', i.e. had put Duns Scotus in the prison at the North Gate (where Cranmer was incarcerated during the Marian reaction); it was from this time that the word 'dunce' came into use – humanists had no use for Duns's philosophizing, if indeed humanism had ever had any. At New College leaves from the manuscripts of the discarded schoolmen fluttered about the quadrangle, to be picked up by a hunting man to stuff the pales of his deer-park, and by others for other uses.

Reform has its losses no less than reaction, and a deplorable loss at this time was Duke Humphrey's library, with all its manuscripts and rarities, which would have been of immense value today; the building itself was left empty and derelict, until Sir Thomas Bodley took it in hand. There were losses from college libraries: some of the books from All Souls ultimately fetched up at the Plantin collection in Belgium. The fact was that humanism had no opinion of medieval scholasticism, any more than the admirers of Renaissance architecture appreciated the rebarbative Gothic of monasticism (the stones of Merton Priory were simply bundled in to make the foundations of Henry's fantasy-palace of Nonsuch).

Cromwell's Injunctions for Cambridge significantly swept aside regulations hindering polite learning and recommended contemporary Rudolph Agricola and Melanchthon along with Aristotle, in place of the schoolmen. Henry VIII, in his last reflective year, founded five Regius professorships at Oxford, in medicine, civil law and Greek, symptomatic of new directions, along with theology and Hebrew, even the last pointing to the direct study of the text of the Old Testament. Edward VI's Commission for Oxford continued the good work. It is noteworthy that several of its members were Cambridge men: both bishops, Ridley and Holbeach; both deans, Cox who had been brought over to rule Christ Church, and Heynes, who had been vice-chancellor over there; the civil lawyer, Nevinson; while Morison, though an Oxford man, was a distinguished humanist of Cromwell's circle.

Humanism, with its emphasis on government service and education to that end, strongly favoured the study of civil law, of growing importance in the relations between states. The commissioners proposed to make All Souls a purely legal college, exchanging the artists there for the jurists at New College; the chantry element at All Souls, with its altars in the ante-chapel, had already been suppressed. New statutes were drafted changing the emphasis in the curriculum, abolishing the study of canon law and the medieval sentences; less logic and more liberal arts, grammar and rhetoric: more useful, at least more appealing, for public speaking. An eminent Latinist, Walter Haddon, was brought over to take the place of the insignificant Oglethorpe as president of Magdalen.

It is evident that the conservatives were strong at Oxford, and with Mary's unexpected accession they had their brief day. Out went Peter Martyr, in came the Spanish friars, Soto and Villa Garcia, to make Cranmer's last days in Bocardo miserable. Cardinal Pole became chancellor – and of Cambridge too – to forward the reaction. In his youth he had been a Catholic reformer, like those others of the old Oxford circle, Colet and More, and like their friend Erasmus. As so often in human affairs – as in France in 1789 or in Russia in 1917 – reform came too late, and in a more uncompromising shape when it did. If only the hopes of Catholic reform could have come about, of Erasmus, instead of a brutal Luther on one side, a brutal Caraffa pope on the other, who even turned on Pole in the end! But not all Mary and Pole's burnings could hold up the movement of the time.

During these sickening years, with the insecurity and persecution, numbers fell off, fewer people took degrees. Nothing that Pole did with his Injunctions, all his labours to root out heresy, could do any good. He encouraged the inclusion of students in the colleges, the increasing authority of their heads – but that was happening anyway. Two new colleges were founded. Sir Thomas Pope was a devout Catholic who had made a large fortune out of the dissolution of the monasteries. In 1555 he bought the site of the dissolved Durham College for his new foundation of Trinity: it began with a president, twelve Fellows and seven scholars, with a preference for those counties where the founder had estates, principally Oxfordshire. (Among these was Wroxton, near Banbury, where the North family resided for centuries, until the social revolution of our time.)

In 1557 Sir Thomas White, a leading Merchant Taylor in London, purchased the site of another monastic college, St Bernard's, to found St John's, the patron saint of tailors. The Blessed Edmund Campion, no more credulous than other persons of the time – at least, not much more – said that the founder had been drawn to the site by a dream of a row of elm trees there; and elms continue in front of the college. The purpose of the founder was 'to strengthen the orthodox faith' and help 'afflicted theology'. Perhaps this was reflected in the large number of Fellows, eight in all, who left for Douai. Their place was taken, more substantially, by further endowments and support from the Merchant Taylors' Company, a more profitable connection. This enabled a further quadrangle to be begun in 1596–8, the remaining three sides of which were to form Canterbury Quadrangle, completed by Archbishop Laud, who was surely orthodox enough in all faith.

The accession of Elizabeth meant a return to the movement of the age – which her father had recognized and released – in its Edwardian form, but rather more conservative and less doctrinal than it would have been if Edward had lived. For Elizabeth was the best Erasmian of them all, moderate, cautious, undogmatic. What stands out from the first is the unquestioned ascendancy of the laity: the Elizabethan age was essentially secular. No more cardinals (the only one, Allen, was an exile); the chancellors were all laymen. It is true that, within the walls, the university was dominantly clerical, but the Church was now subordinate to the State, though still with a sphere proper to itself.

The Elizabethan Visitors proceeded to dock the restored superstitious usages in the college chapels, unfortunately destroying altars, roods, ornaments. (The cultivated queen had been against the destruction of roods, but could not prevail against the returned exiles, infected by Calvinism.) At All Souls her archbishop had to order the college to sell the vestments, missals and other 'trumpery' it had been reluctant to part with and to invest the proceeds in land. This proved a good investment. A small number of heads of colleges and figures identified with the Marian regime withdrew or left for abroad; one or two who had been notorious persecutors, like Nicholas Harpsfield, were imprisoned. There continued a steady dribble abroad, particularly after the critical years 1569–72, when it became clear that there was no further hope for Catholicism in England.

These people were only a small minority. At Cambridge Puritans were far more numerous and far more troublesome. Leicester was the (political) patron of left-wing Protestants; he used his position as chancellor to support them, and occasionally to intrude them, at Oxford. But they were very much in the minority here, and had no such strength as in such Cambridge colleges as St John's, Christ's and Emmanuel. (This was reflected in the large proportion of Emmanuel men who created Harvard in Puritan New England.) The Elizabethan settlement meant consolidation and recovery. By 1566 the number of men taking degrees almost doubled from Mary's time: it jumped from 60 or 70 to 112. The colleges were full: in 1565 Christ Church had 208 persons within its walls, servants included; Magdalen 132, Exeter 113, Balliol 65. Merton, largest of early medieval colleges, now came low on the list with some 50. Elizabethan consolidation may be said to have been celebrated by the queen's visit to Oxford in form, accompanied by the court, in 1566 and to have been marked, more practically, by the Act of Parliament in 1571 incorporating the universities, giving statutory confirmation to their rights, privileges and liberties. Here was the secular recognition of their place in the state.

In this same year Jesus College had its difficult, impecunious beginnings. Hugh Price, treasurer of St David's cathedral, gave an endowment which did not take effect for some time; the queen granted letters patent for the college to absorb a hall on the site, and was willing to be regarded thereupon as foundress. It took the college some time before it got going, but gradually small benefactions from Wales began to come in – including one from Dean Wood who figures so equivocally in Simon Forman's Case Books.* From the first the college had a Welsh character and before long it appealed to Welsh patriotism: a collection was made among the Breconshire squires, and money trickled in from the Welsh gentry and clergy. Welsh civil lawyers from All Souls were its first principals, and a library with many rare Welsh books was built up. There were only eight Fellows and eight scholars, but shortly commoners came in, with their cash, and buildings went up. We recall that when Milton was marrying young Mary Powell up at Forest Hill, her father was supplying the timber from Shotover for the new building at Jesus.

Thus the universities were more closely integrated into the fabric of the more efficient society that accomplished the achievements of the Elizabethan age, not only in thought and religion, in literature, drama and science, but at sea and on land, in all which activities university men were to the fore. There was an increased and closer affiliation with the governing class, which realized that the expanding needs of society required educated men to meet and direct them. Cecil saw that the nobility needed to be educated (not like old days) and sent the young peers who were his wards, the Earls of Oxford, Essex, Rutland, Southampton, to Cambridge. There was thus closer contact at the apex of society between monarch, government and university. Lower down, the sons of gentry and middle classes were coming up in increasing numbers to be taught and disciplined by their tutors in the colleges: 'Young gentlemen had come to the universities to stay' – here was a marked difference from the Middle Ages. The colleges now provided the teaching and most of the lecturing, though exercises and disputations continued in the schools, and the university awarded the degrees. Within the university the heads of colleges had the power. From West-

* Cf my *Simon Forman: Sex and Society in Shakespeare's Age.*

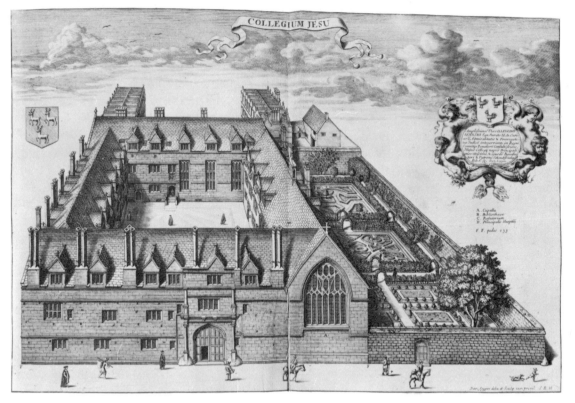

Jesus College, a Welsh foundation in 1571, had 'difficult, impecunious beginnings'.

minster the Tudor State, incarnate in such university men as the Cecils, the Bacons, a Walsingham or an Egerton, watched over the universities as nurseries of the nation's operative agents, not of a rootless intelligentsia without responsibility or a working place in society.

The results were apparent. By the end of Elizabeth's reign the bulk of the clergy were university men, as they had not been before the Reformation. There was an immense expansion in education: by the seventeenth century most of the market towns in most counties were equipped with a grammar school, of which the masters needed to have a degree. The number of members of Parliament with a university education markedly increased: no doubt it made them more voluble and disputatious. But it reflected the growing habit in the upper classes of sending their sons to the university and then on to an inn of court. We can see a long-term effect of this in the number of Parliamentary leaders produced by Oxford – from Job Throckmorton to Sir Edwin Sandys, from Sir John Eliot and

Attorney-General Noy, John Selden, Pym and his step-brother Francis Rous and Strode, to Oliver St John, John Hampden and Sir Henry Vane.

Within Cambridge the Puritan movement was far stronger and more clerical: it found its intellectual leadership, in the Presbyterian form, with Cartwright, who took on Whitgift in voluminous controversy – though Archbishop Whitgift himself was a Calvinist in theology. Predestinarian nonsense prevailed; in the Lambeth Articles put forward by Whitgift in 1595, he allowed that 'God from eternity has predestined some to life and reprobated some to death.' The sensible Erasmian queen refused to have this nonsense promulgated: she 'misliked much that any allowance had been given by his Grace and the rest, of any such points to be disputed, being a matter tender and dangerous to weak, ignorant minds'. True enough; but this did not prevent weak ignorant minds from embracing them. When Puritanism won, in its Presbyterian form, with the Westminster Assembly of divines, sixty-two of them were Cambridge men, and only thirty-four – more than enough – from Oxford.

Already there is appearing a difference of emphasis, with Oxford more interested in a real subject, such as geography. The seminal mind of Richard Hakluyt expounded the subject from Christ Church and attracted like minds to him, with prodigious consequences in the oceanic voyages, the acquisition and spreading of geographical knowledge in an expanding world, and in the colonization of America. The privateering Earl of Cumberland left Cambridge to come to Oxford 'to study geography and especially to consult ancient maps and divers papers'. The promising Renaissance scholar, Stephen Parmenius, came from Hungary to learn what Hakluyt had to teach. With Humphrey Gilbert, another Oxford man, Parmenius went on the Newfoundland voyage, upon which they both perished.

Richard Madox of All Souls went as chaplain on Fenton's voyage, intended to follow up Drake's soundings in the Far East. His diary reveals something of the geographical interest at Oxford, which inspired Anthony Shirley of All Souls to his extraordinary career in the Caribbean, the Levant and Persia. On Gilbert's death, his step-brother Walter Ralegh of Oriel took up his plans of American exploration and colonization. He employed the most brilliant Oxford mathematician, Thomas Hariot – with Viète the greatest algebraist of the age – for many years as his adviser in cosmology and navigation. Hariot's posthumous work on algebra was prepared for publication by another Oxford mathematician, Torporley, a clergyman who did not approve of the religious heterodoxy of the man of genius.

We need go no further; these are merely illustrations, as with the drama, of the more piquant side of the intellectual life of the university, destined to have a better flowering than the theological concerns of more pedestrian persons. How-

Right: A detail from the shrine of St Frideswide in Christ Church Cathedral.

ever, we do not neglect the sound and widespread influence of a truly catholic mind like Richard Hooker, with its comprehensiveness, its essential moderation and tolerance, in creating a *via media* for the English Church, which could recruit to it, after long wandering, such an intellect as John Donne of Hart Hall. The generalized influence of the university in the country at large may be seen in the training and broadcasting of thought in society, the inculcating of a consensus of moral and intellectual standards, a common background of discourse necessary to hold society together in spite of disagreements and disputed points.

The new conception of the role of the university in the state was emphasized by the state visits of the queen, attended by privy councillors, court and ambassadors, when she took part in the disputations and academic exercises, heard the sermons, saw the plays, attended the services and enjoined learning and keeping to their studies upon the scholars. As she mounted Shotover Hill, along the old road to London, on a September afternoon in 1566, she turned to look back on the city, beautiful then with the country up to its walls: 'Farewell, Oxford; farewell, my good subjects! Farewell, my dear scholars: pray God prosper your studies! Farewell, farewell!'

On her last visit in 1592 she was attended, among others, by young Southampton from Cambridge, who proceeded M.A. at Oxford: 'quo non formosior alter' (than whom none more beautiful). We read in his poet's play of next year, *Love's Labour's Lost* – a skit on the young man's bachelor circle by its poet:

> Proceeded well, to stop all good proceeding!

And in *A Midsummer Night's Dream* of the year following, to celebrate the second marriage of the patron's mother, we find just such an academic scene on a royal visit described:

> Where I have come, great clerks have purposèd
> To greet me with premeditated welcomes;
> Where I have seen them shiver and look pale,
> Make periods in the midst of sentences,
> Throttle their practised accent in their fears,
> And on conclusion dumbly have broke off.

We need not doubt that William Shakespeare was present on that occasion, on the familiar route between Stratford and London through Oxford.

Left: The stained glass window of Jonah beholding the city of Nineveh, in Christ Church, the only van Linge window in the Cathedral to survive the nineteenth century.

5
Laudian Oxford

THE finest achievement of seventeenth-century Oxford was the founding and building up of the Bodleian Library, one of the great libraries of the world, with the richest early collections in the English-speaking world, except for the British Museum. The Bodleian has been justly described as 'the greatest single contribution made in Oxford to seventeenth-century culture'. Once more, after the break made by the Reformation, Oxford was brought, as in her brilliant medieval period, 'fully within the orbit of European scholarship'. We may regard it as a late flowering of the Elizabethan age, since the founder, Sir Thomas Bodley, was a complete Elizabethan. He was born in Exeter in 1545, of middle-class parents who, as firm Protestants, sought refuge under Mary in Germany and Geneva. This had the good effect of furnishing their clever son with languages; later on, as Fellow of Merton from 1564, he gave public lectures on Greek. Four years' travel abroad equipped him for public service, nor did marriage to a rich widow disqualify him in any way. He was sent as an envoy to Denmark, and then to the key-post of resident ambassador in the Netherlands. A very intelligent man, he could have been Secretary of State if he had wished; but he had had enough, and by 1596 was determined to retire, to devote himself to the creation of the Library he had long contemplated. It was Bodley's familiarity with the continent that gave him his ideas, enabled him to rise above insularity and set new standards.

He had been a don, he was always bookish; his heart had been touched by seeing Duke Humphrey's big room over the Divinity School 'in every part ruined and waste': he saw a mission for himself, a public need to meet. In the event, though he cannot have conceived the scale the enterprise would reach, the overwhelming collections that would flow in – not only of books and manuscripts, but letters and papers – or the model it would set for others, his name achieved immortality thereby.

It was well deserved, for he devoted the last fifteen years of his life to concerning himself with every detail. His wealth enabled him to buy books; he sent an assistant, John Bill, to go through the Italian cities from north to south making purchases; other agents traversed Europe and even went as far as Syria. He used

Right: Archbishop Laud, greatest of Oxford's benefactors. Portrait at Cambridge from the studio of Van Dyck.

his prestige and diplomatic skill to persuade, and solicit benefactions and bene-factors, and to prevail on others to take part in the work, rewarding them by making their names known in his big benefactors' book. Soon someone was writing, 'Everyman bethinks himself how by some good book or other he may be written in the scroll of benefactors.' Bodley had the scholarly knowledge to know what was required, though he had a fondness for folios as against small books. We need not go into his correspondence about carpenters and locksmiths, shelves and chains, nor the rules and regulations he drew up: he thought of every-thing and saw to everything.

He began in 1598 by restoring the big chamber – shortly it was given the beautiful painted roof we see today; as books and benefactions rolled in, it was necessary to enlarge the library with a transept at either end – Selden End to the west, and Arts End above the Proscholium built on in 1610. This last was the beginning of a whole Schools Quadrangle, dominated by a 'tower of the five orders' with James I in glory at the top. Truly the early seventeenth century was a period of remarkable expansion at Oxford and the discerning eye can still see the two dominant periods that give the university its character, the medieval and the seventeenth century, under the later accretions.

The benefactors Bodley recruited by his drive form a roll-call of late Eliza-bethan society. The 'Wizard' Earl of Northumberland, called so for his scientific interests, gave £100 (multiply, perhaps by fifty, for current value); Lord Mount-joy, from Ireland, £100; Sir George Carew, also in Ireland, £95; Sir Walter Ralegh and Sir Robert Cecil, £50; Sir Edwin Sandys, £20 and later he raised £100 from others. Lord Chamberlain Hunsdon (whose father, the first lord, had Shakespeare's 'Dark Lady', Emilia Bassano, for his mistress), gave 'a hundred new volumes, all in a manner new bound, with his arms and a great part in folio'. Shakespeare's patron, Southampton, gave £100 in 1605; Bodley wrote to the vice-chancellor that he was anxious to have Southampton's gift on record before the king's visit, and that he was procuring books from Venice and Lyons with it. Among the foreign books bought was a first edition of *Don Quixote*.

Bodley did not hold with almanacs, plays and 'riff-raff books', though he was not wholly opposed to plays: 'haply some plays may be worth the keeping, but hardly one in forty'. This would include Shakespeare's First Folio, and it was bought for the library. In the usual way it was disposed of when a later edition, the Third Folio, was received. It makes a good story that eventually in this century, in 1905, the original Bodleian copy returned to its old home.

Southampton's friend and leader, Essex, made a magnificent donation of 'about 300 volumes, of which the far greater part are books in folio'. Many of these had been carried off from the library of the Bishop of Faro, on Essex's return from the capture of Cadiz, where other books had been captured, including those which

Left: Sir Thomas Bodley, founder of 'the greatest single contribution made in Oxford to seventeenth-century culture'. His monument in Merton Chapel.

Sir Arthur Throckmorton presented to Magdalen.★ These Renaissance predators had cultivated tastes, and valued books.

Essex's follower, the deleterious Dean Wood, appears again as a benefactor. He bequeathed a hundred marks, and had been one of the donors of the earliest Chinese books to come to England. Later, the invaluable papers of Simon Forman came to the university through Ashmole, from Sir Richard Napier of All Souls. A letter from Napier as an undergraduate gives us a revealing glimpse into the interior of the library in early days.

I have made a fair way to go into the Library privately when I please, and there to sit from 6 o'clock in the morning to 5 at night . . . I have made the second Keeper [Verneuil] my friend and servant, who promised me his key at all times to go in privately; when as otherwise it is not opened above four hours a day. He hath pleasured me so far as to let me write in his counting-house, or his little private study, in the great public Library, where I may very privately write, and lock up all safely when I depart thence.

This studious young man had certainly circumvented Bodley's regulations, though after Sir Thomas's death.

The founder was faithfully supported by west country friends and relations. His brother, Captain Josias Bodley, gave an astronomical sphere and scientific instruments. Another brother, Laurence, a canon of Exeter, gave thirty-seven 'very fair and new bought books in folio', and later added £20; best of all, he persuaded the dean and chapter to give eighty-one of their most valuable manuscripts – which otherwise might have been lost in the Civil War, or sold away in our time – including, among Bishop Leofric's books, that to which we owe some of the best Anglo-Saxon poetry. As speedily as 1602 the library was ready for opening, and Bodley could write: 'Now methinks my long design is come to some perfection.' When he died in 1613 it was already the talk of England; unkind tongues said that he was 'so drunk with the applause and vanity of his Library' that he left little for his family. But they would not have achieved anything anyway; Bodley had won an immortal name for himself.

Bodley's will provided in part for a picture gallery, and gradually there was collected a splendid series of portraits, often historically interesting even if no great works of art. Thus was formed the earliest public picture gallery in England. In addition there has only recently been rediscovered – what had been obliterated by Victorian whitewash – a painted frieze of portraits to illustrate the whole history of European learning. The richest benefactions came between Bodley's death and the ruinous Civil War. In 1628 Sir Thomas Roe, who had been in India and the Levant, presented nearly thirty Greek manuscripts. Next year the chancellor, the Earl of Pembroke, whom we see in Le Sueur's bronze statue outside

★Cf my *Ralegh and the Throckmortons*.

The Bodleian picture gallery in 1829, showing the Earl of Pembroke's statue (now in the quadrangle), the original ceiling destroyed in 1830 and the painted frieze rediscovered under Victorian whitewash in 1949.

the entrance today, made a munificent gift of the Barocci library from Venice, some 242 volumes, mostly Greek. It was Laud who inspired Pembroke to this act of generosity, as also Sir Kenelm Digby to present Thomas Allen's valuable library, containing manuscripts of medieval science and the earliest copy of the *Chanson de Roland* from poor ruined Osney. When Laud became chancellor he proved himself one of the most generous patrons the Bodleian, or Oxford, ever had. Before his troubles fell upon him – simply for doing his duty for the Church – he had presented some 1,300 manuscripts in many languages. Among numerous treasures was a most valuable text of the *Anglo-Saxon Chronicle*, an early Irish manuscript with Cormac's Glossary, and ancient poetry; books from Würzburg rescued from the devastation of the Thirty Years' War in Germany. To these treasures Laud added a collection of rare coins, an astrolabe and the bronze bust of Charles I one sees on entering 'Duke Humphrey'.

It was fortunate that Bodley was not there to reject the bequest of Robert Burton, author of *The Anatomy of Melancholy*; for this rag-bag of a mind had got together a wonderful collection of miscellanea, 'baggage books', plays, pamphlets, newsprints and jestbooks, items of contemporary literary value – works of Elizabethan poets – and for the social life of the time. Already the foundations were being laid of the oriental collections which would be immensely enriched later in the century. And in the issue of its printed catalogues the Bodleian was to remain unsurpassed, thus encouraging the resort of European scholars to Oxford.

With the beginning of the Civil War progress was suspended; Charles I was reduced to borrowing £500 from the prosperous library chest – it was never repaid. When Oxford surrendered in 1646

the first thing General Fairfax did was to set a good guard of soldiers to preserve the Bodleian Library. He was a lover of learning and, had he not taken this special care, that noble library had been utterly destroyed, for there were ignorant senators enough who would have been contented to have had it so.

Perhaps this was unfair, for there were friends of learning on the other side. Bodley's second librarian, John Rous, was a friend of Milton, who had given a copy of his *Poems* of 1645; this was lost, and to replace it Milton gave another with a long Latin ode to the librarian. It makes one wonder what would have eventuated if Milton had come to his father's university – the Miltons were an Oxfordshire family – instead of going to Puritan Cambridge: perhaps he would not have been so bitterly hostile to the Laudian Church which was trying to restore order and beauty and music in the churches – regrettable in one so much of an aesthete!

When the Commonwealth came to an end in disillusionment and despair for such as he, another man of genius who had been earlier critical of royal government but then learned that Parliament was no better, John Selden, left his magnificent library of 8,000 volumes to the Bodleian. The largest collection to come in for two hundred years, it reflected the extraordinary width of Selden's interests in many subjects and languages. Selden was the first to collect Caxtons; the most admired of English scholars received autographed copies from the first writers of the age at home and abroad. Perhaps most remarkable were the early Mexican books and codices. The weight of Selden's books shortly necessitated the strengthening of Duke Humphrey's buttresses by Wren. The books came in as Charles II came back.

Meanwhile, Oxford was flourishing in other ways: by the founding of new colleges; the creation of that admirable institution, the Botanical Garden; the building of new college chapels, beautifying them with good woodwork and stained glass again after the philistine devastation of the Reformers; the strengthening of order and decency and discipline under the leadership of Laud as president of St John's, then his fostering care as chancellor when, in addition to everything else on his shoulders, he carried through the codification of the university statutes, by which it was governed for most of the next two centuries.

In 1609 Nicholas Wadham, of an old Somerset family, died; he had married Dorothy Petre, of that family erected on church lands, which had remained Catholic. One sees the couple today on their fine tomb in Ilminster church. Since they were childless they were able to do good works and found Wadham College. In 1610 the site of the Austin Friars was purchased from the city. The large sum of £11,000 was spent on its beautiful buildings, to a uniform design like a Somerset manor house. The college indeed had strong west country affiliations. Among its early undergraduates were Ralegh's son, Carew; Nicholas Monk, brother of the Devonshireman who managed the Restoration; the Commonwealth Admiral, Robert Blake; Sydenham, the brilliant doctor, from Dorset; John Mayow, physiologist and chemist, from Cornwall. John Gauden was an Essex man, but he was rewarded with the see of Exeter at the Restoration for his *Eikon Basilike*, which contributed so largely to the cult of the royal martyr after his execution. Somewhat unexpectedly, Wadham's most brilliant period, that of its most fruitful contribution to the nation, was to come during the Commonwealth.

The long internal peace was a prosperous time and the 1620s one of rapid expansion. An Abingdon merchant intended a handsome benefaction to Balliol, which much needed it; another Abingdon merchant came up with an offer, but the corporation of the town seem to have been too anxious to confine the endowment to townsfolk and scholars of Roysse's school there. Somehow, rather uncharacteristically, Balliol lost its chance. People seem to have thought that a new foundation was justified; fifty contributors added their cash, and the well-known Broadgates Hall was converted into a college, and given the chancellor's name with hopeful expectations. (No doubt Pembroke thought he had done enough in giving the Barocci library, which cost him £700, and he was rebuilding Wilton.)

In pursuit of his policy of restoring crown livings impropriated from the Church Charles I gave the neighbouring living of St Aldate's, and later added three Fellowships for Channel Islanders, one each for Pembroke, Exeter and Jesus. Broadgates Hall had been favoured by west country people, like Richard Carew of the *Survey of Cornwall*, for residence when members of Christ Church across the road. John Pym had been at Broadgates; now at Pembroke he was followed by his step-brother, Francis Rous – that Cornish family spelt themselves interchangeably Rous, Rouse or Rowse. Francis was a very prolific Rous, on

The Physic Garden in 1856. The oldest of its kind in Britain, it was founded under the shadow of Magdalen Tower to further learning – especially the faculty of medicine.

boring Puritan subjects; a Cromwellian, he was Speaker of Barebone's Parliament and, better, was provost of Eton. Better still he left three scholarships, but they were to be in divinity and for members of the Rous family or Eton. This college, like Wadham, was always poor but hardly less attractive – it was indeed pretty with its three early gardens.

In these same years the Botanical Garden was taking shape, the oldest of its kind in Britain. Henry Danvers, later Earl of Danby, had been Southampton's intimate friend – he remained always unmarried and so was able to be a public benefactor. In 1621 he was 'minded to become a benefactor to the university, determined to begin and finish a place whereby learning, especially the faculty of medicine, might be improved'. So the intention was originally to help medicine, growing suitable herbs and plants, and the proper name of it the Physic Garden. A beautiful site was chosen, on the Cherwell below Magdalen Bridge. Admirable walls were to be built, 'of the fairest for truth and beauty', to enclose what had been the medieval Jews' burying ground. Nicholas Stone built three fair portals, and the splendid entrance portico, after an Inigo Jones design.

And so came into being this exquisite place under the shadow of Magdalen Tower, its shady walks under the rare and feathery trees – gingko and pawlonia, arbutus and ailanthus, the service trees shedding their fruit, ruddy and gold, on the grass in autumn, the dark umbrella pines recalling the pines of the Pincio in Rome. Henry Danvers would have known the Jardin des Plantes at Paris, founded in 1597 while he was in exile with his brother. He spent some £5,000 on his project and, having failed to entice John Tradescant, the king's gardener, he at length got a veteran of the German wars as keeper. By the end of the Civil War Jacob Bobart had collected 1,600 plants, species and varieties; the fruit he grew helped to support him in the bad time. His cottage still survives, and the professor of botany's chair is made from the wood of one of his pear-trees. Henry Danvers – whose bearded bust we see above the portico, like a Roman emperor – lived to see his dream come true but he cannot have imagined its subsequent extensions, the Genetic Garden in the Parks, and the Arboretum at Nuneham Courtenay looking down upon the curve of the Thames below.

A characteristic book of the Jacobean time, and a very Oxonian work, is Robert Burton's *Anatomy of Melancholy*, 1621. He dated it 'from my study in Christ Church', which he described as 'the most flourishing college of Europe'. Wishing to write 'something worthy so noble a society', he had meant to write in Latin, but found the publishers reluctant to publish it. This was fortunate for him as an English author, for it became something of a best-seller, with a number of editions, to each of which Burton added. There arose a veritable cult of him and his book, particularly among the lovers of old and old-fashioned books. This continued as long as there was a culture based on the classics; for Burton had an enormous range of out-of-the-way classical reading, and his book is studded with Latin quotations not so accessible to us.

Nevertheless, he was a precursor too in a way, for he stands at the beginning of modern psychology with his acute observations of the phenomena not only of melancholy but of almost everything else in the human spirit – discontents, envy, love, jealousy, hate, anxiety, depression, even suicide, a subject which his fellow Oxonian, the poet Donne, was treating contemporaneously in his *Biathanatos*. Burton, indeed, is said to have investigated the subject practically, with an attempt at suicide. Describing himself as leading a solitary, silent life – though, as vicar of St Thomas's, he built the south porch there – he found it a source of amusement to go down to Folly Bridge to hear the bargemen swearing, 'at which he would set his hands to his sides and laugh most profusely'.

For himself there was travel in the realms of the mind, like his predecessor at Christ Church, Richard Hakluyt: 'He traversed desolate seas in search of fabled lands; he trod the Wall of China; off the coast of Madagascar he watched for the great Ruck; he penetrated the inner parts of America to discover the great city of Manoa, or Eldorado', like that Oriel man, Sir Walter Ralegh, who actually attempted it. His suggestion of merry company and bachelor mirth as a cure for melancholy may be said to have been taken up in the next generation by Aldrich and his friends making music together. Burton's suggestion of a college where discontented old maids might live was not followed up till the days of Miss Moberley and Miss Jourdain – who certainly made a literary sensation with the ghosts they saw at Versailles.

At length Burton reached the age predicted by his calculation of his own horoscope and incontinently died, leaving £100 for books for the Bodleian, and another £100 to Christ Church, which was to choose books from his own library. There they stand in a section on their own, brought together by a sympathetic fan of Burton: Sir William Osler, wisest and most beloved of physicians.

These were wonderful years at Oxford, with dismal Puritanism retreating within the university before the advance of younger men of wider views, more sympathetic to the refinements of culture. (What more proper to a university? Though it is culture that is in retreat today.) The active leadership was taken by Laud, who in 1606 defended the Catholicity of the English Church in a university sermon; for this he was delated by the Calvinists. But in 1611 he became president of St John's, and younger, civilized persons fell in behind him; he went on to become leader of the Church, with the full support of Charles I – though it was a pity that Archbishop Abbot lived so long, or Laud would not have been so pressed for time for his good work.

Sir Henry Savile founded two professorships, in the expanding subjects of astronomy and geometry; one White, a chair of moral philosophy. More attractively – and, in a sense, more real – the eminent historian Camden founded the professorship of ancient history, and Dr Heather that of music. We are reminded that the school of music possesses a striking portrait of the most brilliant performer among Elizabethan musicians and a composer of genius for the keyboard, Dr John Bull. He took his bachelor's degree in 1586, but his doctor's not until 1592: Anthony Wood says that the delay was caused by 'the rigid Puritans there that could not endure church music'. It is true that they hated the divine music the Elizabethan composers wrote for the Church. An Oxford scholar of cultivated tastes, Dr John Case, dared to take up the defence with *The Praise of Music*, and a subsequent Latin tract, for which the noblest of English composers, William Byrd, expressed his gratitude. We remember also that Byrd's successor as composer of church music, Orlando Gibbons, was born in Oxford, the son of a citizen. John Case was a friend of the artistic connoisseur, Richard Haydock of New College, who translated Lomazzo's standard work on the art of painting, and himself executed a number of incised emblematic brasses still in the chapels and churches at Oxford.★

★Cf my *The Elizabethan Renaissance: the Cultural Achievement*, pp. 86, 177–9.

Leicester had encouraged the revival of the University Press. A book had been printed at Oxford as early as 1478, only two years after Caxton's introduction of printing at Westminster in 1476. After 1519 printing at Oxford fell into desuetude, and London printers were anxious to keep a monopoly of the art. Printing was not resumed at Oxford till 1584, by Barnes the bookseller, with Leicester's encouragement and a loan of £100 from the university. It is pleasant to record that Dr John Case's book was the first to be printed. In 1633 Laud obtained a charter for Oxford's press, securing it rights and privileges; an excellent scholar himself, he was keen to see important manuscripts in the libraries put into print. An unforeseen result of the extension of printing was that, during the Civil War, Oxford was able to speak up for the king's cause and become the centre of royalist propaganda, publishing newsheets and papers, pamphlets, satires, squibs, ballads, as well as books.

Buildings sprang up everywhere before the disaster. At Wadham the chapel was finished with a big east window, signed 'Bernard van Linge, 1622': scenes of the life of Christ in emphatic colouring with bulky Flemish figures. In the lower lights of the windows a scheme was followed of Old Testament prophets on one side, apostles on the other: dated 1616. At Lincoln a similar scheme was followed for the chapel windows by Linge in 1629–31. At Christ Church work went forward, buildings extended in Canterbury and Peckwater, the splendid fan-vaulting of the hall staircase finished; in the cathedral van Linge windows were put up, of which the Victorians left only one specimen, the striking picture of Jonah beholding the city of Nineveh.

The earliest of these buildings was Savile's Great Quadrangle at Merton, built with exceptional speed in 1610, the tower of the four orders completing it in 1625–6. In 1618 Sir John Acland of Devonshire gave the money for the grand hall at Exeter, with its noble roof and ornamented screen. The rebuilding of Oriel was begun in 1619 and finished, hall, chapel and all, on the eve of the Civil War, in 1642. University College began, too late, in 1634; the work was held up by the war and completed after it. At Jesus Sir Eubele Thelwall, of an old Welsh family, finished the quadrangle with hall, chapel and charming lodgings for himself as principal, and built a library in what became the inner quadrangle later in the century. Magdalen put up new buildings for commoners beside the Cherwell, and in 1635 a fine portico in Inigo Jones style facing the chapel, making a proper logical entrance – a scheme ruined by the Victorians.

St John's the most beautiful of all these Caroline buildings was the work of Laud: he finished the Canterbury Quadrangle with two Renaissance colonnaded ranges, roundels with busts of the virtues such as Justice, Temperance, Charity – which were singularly unrepresented in the life of the time, while there was all too much Faith and Hope. Laud himself came to exemplify Fortitude, rather than

Prudence. There was a splendid classic gateway on either side, Corinthian columns and pediments, with niches for grand busts of Charles I and Henrietta Maria by Le Sueur. The east range, with its endearing garden front, formed the library, which Laud furnished, while much besides had been accomplished for chapel and president's lodgings. Truly, the clothier's son of Reading was a prince among benefactors.

The triumph of Caroline culture over dreary Calvinism was celebrated by a three-day royal visit in 1636, with plays, processions, convocation, bell-ringing, banquets. Young Prince Rupert of the Rhine was made a Master of Arts – with no thought of Marston Moor or Naseby. Cartwright's *Royal Slave* was produced at Christ Church, with scenery by Inigo Jones, music by Henry Lawes. Another play was put on at St John's at Laud's expense; indeed he spared no expense for all these works, which have lived on after him. He cared nothing for feasts and banquets himself; a mean-spirited comment on him by an historian of not much aesthetic appreciation emphasizes Laud's relief that only two spoons were found missing. In a similar spirit the odious Henry Burton attacked the archbishop in his *Divine Judgment upon Sabbath-Breakers*, for 'feasting and profane plays at Oxford'. While the beautiful baroque porch at St Mary's with madonna and child, executed by Nicholas Stone, was made a charge against Laud drawn up by the horrible Prynne, hounding him to his death in the Tower.

Archbishop Laud was killed by the Puritans for his good works.

Before that catastrophe much had been accomplished, of which we can enjoy the fruits, if much has been spoiled by changes of taste. The Laudian work in the chapel at St John's was thrown out for early nineteenth-century Gothic; the library was similarly spoiled. Fortunately the Caroline chapels of Lincoln and Oriel remain with their admirable rich woodwork. And even if many medieval brasses were ripped up during the Reformation and after, the Caroline monuments remain: a singularly chaste, and precociously classic white marble at Magdalen to two Lyttelton youths drowned in the river; the fine, if complex and allegorical, monuments to Sir Henry Savile and Sir Thomas Bodley at Merton. All three by Stone, while the grand Portman monument at Wadham, to my eye, looks like his handiwork too.

If we want to know what life was like from an (intelligent) student's point of view we have John Evelyn's. At sixteen and a half he was admitted a fellow-commoner at Balliol in the glad maytime of 1637. His father had arranged for George Bradshaw to be his tutor, whom Evelyn thought to have parts enough, but that 'his grudge' to the master 'took up so much of his time that he seldom or never had any opportunity to discharge his duty to his scholars'. With the Parliamentary Visitation after the Civil War, Bradshaw succeeded in supplanting the

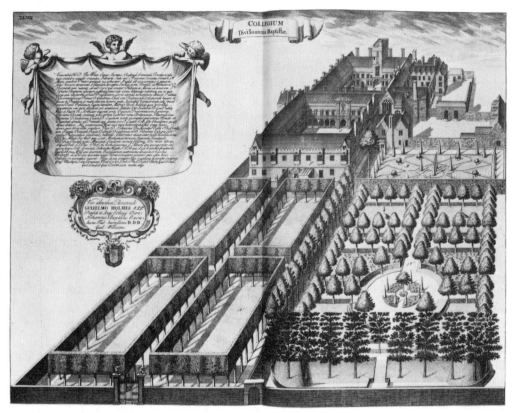

St John's College, the Caroline buildings of which were the work of Archbishop Laud, showing the formal gardens.

master. Young Evelyn spent his first week visiting the colleges and their rarities – we see that he was exceptional, his sensibility already aroused to such things, not just an ordinary student. In a week at the end of term he first answered an opponent at a Latin disputation in hall, two days later declaimed in chapel, and four days later first 'opposed' in hall. At Christmas Exeter presented a comedy, at which there was such a press that Evelyn injured a leg, which took till Easter to cure. In 1639 he 'began to look upon music' and was confirmed, at nineteen. Next year his father died and he did not return.

He tells us that he first saw coffee drunk there by a distinguished Greek, Canopios, who became a chaplain at Christ Church and was known for his musical compositions – expelled, of course, in 1648. Discipline had been very remiss at Balliol until the mastership of Parkhurst 1617–37. But the university was 'exceedingly regular under the exact discipline' of Laud as chancellor. 'At this time was the Church of England in her greatest splendour, all things decent and becoming the peace and the persons that governed.' Evelyn's phrase for it was 'that halcyon time'.

There is a classic account of these halcyon years, before the storm burst upon the country, in Clarendon's autobiography. Young Edward Hyde had been recommended for a demyship* at Magdalen by King James, but the president made a mistake in not admitting him and Hyde became a commoner of Magdalen Hall. His friends were all members of the famous circle around Lord Falkland at Great Tew, poets, philosophers, wits, divines – one of the most attractive groups of men ever to adorn the English scene, though not the most fortunate, for they were torn apart and dispersed by the war. Falkland's house,

where he usually resided – Tew, or Burford, in Oxfordshire – being within ten or twelve miles of the university, looked like the university itself, by the company that was always found there. There were Dr Sheldon, Dr Morley, Dr Hammond, Dr Earle, Mr Chillingworth, and indeed all men of eminent parts and faculties in Oxford, besides those who resorted thither from London.

Among these were poets like Sidney Godolphin and Edmund Waller, scholars like John Hales of Eton, country gentlemen of cultivated tastes like Sir Francis Wenman of Thame, and the humorous, crusty philosopher Hobbes.

Falkland kept open house:

All found their lodgings there as ready as in the colleges. Nor did the lord of the house know of their coming or going, nor who were in his house, till he came to dinner or supper, where all still met. Otherwise, there was no troublesome ceremony or constraint to forbid men to come to the house, or to make them weary of staying there. So that many came thither to study in a better air, finding all the books they could desire in his library, and all the persons together whose company they could wish, and not find in any other society.

Thus Chillingworth's famous book, *The Religion of Protestants a Safe Way to Salvation*, was thought out and formed in this atmosphere of philosophic discussion. Chillingworth was the son of an Oxford citizen, and a godson of Laud. But his mind was of a sceptical cast, and at one point he popped over to Rome. Laud brought him back to the safer way – nevertheless one of the charges against Laud was that he was secretly a Papist, simply because he wished for the reunion of Christendom. When Chillingworth fell mortally ill after his capture at Arundel Castle, his last days were tormented by the persecutions of a Puritan 'divine', Cheynell, who on Chillingworth's death flung a copy of his book into the grave that it might 'rot with its author and see corruption'. Cheynell was chagrined at making no headway with a superior intelligence.

*A kind of scholarship.

Sheldon from All Souls and Hammond from Christ Church would go out to Great Tew in the good days; when the bad days came and the king was defeated, they were allowed to attend him at Hampton Court, as Laud's friend and successor at St John's attended him on the scaffold and buried the body at Windsor. Clarendon gives us a faithful portrait gallery of these personalities: Sheldon, 'born to be Archbishop of Canterbury', who repaired the damage to the Church after the Restoration. There was witty Dr Morley of Christ Church who, when asked what the Arminians held, answered, 'all the best bishoprics and deaneries in England'. (This was what infuriated the Calvinists.) The answer somewhat retarded Morley's preferment; but he lived on till, after the Restoration, he was able to build the fine bishop's palace at Winchester. Dr Earle, author of the famous *Microcosmography*, a book of characters, was 'of a conversation so pleasant and delightful, so very innocent and so very facetious, that no man's company was more desired and more loved'.

Of Sidney Godolphin, 'There was never so great a mind and spirit contained in so little a room, so large an understanding and so unrestrained a fancy in so very small a body.' There was in him a touch of genius, as we can see from his *Poems*, published at Oxford in our time. He was killed in a skirmish at Chagford in 1643. He left a legacy to Hobbes, who dedicated the *Leviathan* to his memory. Hobbes wrote the great book in exile; when he saw how hopeless things were, with the meeting of the revolutionary Long Parliament, Hobbes was philosopher enough to skip over to Paris and stay there while the fighting fools fought it out. Like Clarendon he had been up at Magdalen Hall, and considered those earlier years the happiest in his life – compare Clarendon's celebrated apostrophe:

O fortunati nimium, bona si sua norint!★

In this blessed conjuncture . . . a small, scarce discernible cloud arose in the North, which was shortly after attended with such a storm that never gave over raging till it had shaken, and even rooted up, the greatest and tallest cedars of the three nations, blasted all its beauty and fruitfulness, brought its strength to decay and its glory to reproach, and almost to desolation. . . .

★'O too fortunate, if only you had known how happy you were!'

THE AGREEMENTS
MADE BETWEEN
HIS MAIESTY
AND THE
KNIGHTS, GENTLEMEN,
Free-Holders, and Inhabitants of the
County of OXFORD, for the better
Provision and Ordering of His
MAJESTIES Army.

AND
A DECLARATION
Of His MAJESTIES gratious
Acceptation thereof;

AND
His Royall Proclamation commanding the due observation
thereof in all Parts.

Printed by His MAJESTIES Command
At OXFORD, Sept. 30.
By LEONARD LICHFIELD, Printer
to the Vniversity. 1643.

6
Royalist Capital in the Civil War

NEVER was Oxford more important in the life of the nation than during the Civil War, when for four years it was the king's capital, the pivot of the Royalist cause, the centre to which his supporters throughout the country looked and to which many came, from which went out the defence of his cause, news and propaganda. Never was the city so crowded with grandees, important persons in state and church and army, with envoys and commissioners engaged in negotiations. Since it was the residence of the court there were the king's ministers and royal officials; the royalist Parliament met here, a majority of the Lords with perhaps a third of the Commons. Then there was the usual penumbra of a court, the hangers-on, the naughty ladies and dissolute men, the duellists and gamesters, poets and playwrights and journalists (a new profession). And at least two men of genius: Clarendon to write it all down in his *History*, and William Dobson, the first of English painters to date, who painted their portraits, in which we can still see the mingled strain and bravery of it all, the brief brilliance and sombre tragedy.

The sympathies of the citizens, like those of most of the middle-class townsfolk throughout the country, were with Parliament – as were apt to be those of the lesser gentry in the counties: they had something to be jealous of. On the king's side, on the whole, were the nobility and greater gentry, with their tenantry and retainers and, of course, the Church. Thus the university was overwhelmingly royalist – Puritan sympathies were relegated to a few colleges, like Exeter, and mostly to the remaining halls, like New Inn Hall.

In May 1642 young John Aubrey, at seventeen, went up to Trinity.

Peace. Looked through Logic and some Ethics. 1642, *Religio Medici* [Sir Thomas Browne's] printed, which first opened my understanding. But now Bellona thundered, and as a clear sky is sometimes suddenly overstretched with a dismal cloud and thunder, so was this serene peace by the civil wars, through the factions of those times – *vide* Homer's Odyssey. In August following my father sent for me home for fear.

Upon the outbreak of war in August 1642 Sir John Byron brought a body of troopers into Oxford to recruit among the scholars for the king. The city authorities applied to Parliament for support. In September Lord Saye and Sele ('Old

Left: A poster from the Civil War when, as the royalist capital, Oxford was 'never more important in the life of the nation'.

Subtlety') arrived with troops. A collateral descendant of William of Wykeham, he was a complete Wykehamist and, as founder's kin, a perpetual Fellow of New College. He had spent much time at Geneva, 'where he improved his disinclination to the Church, with which milk he had been nursed', and had married the daughter of Sir John Eliot, who had martyrised himself for parliamentary rights. However, Lord Saye did not wish to damage his old university, though his soldiers marvelled at 'the painted idolatrous windows' at Magdalen, and fired at Nicholas Stone's statue of the Virgin at St Mary's, to break her head and that of the child. 'Popish' books and pictures out of the churches were burned. However, Old Subtlety decided that Oxford could not be held, and moved out.

After his victory at Edgehill the king made a state entry into the city, attended by the princes, and someone of more value than they. This was William Harvey, discoverer of the circulation of the blood. He had been present at the battle, but had very sensibly read a book under a hedge, while the fighting fools fought. He was the king's doctor and, at the end, since there was nothing else to reward him with, Charles made him, a Cambridge man, warden of Merton. While he was away from Whitehall his lodgings were plundered by the rebels; his work on insects with its anatomical observations, on which he had been working for years, was lost. Harvey, who lived for research and to add to knowledge – a rather solitary worker – would say, ''Twas the greatest crucifying to him that ever he had in all his life.' One more among the losses of that appalling time.

Clarendon says of the king's reception that Oxford was 'the only city of England that he could say was entirely at his devotion; where he was received by the university to whom the integrity and fidelity of that place is to be imputed, with that joy and acclamation as Apollo should be by the Muses'. Convocation conferred degrees on the king's Palatine nephews, the Elector and Prince Rupert. Leading royalist churchmen returned, Dr Samuel Fell, dean of Christ Church, the president of Laud's St John's, and others. No one could have expected that this was the beginning of four years of resistance to the immensely superior resources of Parliament in men and money – with London and the eastern counties behind them they were certain to win in the end.

However, the king now had a capital – well situated strategically – to which his supporters flocked, where he could be 'in good ease', to which an army could be recruited and quartered round about. Meanwhile the sick and wounded from Edgehill were brought in, as also the body of the king's young cousin of the Lennox family, Lord d'Aubigny,

A gentleman of great hopes, of a gentle and winning disposition, and of very clear courage. He was killed in the first charge with the horse ... His body was brought off and buried at Christ Church. His two younger brothers, the Lord John and the Lord Bernard Stuart, were in the same battle and were both killed afterwards in the war.

There is a famous Van Dyck of two of these handsome young brothers in all the pride of aristocratic youth. The eldest of these three was given a grand funeral in the cathedral on 13 January. A week later Prince Rupert was able to depart with an army of some seven thousand.

During these months there had been drilling in Christ Church Meadows, on Bullingdon Green and in the New Parks out beyond Wadham. The citizens and county trained bands had been disarmed, a regiment formed out of them for the king's service, and two regiments out of university recruits. 'The great want at Oxford,' Clarendon tells us, 'if any one particular might deserve that style where all necessary things were wanted, was ammunition.' The town's supply of arms was taken and stored in the top story of the schools tower. As the university emptied of students for the benefit of war the various schools became warehouses and magazines; so did the neighbouring Brasenose gate tower, and the cloisters and tower of New College (thus it was that one of Haydock's incised brasses was destroyed).

To purchase ammunition the king was forced to 'borrow' £2000 from the university, and £2000 from the city – to which the city fathers added £500 *ex gratia*. (We see that the country had been prosperous, before its folly.) In January 1643 the mint arrived from Shrewsbury, and the king was reduced to requisitioning the plate of the colleges, besides what they had already sent him. Altogether some 1,610 pounds of plate was raised, the leading contributors being Magdalen with 296 pounds, and All Souls with 253 pounds; there follow Queen's, Trinity, Christ Church, Brasenose, each with over 100 pounds. St John's offered £800 to save its plate, then had to yield it up in addition. Communion plate was exempt; but two colleges managed to save more of their plate – thus it is that Corpus and New College have more medieval plate to show than any others.

Now the Oxford mint could begin to operate in empty New Inn Hall, and beautiful work it put out. The Oxford coins, *Exsurgat Deus*, were never debased (unlike our coinage today), and some of the pieces, especially the crown-piece, were of exquisite workmanship. So, too, were the medals struck to celebrate special occasions – the Kineton Medal for the meeting of Charles and Henrietta Maria above Edgehill in July 1643, and that commemorating Prince Rupert's taking of Bristol.

In February a commission from Parliament came to negotiate terms of peace; it was headed by Northumberland, and included Bulstrode Whitelocke, who describes it for us.

The commissioners were admitted by the lords, two with each lord in their coaches, which were with six gallant horses in every coach, and a great number of their servants on horseback to attend them. Some of the soldiers and of the rascality of the town, and others of better rank though of like quality, as we passed by, reviled us with the names of

Edward Hyde, first Earl of Clarendon, historian and bene-factor to the university.

'Traitors' and 'Rebels', but we took no notice of them. Only we acquainted some of the King's officers therewith, who seemed to be very angry at it.

We had our first access to the King in the garden of Christ Church, where he was walking with the Prince, and divers of the lords attending him. All of us kissed his hand ... according to our several degrees ... Mr Waller was the last. The King said to him, 'Though you are the last, yet you are not the worst, nor the least in my favour.' After we had all kissed the King's hand, the Prince gave us his hand to kiss.

The Earl of Northumberland read the Propositions to the King with a sober and stout carriage.

When the king questioned a point, Northumberland's Percy blood rose, and he said, 'Your majesty will give me leave to proceed'. The king said, 'Aye, Aye,' and the earl read them all through to the bitter end.

Whitelocke says that

the King used us with great favour and civility; his General, Ruthven, and divers of his lords and officers came frequently to our table. The King himself did us the honour sometimes to accept of part of our wine and provisions, which the Earl sent to him, when we had anything extraordinary.

Whitelocke later set down his impression that in the negotiations

the King manifested his great parts and abilities, strength of reason, and quickness of apprehension, with much patience in hearing what was objected against him; wherein he allowed all freedom and would himself sum up the arguments and gave a most clear judgment upon them. His unhappiness was that he had a better opinion of others' judgments than of his own, though they were weaker than his own.

Actually Parliament expected the king to give way on all the main points; Clarendon thought he should have made some concessions, and in the end the negotiations came to nothing.

The war went on.

That February, while the commissioners were there, we learn from Aubrey,

with much ado I got my father to let me to beloved Oxon again, then a garrison *pro rege*. I got Mr Hesketh, Mr Dobson's man [evidently the painter's] to draw the ruins of Osney three or four ways before 'twas pulled down. Now the very foundation is digged up. In April I fell sick of the small pox at Trinity College, and when I recovered, after Trinity week, my father sent for me into the country again.

Aubrey did not return until the war was over. In November 1646 he got back to college 'to my great joy, was made much of by the Fellows, had their learned conversation, looked on books, music'. He remained till Christmas 1648, when his father fell sick and Aubrey had to take over the encumbered estate.

It is to these periods of broken residence that we owe his vivid pen-pictures of what Oxford was like during the Civil War, its denizens and characters with their oddities. He had a sharp eye for quirks of personality, and his portrait of the president of Trinity, Ralph Kettell, is as vivacious as it is endearing.

He was irreconcilable to long hair, called them hairy scalps. When he observed the scholars' hair longer than ordinary, he would bring a pair of scissors in his muff, which he commonly wore, and woe be to them that sat on the outside of the table. I remember he cut Mr Radford's hair with the knife that chips the bread on the buttery-hatch.

This, while the old boy sang a refrain from *Gammer Gurton's Needle*.

Naughty court-ladies would come to tease the old Doctor.

Our grove was the Daphne for the ladies and their gallants to walk in, and many times my Lady Isabella Thynne would make her entry with a theorbo or lute played before her. I have heard her play on it in the grove myself, which she did rarely [i.e. exceptionally well]: for which Mr Edmund Waller hath in his Poems for ever made her famous ... She was most beautiful, most humble, charitable, etc., but she could not subdue one thing. I remember one time this lady and fine Mistress Fanshawe (her great and intimate friend, who lay at our college) would have a frolic to make a visit to the President. The old Doctor quickly perceived that they came to abuse him. He addresses his discourse to Mistress Fanshawe, saying, 'Madam, your husband and father I bred up here, and I knew your grandfather; I know you to be a gentlewoman, I will not say you are a whore, but get you gone for a very woman.'

Many were the tricks put upon the Doctor. He dragged his foot a little, 'by which he gave warning, like the rattle-snake, of his coming'. One of the Egertons, 'a good mimic, would go so like him that sometimes he would make the whole chapel rise up, imagining he had been entering in'. The old boy sang 'a shrill high treble; but there was one who had a higher, and would play the wag with the Doctor to make him strain his voice up to his'. He was a good Church of England man, and preached every Sunday at his parsonage at Garsington.

Upon Trinity Sunday, our festival day, he would commonly preach at the college, whither a number of the scholars of other houses would come to laugh at him. He was a person of great charity. Where he observed diligent boys that he guessed had but a slender exhibition from their friends, he would many times put money in at their windows, that his right hand did not know what his left did. Servitors [poor scholars that waited at table] that wrote good hands he would set on work to transcribe for him and reward them generously.

Aubrey concludes,

'Tis probable this venerable Doctor might have lived some years longer and finished his century, had not those civil wars come on: which much grieved him, that was wont to be absolute in the college, to be affronted and disrespected by rude soldiers. I remember, being at the Rhetoric lecture in the hall, a foot-soldier came in and brake his hour-glass ... The dissoluteness of the times grieving the good old Doctor, his days were shortened.

A consequence of the failure of the Oxford negotiations was to strengthen Parliament's determination to prosecute the war, and something that took place at Oxford came to the hand of that expert politician, John Pym, who well knew how to make the most of it. The poet Waller, who had been in the negotiations, was all in favour of peace, and realized well that it was the extremists on both sides who were making peace impossible. When he returned to London he openly aired his views – a poet, he was too expressive for a politician. He was betrayed by a servant to Pym, who had a good intelligence service. At the same time Lord d'Aubigny's widow came down with a pass to settle her husband's affairs with the king, and was by him entrusted with a small box to deliver – it was thought to Waller, who often visited her. Clarendon himself never knew the inwardness of Waller's plot; but Pym used it to scare people with, in the manner with which we have been made so familiar in our time.

Pym used the scare to drive on the war, and shortly brought off his masterpiece, the Scottish alliance, by which the Scots turned the scales in the war (they repented of it shortly) in return for the imposition of their Presbyterian Covenant, quite unrepresentatively, upon the English at large.

At Oxford the fortifications were strengthened. In March 1643 the Cherwell

Right: Edward III granting a charter of privileges to the Chancellor of Oxford University.

Privilegia concessa Vniuersitati Oxon. Dno nostro rege Edwardo tertio. Infra villam Oxon. et suburbijs eiusdem. et in pndreto extra portam borialem. Scripta p Willm Wiston Cancellar prediat vniuersitatis. &c. mo. smo.

Anno dni millesimo ccc lxv. qnto

Edwardus dei gracia rex Anglie et Francie et Dominus hibernie Archiepis epis Abbatibus prioribus Comitibus Baronibus iusticiarijs vicecomitibus ppositis ministris et omnibus Ballivis et fidelibus suis Salutem. Inspeximus magnam cartam confirmacionis cui nup fieri fecim in hec ita Ed Wardus dei gra rex Anglie Dominus hibernie et Dux Aquit Regnis epis abbatibus prioribus Comitibus Baronibus iusticiar vicecomitibus ppositis ministris et omnibus Ballivis et fidelibus suis cariatem Inspeximus litteras patentes confirmacionis Edwardi nup Regis Anglie pris nostri in hec ita Edwardus dei gra rex Anglie Dominus hibernie et Dux Aquit Omnibus ad quos psentes liae puenerint Salutem Inspeximus litteras patentes quas Dominus H quondam Rex Anglie Auus nr fecit Cancell et vniuersitati Oxon in hec ita H dei gra Rex Anglie Dominus hibernie Dux Normann Aquit et comes Andeg Omnibus ad quos psentes liae puenerint Salutem Nouerit nos p quiete vniuersitat studencium Oxon de gra qua nra concessisse Cancell et vniuersitati pdce qd nundum nobis placuerit in causis excitor cuprinitus liatis aut ieceptis aut tapacionibus seu secacionibus Domor aut equor conductis veudicis seu comedatis seu pannis et victualibz ortum sentibz seu alijs quibzdam rerum mobilium comitibus in municipio aut cuibus Oxon fatris nra phibito non aperat Et huiuscausae toiam Cancell et vniuersitati Oxon non obstante phibicoe nra Deleant In cuius rei testimon has liae nras fieri secim patentes teste me ipo apud Ledyng iij die may Anno regni nri xviij Inspeximus etiam quasdam alias litteras patentes quas Wen Auus noster fecit pdce vniuersitati in hec ita H dei gra Rex Anglie Dominus hibernie Dux Normann Aquit et comes Andeg Omnibus ad quos psentes liae puenie Salutem Sciatis quod ad tranquillitatem et vtilitatem tam magior et scolarium vniuersitatis Oxonie quam burgencium et aliorum eadem villa Domos Benum concessimus eadem vniuersitati qd de teto omis Domus eiusdem. villae Oxonie et scolaribz inhitate et inhitande de attingnemento in attingne uiri jetapentur secundum arbitrium tapator excitor et laicor eiusdem pte ligator. Et nolumus qd ista jetapacio incipiat a tempe confeccionis psentium liam. eu cuius rei testimon has liae nras eadem vniuersitati fieri secim patentes. T me ipo apud Wodestok. ij die ffebro Anno regni nri quadragesimo Inspeximus etiam quasdam alias lias quas Wen Auus nr fecit dce vniuersitati in hec ita H dei gra Rex Anglie Dominus hibernie et Dux Aquit Omnibus ad quos psentes lae puenint Salutem Inspeximus lias quas vniuersitat scolarium Oxonie fieri secim Anno regni nri tricesimo nono sub sigillo nro quo tunc utebamur in hec ita H dei gra Rex Anglie Dominus hibernie Dux Normann Aquit et comes Andeg Omnibus ad quos psentes lie puenint Salutem Sciatis qd ad pacem et tranquillitatem necnon vtilitatem vniuersitatis scolarium Oxonie puidim et concessimus qd quicumque Aldermanni fiant in Oxon et viri de discrecioribus et legalioribz burgens eiusdem villae asspaciantur ipsis Aldermannis qui omnes iurent nobis fidelitatem et eam asspicientes

V. p. 73. 2

was dammed to render the city unassailable from the east; it is probable that the raised walk at Magdalen now known as Addison's walk, with its water-ditch, was made at this time, for it leads to a bastion commanding the Cherwell at the end. This was called Dover Pier, from its being commanded by the Earl of Dover. On the south and west river and marsh protected the city. On the north a series of defences were made, ditches dug, bulwarks thrown up, the outermost north of St Giles's church; one can still see a remnant of bulwark in the raised walk in the Fellows' garden at Wadham. In a sortie by Prince Rupert there happened what was equivalent to a royalist victory: John Hampden was mortally wounded on Chalgrove Field. I often think of it, driving out from Oxford across the great open field, and of that figure that was observed 'to ride off the field before the action was done, which he never used to do, with his head hanging down and resting his hands upon the neck of his horse'. The king directed the parson of Chinnor to inquire after him. But the wound was fatal: Hampden died in the Greyhound Inn at nearby Thame. He was a sad loss to the country: 'a very wise man and of great parts, and possessed with the most absolute spirit of popularity, that is, the most absolute faculties to govern the people of any man I ever knew'. This is a tribute from an opponent, Clarendon. But, indeed, if Pym and Hampden had lived, with their abilities and prestige, there would have been a civilian settlement, instead of the military dictatorship that eventuated.

Meanwhile the spirited queen had made her way back from the continent, where she had been buying arms and ammunition with the proceeds of the crown jewels, landed in the north and was approaching the city with a convoy. Charles went out to meet her on the ridge above Edgehill; together they were received with bell ringing, poems, a medal struck, bonfires to celebrate royalist successes in the west. Henrietta Maria took up her residence in Merton; a postern was cut in the wall of a canon's garden at the back of Christ Church – one can still see the spot – so that Charles could have private access to her.

That summer of 1643, with the royal cause at its height, three influential earls sought to work their way back, in particular, the Earl of Holland.

He came frequently in the afternoon to Merton College, where the Queen lay and where the King was for the most part at that time of the day, and both their majesties looked well upon him and spake to him in public as occasion was administered. Sometimes the King went aside with him to the window in the same room, where they spake a quarter or half an hour together, out of the hearing of anybody; which the Queen did oftener, in the same manner.

What Holland was after was an office in the household; but the king regarded him coolly, and was under pressure from the Marquis of Hertford who came to Oxford to claim the post. Seeing how the coast lay, Holland took the oppor-

Left: Christ Church kitchen by Ackermann.

tunity of a dark night and a good guide to steal away into the enemy's quarters and make his peace with Parliament. When examined before it, this disingenuous politician pleaded the excuse that 'after he heard of the cessation in Ireland [i.e. Ormonde's truce with the Catholics] his conscience would not give him leave to stay any longer with them at Oxford.'

Nevertheless, Clarendon was of the opinion that the approaches of these earls should have been received more favourably: to have given one or other of them office would have divided opponents, while the impression was fostered that the king and all about him were implacable.

The war went on.

It is not our business to describe it, merely to keep our eye on Oxford. The queen's presence was not an unmixed blessing. She was temperamental in her likes and dislikes, always a liability to Charles. She disliked his greatest servants, Laud and Strafford; she undermined the archbishop's position by her proselytizing Catholicism at court and exposed him to his enemies as a crypto-Catholic, which he never was. Having no good judgement, she preferred sycophants and light-weights like Henry Jermyn. The only good thing to be said about her was that she had courage, and great taste. But faction raged round her:

The temper of the Court was no better than that of the Army, and the King was so much troubled with both that he did not enjoy the quiet his condition required ... All this wonderfully indisposed the lords and persons of quality in the town who did not wish to see the Court as it had been, or the Queen herself possessed of so absolute a power as she had been formerly.

There were quarrels and disputes, receptions and ceremonies, duels and frolics, weddings and funerals to variegate the scene, while the more numerous parliamentary armies threatened and withdrew – for they too had their differences and conflicts of person and policy; their General, Essex, was a military incompetent with only a famous name to commend him. In December 1642 the Spanish ambassador was received; in October 1643 the French, the Comte d'Harcourt, of the family that gave its name to Stanton Harcourt and is still there today. On Maundy Thursday the traditional rite of washing the feet of twelve poor men was performed in Christ Church hall. The Marquis of Hertford was made chancellor of the university in place of the renegade Pembroke and Montgomery.

Death was beginning to take its toll in various ways. Sir Arthur Aston, governor of the city – and a very unpopular one – was attacked one dark winter's night in a side street; later he broke a leg, had to have it amputated and was relegated. Sir Thomas Byron, who commanded the Prince of Wales's regiment, 'a very valuable and experienced officer', was fatally wounded by one of his own captains over a pay-dispute. The captain was shot to death at 'Mr Napper's barn'; the

Nappers owned Holywell manor, so that is where the execution took place. Sir Thomas died of his wound in February, and was buried in the cathedral beside Lord Grandison, who had been mortally wounded at the siege of Bristol. This handsome young Villiers, of that singularly beautiful family, had been painted by Van Dyck, but is more remembered as the father of Barbara Castlemaine, who gave so much trouble (and so many bastards) to Charles II. He must have provided the money later on for the chaste white marble monument over her father's grave.

By now camp fever was raging in the overcrowded town. That summer the son of the great scholar, Sir Henry Spelman, died of it and was given a stately funeral in St Mary's, with a sermon by Archbishop Ussher. This was Sir John Spelman, a Cambridge follower of the king, who was engaged in publishing his father's works. The king called him to Oxford, made him a member of his privy council, and intended him for a secretary of state. He had been given a room in Brasenose. Secretary Nicholas had his lodgings at Pembroke, which was crowded with a hundred guests. Clarendon, then Sir Edward Hyde, as chancellor of the exchequer, lodged at All Souls, which before the end was down to one meal a day.

Among those who died of camp fever was the promising poet and dramatist, Thomas Cartwright of Christ Church, at thirty-two. We have met him as the author of the *Royal Slave* in the good times – the famous headmaster of Westminster, Busby, had acted in it as a youth. Lord Saye and Sele had imprisoned Cartwright briefly, for he had much influence as 'the most florid and seraphical preacher in the university'. Recently he had written his fine elegy for Sir Bevil Grenville, killed at Lansdown. Now the king was to wear black for him; when asked why, Charles said, with his usual grace, that 'since the Muses had so much mourned for the loss of such a son, it would be a shame for him not to appear in mourning for such a subject'.

From Cambridge there arrived such Royalists as the poets Crashaw and Cowley. The delicate sensibilities of Crashaw had been revolted by the rising spirit of Puritanism; his college was Peterhouse, where Laud's example and precepts were followed, and so the beautiful chapel, which had inspired poems, was sacked. When the Presbyterian Covenant was imposed on Cambridge, six Fellows of Peterhouse alone were expelled, among them another young poet, Joseph Beaumont of that celebrated family. Crashaw stayed briefly at Oxford, on his way abroad and into the Roman church. His friend, the much admired Cowley, expelled from Trinity, followed him to Oxford; Cowley was given hospitality at St John's, where he became friendly with sympathetic spirits of the Falkland circle. Alas, that the one to become the greatest poet of them all was on the unpoetic side!

Others went about their work. John Birkenhead, a bright young scholar, whom Laud had recommended to All Souls for a Fellowship, devoted himself to writing the royalist newspaper, *Mercurius Aulicus*. Thomas Willis, the famous doctor to be, whose father was killed in the defence of Oxford, served in the king's regiment, studying medicine the while and later set up in Merton Street, whence he wrote his treatises on fevers. Archbishop Ussher, good man, was not to be deflected from his scholarly work, though preaching regularly at St Aldate's and All Saints. A moderate Calvinist, he was in favour with Parliament and was summoned to the Westminster assembly of divines. A better scholar than any there, i.e. John Selden, said of him, 'they had as good inquire whether they had best admit Inigo Jones, the king's architect, to the company of mouse-trap makers'. Ussher made it clear that he regarded the assembly as illegal, where-upon Parliament confiscated his library. Sir William Dugdale took his opportunity to get forward with his antiquarian researches in the Bodleian.

At New Year 1644 the king summoned the royalist Parliament to Oxford: they responded well, for the letter they addressed to the Parliament at West-minster was subscribed by forty-three 'dukes, marquises, earls, viscounts and barons of the House of Peers, and 118 members of the House of Commons'. The king addressed both Houses in Christ Church (was he audible, one wonders, with the impediment in his speech?); they then adjourned, the Commons to the Divinity School, the Lords to the Convocation House recently built under Laud's chancellorship. Nothing came of these approaches: Westminster was determined to win and, with the aid of the Scots' army, was certain to do so. The law courts were similarly divided. The king had adjourned them to Oxford. Lord Keeper Littleton followed his command and kept his court of chancery in the Convocation House; here he died in the summer of 1645 and was buried in the cathedral, where a grand monument was erected – Ionic columns, pediment and urn – after the Restoration. Sir John Bankes, Chief Justice of Commons Pleas, had died the year before and was buried nearby. The court of requests sat *pro forma*, under Sir Thomas Aylesbury, in the school of natural philosophy. But there was little point in these proceedings: only the arbitrament of war would decide.

That winter very large forces were raised by the Parliament in London with the intention of reducing Oxford in the spring. By April the queen was within a month of bearing a child,

which wrought upon her majesty's mind very much, and disposed her to so many fears and apprehensions of her safety that she was very uneasy to herself. She could not endure to think of being besieged there, and resolved not to stay there but to go into the West; from whence, in any distress, she might be able to embark for France.

The king escorted her out of the city as far as Abingdon, where he took leave of her, never to see her again. She journeyed to Exeter where, after a dangerous delivery, her last child was born, Charles II's favourite sister, Minette. Charles returned to Oxford to prorogue his Parliament, to put his case in the counties; they were to meet again in October.

Parliament's armies under Essex and Waller drew near the faithful city. Lady Fanshawe's memoirs tell us what a dispiriting time it was: 'We had the perpetual discourse of losing and gaining towns or men; at the windows the sad spectacle of war, sometimes plague, sometimes sicknesses of other kind, by reason of so many people being packed together.' She lost her brother thus, William Harrison, buried in Exeter chapel. She herself, who had been brought up in a spacious country house, was packed into 'a baker's house in an obscure street and, from rooms well furnished, to lie in a very bad bed in a garret, to one dish of meat and that not the best ordered, no money – no clothes more than a man or two brought in their cloak bags'. Yet war has always been propitious to love. In maytime 1644 she was married to young Richard Fanshawe, who had just been appointed secretary to Prince Charles, out at Wolvercote beside the upper Thames. 'None was at my wedding but my dear father who, at my mother's desire, gave me her wedding ring, with which I was married; and my sister Margaret, and my brother and sister Boteler, Sir Edward Hyde, afterwards Lord Chancellor, and Sir Geoffrey Palmer, the King's Attorney.' Even the sad and sober king managed to get a little relief from his troubles: a visit to Mr Edwards' tennis court with Prince Rupert (for the game of real, or royal, tennis); an occasional day's hunting in his own park out at Woodstock.

Early in June the Parliament's armies converged upon Oxford, and the king was nearly shut up there. His foot were quartered towards the Cherwell, the horse near the Isis, with orders to prevent the crossing. But Essex got across at Sandford ferry on the lower Thames and was able to post himself at Islip. Charles stole out of the city by night, made a rapid march across the Cotswolds with Waller in pursuit, and reached Worcester. He was able to collect an army, while Waller's forces, frustrated, melted away. In the city the citizens raised a regiment; the gentry and their servants, with the scholars, two more, and did duty till the king's return. In July the whole of the north was lost to him by the disaster of Marston Moor – bonfires were lit in Oxford on the false news of a victory. Essex made the mistake of marching west into Cornwall, where the king followed and forced the surrender of his army, though the horse escaped. More bells, bonfires and shooting of cannon in Oxford for victory. Meanwhile, gallant Colonel Gage had forced the surrender of moated Boarstall House below Brill, which guarded the eastern approach and ensured the levying of contributions in money, food and fodder upon the borders of Buckinghamshire. One sees the evidences of the fighting there today – the noble gate-house tower remains, but the church was so damaged that it had to be rebuilt, and the great house is gone.

In August sixteen cartloads of sick and wounded soldiers were brought into the city. In October the Parliament's forces occupying Abingdon got as near as Botley in the suburbs, where they fired the mill, given over to powder-making. At the same time a fire consumed a section of the city around present-day George Street. On his way back from his victory in Cornwall the king's army was engaged by that of Manchester and Cromwell at the second battle of Newbury. At the first, in 1643, Falkland, despairing of peace, had thrown away his life, deliberately riding into the *mêlée*. The second was followed by a violent quarrel between Manchester and Cromwell, who considered that the Earl had consciously refrained from crushing the king's forces. It was followed by the rise of Cromwell and the New Model Army: a portent.

Charles returned safely to winter quarters at Oxford, his army lying about Faringdon. He entered 'to the universal joy on 23 November, a season of the year fit for all the troops to be in their winter quarters. The king was exceedingly pleased to find how much the fortifications there had been advanced by the care and diligence of the lords, and was very gracious in his acknowledgment of it to them.' Colonel Gage, who had done so well at Boarstall, was knighted – and early next year was mortally wounded near Culham, a marked loss to the army and the city, where he was very popular. In London the evil Prynne drove on his campaign against Laud to the death. On the eve of the war the archbishop had taken leave of the university he loved so much, and for which he had done such great things, and resigned his chancellorship since he could do no more for them. Impeached by Parliament, he defended himself with such ability, acquitting himself in the eyes of all fair-minded persons, that his enemies were reduced to killing him by attainder, i.e. by act of Parliament. 'And so, without troubling themselves farther, they gave order for his execution', though no guilt could be found in him. The archbishop had long been sick of the folly of the world, and was glad to leave it; though he had fainted away at the spectacle of his friend Strafford going to the scaffold, he faced his own death without faltering. Laud's only crime was that he had no gift for popularity – though we should know, if only from this story, what that is worth.

This criminal execution, which came to be rightly regarded by the Church as a martyrdom in its cause, was no good omen for the peace negotiations at Uxbridge in February 1645. Parliament had sent the Earl of Denbigh with its reiterated propositions to Oxford in November. The king received him in Christ Church garden. Denbigh was a man torn between two sides: his family were Royalist, his father and uncle were both killed fighting for the king. He had opted for Parliament out of ambition, though his mother adjured him 'to leave that merciless company which was the death of his father'. He was appointed to lead the parliamentary commissioners at Uxbridge; where, Clarendon tells us, he showed 'much greater parts and saw further before him into the desperate designs of that party that had then the power than either of the other three' – Northumberland, Pembroke or Salisbury.

A fundamental issue in dispute was the Church, and Charles appointed a strong body of Oxford divines, headed by Sheldon and Hammond, to defend its position. They took a conciliatory line, arguing for the retention of episcopacy as the guarantee of order, but shorn of coercive powers (though the whole moral of the disorder of the time showed that these were necessary enough). For example: the king's commissioners on arriving at Uxbridge were surprised by an inflammatory sermon from a young minister who accompanied Parliament's commissioners, telling the people that the men from Oxford were 'men of blood' (the usual Puritan jargon) who were sent only to amuse them until they could do some mischief to them. This young man, inciting the people to mutiny was inappropriately named Love. A few years later, Oliver Cromwell – whose instinct for power was infallible and would not put up with nonsense from a young sectary – 'had his head cut off upon Tower Hill for being against the army'.

Alexander Henderson, the leading Scotch divine, was not much better: he harangued the commissioners, 'rather with rhetoric than logic', urging a complete change in the English Church to a Presbyterian basis. He was so much out of touch with reality that he never realized how small a minority of the English people would welcome such a delightful transformation. Charles I, though a Scot, knew better than that and in his heart never accepted Presbyterianism for England. Later on Henderson had the conceit to think that he could bring the king over to his ludicrous point of view; when he found that Charles held firm to his own position, Henderson went home to Scotland broken-hearted.

It is hardly surprising in these circumstances that no progress was made. Clarendon learned a good deal of the differences and disillusionments on the other side. Denbigh privately 'informed him more fully of the wicked purposes of those who then governed the Parliament than others apprehended or imagined, and had a full prospect of the vile condition himself and all the nobility should be reduced to; yet thought it impossible to prevent it by any activity of their own'. To such a pass things had come. When the commissioners came back to Oxford the king 'received them very graciously and thanked them for the pains they had taken'. But he 'spake to those he trusted most at that time with much more melancholy of his own condition and the state of his affairs than he had used to do'. Henceforth there was confusion and growing despair; only the divisions on the other side gave any ground for hope. Only power, the arbitrament of force, would settle men's fatuous disputes of opinion.

That same month the House of Lords in London assented to the New Model Army – with all the energy and force of Oliver Cromwell behind it.

The Negative Oath,

I A. B. Do fwear from my heart, that I will not d'reċtly nor indirectly adhere unto or willingly affıſt the King in this Warre, or in this cauſe againſt the Parl. And I do likewiſe ſwear that my comming and ſubmitting my ſelf under the power and proteċtion of the Parl, is without any manner of deſigne whatſoever, to the prejudice of the proceedings of the two Houſes of this Parl. and without the direċtion, privity, and advice of the King, or any of his Councell, or Officers, other then what I have now made known, So help me God, and the Contents of this Book.

1646.

The King Eſcapes out of Oxford in a diſguiſed maner

Ordered that whoſoever conceals the Kings perſon, ſhall be a Traytor. *A Letter concerning the Kings coming to the* Scots *Army May* 5. 1646.

A page from Clarendon's *History* illustrating King Charles's escape from Oxford.

At Oxford it was resolved to send the Prince of Wales, with an independent command, into the west. The western leaders came to the city to urge a western association, of Dorset, Somerset, Devon and Cornwall, on the model of the eastern counties association. A chapter of the Order of the Garter was held at Christ Church, no doubt to raise spirits. Upon that the king adjourned his Oxford Parliament – his real sentiments about which were revealed after Naseby when his secret correspondence with the queen was deciphered: 'I being now freed from the place of base and mutinous motions (that is to say, our Mongrel Parliament here) as of the chief causers – for which I may justly expect to be chidden by thee – for having suffered thee to be vexed by them.' This did much damage among the Royalists when revealed.

After Charles had left Oxford and was with the Scots at Newcastle, Henrietta Maria – 'who was never advised by those who either understood or valued his true interest,' said Clarendon – sent an envoy to him urging him to sacrifice the Church in order to come to terms with Parliament. Clarendon regarded the messenger as no more suitable than the message. For this was Sir William Davenant, 'an honest man and a witty, but in all respects inferior to such a trust'. Davenant was born at Oxford, his father the keeper of the Crown Tavern, his mother 'a very beautiful woman, and of a very good wit, and of conversation extremely agreeable'. Davenant liked to think that he was a by-blow of William Shakespeare, on his way through Oxford between Stratford and London. This is not at all improbable – there are one or two indications that it was so.

The king 'knew the person well enough under another character than was like to give him much credit in the argument in which he was entrusted', i.e. regarded him as a lightweight. It was Jermyn and Culpepper, whose judgments also were of no gravity, who had advised Henrietta Maria; but when Davenant dared to add his own opinion to theirs, 'his majesty was transported with so much passion and indignation that he gave him more reproachful terms, and a sharper reprehension, than he did ever towards any man, and forbade him to presume to come again into his presence.'

Meanwhile Cromwell was drawing closer to the city. In April he raided Islip and captured a hundred horse, besides the slain – including one of the Wilmots, the Earl of Rochester's family. Next day Cromwell summoned Bletchingdon House to surrender. It was held by Colonel Windebank, a son of the secretary of state who early absconded abroad, as a crypto-Catholic, to avoid impeachment. The old romantic tradition at Oxford is that young Colonel Windebank had married, was entertaining a wedding party and that the house was full of women – hence his surrender without resistance. For this he was tried by court-martial and sentenced to death; again, the tradition is that he was shot against the city wall outside Merton – the section near Christ Church known as 'Colonel Windebank's wall'. But it would seem that he was shot to death within the Castle. The summer before a more eminent colonel on the other side had been exchanged after a brief imprisonment there: this was the well-known republican, Ludlow.

That summer saw the ruin of the royalist cause with the disaster of Naseby, Prince Rupert's surrender of Bristol, the defeats, the long-contested retreat and final break-up in the west. Not all the ordnance shot off in Oxford for Montrose's Pyrrhic victories in Scotland, nor rumours of local successes in the west, afforded any ground for hope. The long convoys bringing cattle, sheep and provisions to Oxford could only be for the purpose of a siege. The case really was, as a royalist commander put it: 'You may go play now – unless you fall out among yourselves.' This, of course, was precisely what happened: it was largely the divisions on the dominant side that enabled the weaker to hold out as long as it did.

At New Year the king was negotiating desperately with Parliament. The French ambassador, Montreuil, was in Oxford that winter, playing an ambivalent role; the king hoped for an arrangement through him with the Scots, now disillusioned with the army and its patronage of the Independents against pure milk-of-the-word Presbyterianism. A final jollity was the marriage, in the choir of the cathedral, on 26 February, of a groom of his majesty's bedchamber to Mary Townsend: 'The King gave her, she being the admired beauty of the times.' This must have aroused sad memories, for she was the daughter of the court poet, Aurelian Townsend, who had written the words for Inigo Jones's fabulous masques in happier days, *Albion's Triumphs* and *Tempe Restored*. In the confusion of the war the poet disappeared; his beautiful daughter, who had been mistress to Rupert's elder brother, the Elector, and to the Earl of Dorset, was now provided for. A fortnight later the tragedy of the time was brought home by the body of Lord Bernard Stuart being brought from Chester, where he had been slain, to be buried by his brothers in the cathedral, Lord d'Aubigny and Lord John. There these three handsome youths lie together.

By April fool's day the end at Oxford was in sight. Montreuil left to go to the Scots, the king placing his hopes on him – though the interest of the French was to keep the broils in England going. In mid-April an attack in force on the king's house in Woodstock Park was beaten off, but the place surrendered before the end of the month. Prince Rupert's troops were disbanded, but 600 foot arrived with their arms from loyal Exeter upon its surrender. Oxford was now a beleaguered fortress with the enemy all round; the soldiers were convinced that they could hold it, the lords of the council disagreed, but they were opposed to the king's desperate resolve to leave the city and go to his own people, the Scots, who in the event betrayed him.

We can follow these last days in Oxford as the royalist capital in some detail from Sir William Dugdale's Diary. The king's determination was not to fall into the hands of his enemies as a prisoner upon the capture of the city. He had paid his last visit to his Parliament in the Schools in February. Before the end all the records of its transactions were burned by the lords of the council – to the loss of the historian. On 27 April, 'this morning about one of the clock the King with Mr. Ashburnham and Mr. Hudson, a divine, went out of Oxford disguised towards the Scots' quarters then at Southwell'. At parting Sir Thomas Glemham, the governor of Oxford, letting the forlorn party out at the gate over Magdalen

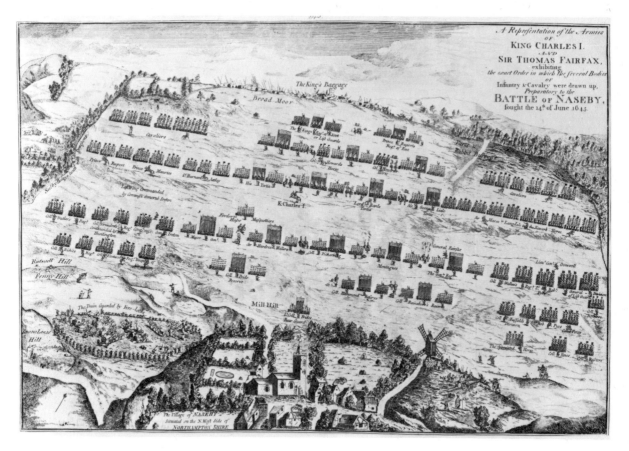

The battle of Naseby (1645) – 'the ruin of the royalist cause'.

bridge, said 'Farewell, Harry'. The king, who all his life had been served with such ceremony and kissing of hands, went as faithful John Ashburnham's servant. Hudson knew the route, the roads and by-ways. But the whole adventure, like so much in Charles I's life – ever since the journey with Buckingham to Madrid to fetch home the Infanta – was misconceived.

Two days later, when the news broke upon the astonished city, there was 'a solemn fast and prayer for the safety of the King's person and good success in his journey'. On Mayday Fairfax's horse appeared in the fields east of the city and the Lord General took up his quarters at Holton. The foot now appeared in all the adjacent villages and the rebel headquarters were advanced to Headington, whence it could look down on the faithful city – cannon shot fell first in Christ Church meadow. The lords of the council began to treat with Fairfax, against the

ARCH BISHOP SHELDON

Archbishop Sheldon, a great benefactor to the university.

wishes of the military, whose obstinacy would have subjected the city to storm-ing, which the humane Fairfax wished to avoid.

In the midst of the negotiations there was a touch of romance on the part of the Ironsides, when up at Holton Henry Ireton, the very able lawyer turned soldier who was seconding Cromwell in them, married the great man's daughter, Bridget. The wedding took place in Lady Whorwood's house on the hill above Oxford. The new relationship in which Ireton stood much strengthened his influence with Cromwell; Whitelocke says, 'No man could prevail so much, nor order Cromwell so far, as Ireton could.' He was an Oxford man, having been a

Right: Le Sueur's statue of Charles I in Canterbury Quadrangle, St John's College.
Overleaf: Standards and banners from the Civil War.

The DEVISES, MOTTO'S &c. used by the V...
&c. in the late CIVIL WARS; taken from an Orig...
ja.ⁿ Cole of Oxford. Published at y Desire of divers G...

Orа et Pugna Iuvet et Iuvabit JEHOVAH

Maj.ᵗ Skippon one of the Comittie for y Militia and Cap.ᵗ of a Troop of Horse 1642

Lex — Suprema — Salus — Patriæ

Cap.ᵗ Harvie Cap.ᵗ of the City Traind bands and Cap.ᵗ of a Troop of Horse 1642

Only in Heaven

Cap.ᵗ Mannaring one of y City Cap.ᵗ and Cap.ᵗ of a Troop Horse 1642

Cap.ᵗ Brown a Draper by S.ᵗ Austins Gate London

Ut Rex Noster Sit Noster Rex

Cap.ᵗ Gold

DEUS ... *Sic Pacem Qtær'mus*

Cap.ᵗ Massingberd

Propter De... um Conventu... Evangelium

Cap.ᵗ Creed Cap.ᵗ of a Troop of Horse 1643

Exurgat De... us Dissipentur Inimici

Coll. Ridgely

Fructus Virtu...

S.ʳ William Waller

Fides Temerata Cogit

Cap.ᵗ Trenchard on his Expedition to Ireland 1642

Only in Heaven

S.ʳ Arth. Haslerig

*If God be w.ᵗʰ i...
who shall be...
against us*

Cap.ᵗ Duglas 1642

...ment Officers *on* STANDARDS, BANNERS,
...anuscript done at ij time now in ij hands of Ben
...n to be Bound up w.th ij Lord Clarendon's Hist.ry

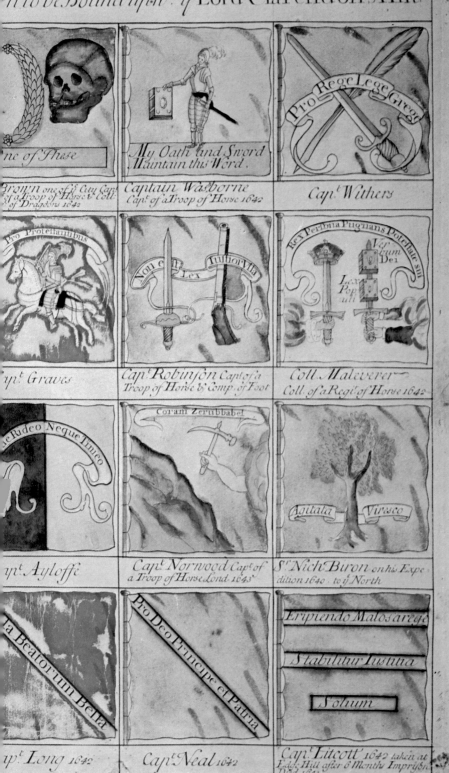

ne of These

My Oath and Sword
Maintain this Word.

Pro Rege Lege Grege

...rown one of ij Citty Cap.t
of a Troop of Horse & Coll.
of Dragoons 1642

Captain Washorne
Cap.t of a Troop of Horse 1642

Cap.t Withers

Pro Protestantibus

Non est Lex — Justior Illa

Rex Perbria Pugnans Potestate sua
Verbum Dei
Lex Populi

...p.t Graves

Cap.t Robinson Cap.t of a
Troop of Horse & Comp. of Foot

Coll. Maleverer
Coll. of a Reg.t of Horse 1642

...e Rideo Neque Timeo

Coram Zerubbabel

Agitata — Viresco

...p.t Ayloffe

Cap.t Norwood Cap.t of
a Troop of Horse Lond. 1643

S.r Nich. Biron on his Expedition 1640 - to ij North

...a Beatorum Bella

Pro Deo Principe et Patria

Eripiendo Malos a rege

Stabilitur Justitia

Solium

...p.t Long 1642

Cap.t Neal 1642

Cap.t Litcott 1642 taken at
Edge Hill after 6 Months Impriss...
Died 1643

Magdalen College Oxford

gentleman-commoner of Trinity; as such it is curious that Aubrey has no mention of him in his *Brief Lives*.

Cromwell moved down to Marston, where negotiations proceeded in Mr Crooke's house, the manor which still in part remains. At the end of the month, negotiations hanging fire, Fairfax sent a trumpet into the city with his terms, and the course of the Isis, which came to the castle mills, was diverted back to Hinksey and Botley. A sally out at the east port, of a hundred horse, in the hope of capturing grazing cattle, was driven back. Fairfax enforced the point with a handsome present of bucks, lambs, veals, capons to the king's younger son, James, Duke of York, left behind in the city. At the gates the soldiers of both sides fraternized, while now, within, the Church authorities were protesting that their interest and well-being were being disregarded in the terms of surrender. Ill feeling was aroused between the negotiating councillors and a mutinous soldiery: it was high time to surrender, and at last the king's permission to do so was received.

On 21 June the Lord Keeper summoned a meeting of leading Royalists in the audit house at Christ Church, where the king's letters were read in form. At the news that the Scots were pressing the king for a religious settlement against his conscience, upon which he had withdrawn to weep, the Lord Keeper faltered and shed tears at his fate.

Next day the Princes Rupert and Maurice – heroes of so many gallant fights, and responsible for not a few of the king's troubles – were permitted to leave the occupied city with some three hundred Cavalier gentlemen of quality. Among them was a painter of genius, of greater promise than any English painter yet to appear: William Dobson. It is in his canvases that we see the transition from the romance and fantasy of Van Dyck, the fabled world of Inigo Jones and the court masques, to the storm and stress of the war, the sense of strain upon the faces of the sitters in the uncertainty of the time; buff-coats, crimson sashes and swords against the lowering clouds and the glow of lurid skies. There they are, these figures we know in their actions and the parts they played – Prince Rupert with Colonels Russell and Murray; John, Lord Byron, moustachioed and scarred, pointing to the field of battle; an unknown officer with a page; Sir Charles Lucas who was to be shot to death at Colchester.

Within the year this foremost hope of English painting was himself dead, still young, in poverty and despair, his world – like the king's – in ruins.

Left: All Souls College by Rowlandson (mistakenly described as Magdalen).

7
Recovery: Commonwealth and Restoration

AFTER all this, surprising as it may seem, we are on the threshold of the most brilliant decade, intellectually, that Oxford has ever enjoyed, especially in the realm of science. In the 1650s Oxford was, according to an American scholar, 'the scientific centre of the nation'. There were certain special reasons for this, such as the organizing genius of John Wilkins, drawing a remarkable group of men around him, from which flowered, immediately and directly, the Royal Society. Even before the Civil War, in the 1620s and 1630s, 'in mathematics and astronomy, in particular, Oxford offered the most advanced instruction in the country'. This was the result of Sir Henry Savile's foundation of the two professorships in those subjects, followed by the bequest of his scientific library to the Bodleian. There was a regular flow between the universities and Gresham College in London – the chairs there were equally divided between Oxford and Cambridge men; it was now worth while for Gresham professors to come to Oxford, whether a Cambridge man like Rooke, or one who had been at Oxford like Wren.

Wilkins' group of gifted men centred upon the new college of Wadham, of which he became warden, where he kept open house for his scientific friends, and fostered promising students. But Wadham was not the only centre, nor was the new philosophy, theoretical and experimental, the only subject to make remarkable progress. Medicine was hardly less notable, with such figures as Willis at Merton, Sydenham and Mayow at All Souls, Lower and the young Locke at Christ Church. Robert Boyle, though persuaded to come to Oxford by Wilkins, was an independent power, as a rich aristocrat living out of college in his house opposite All Souls in the High, able to run his own laboratory for experiments with the aid of a young man of genius, Robert Hooke. Meanwhile, the university recovered its prosperity and advanced under the Commonwealth, as even Clarendon allowed; on the whole, it continued in the traditional ways – except for its religious services – and the fact that discipline was more strict had a beneficial effect on the students. Again, we may say that there was rather less concentration on the excruciating delights of theology; new subjects were being opened up more profitably. Even so, poor Archbishop Laud's devotion and patronage

Right: John Wilkins, who drew a scientific group together at Oxford, out of which came the Royal Society.

were to bear fruit in the achievements of the greatest orientalist of the age, Edward Pococke, whom Laud had backed before the catastrophe.

One of Laud's talents had been for spotting able young men. The archbishop, as Visitor, had forced Jeremy Taylor, a Cambridge man, on All Souls against the wishes of Warden Sheldon and the statutes. But had not Laud been right? Jeremy Taylor turned out one of the most famous Fellows the college has ever had, its finest preacher and prose writer; his portrait now hangs proudly here in hall. It is a further irony that it fell to Sheldon to restore the Church, after the collapse of the Puritan revolution, in conformity with Laud's ideas of hierarchy: nothing else was consonant with law and order.

But there was all the confusion and chaos of the Revolution to get through before that desirable consummation, when people returned to their senses.

When the Cavaliers left the surrendered city in 1646, there went with them artists like Dobson, poets like Lovelace, some to face imprisonment, or to fight beyond the seas, many to die in exile. Meanwhile they consoled themselves with writing, as Clarendon did, immortal prose, or Lovelace in verse:

> Stone walls do not a prison make,
>   Nor iron bars a cage;
> Minds innocent and quiet take
>   That for an hermitage:
> If I have freedom in my love
>   And in my soul am free,
> Angels alone that soar above
>   Enjoy such liberty.

Or, 'To Lucasta going beyond the Seas':

> If to be absent were to be
>   Away from thee,
>   Or that when I am gone
>   You and I were alone:
> Then, my Lucasta, might I crave
> Pity from blustering wind or swallowing wave ...

Meanwhile, at Oxford there was a good deal to put up with, though it might have been worse. The ghastly Prynne came back to gloat, as a Parliamentary Visitor, in the seat of the martyred Laud. The frightful Cheynell, who had tormented Chillingworth's last days, came back to take the place of Laud and Juxon at St John's – observers thought he had 'the face of a fiery fury'. An astonished congregation at St Mary's heard the notorious Hugh Peters, Cromwell's chaplain, preach; he was not a bad man – and was, somewhat unfairly, hanged for a regicide at the Restoration – but he was a vulgarian, whose antics in the pulpit would not have commended him to the Anglican succession of preachers, like Hooker, Lancelot Andrewes, Donne, Jeremy Taylor. With the country at sixes and sevens, the university, under its royalist leadership, organized complete passive resistance.

Clarendon celebrates in memorable language the united front put up by Laud's university:

The whole body of the university met in their Convocation and, to their eternal renown – being at the same time under a strict and strong garrison put over them by the Parliament, the King in prison, and all their hopes desperate – passed a public act against the Covenant, with such invincible arguments of the illegality, wickedness and perjury contained in it that no man of the contrary opinion, nor the Assembly of Divines (which then sat at Westminster forming a new catechism and scheme of religion) ever ventured to make any answer to it.

This is hardly surprising, for the absurd Scotch Covenant never had meant anything to the mass of Englishmen: it had been only a political necessity forced on Parliament to gain the alliance of the Scots against their king – as their emissaries to the Westminster Assembly found, and returned home disillusioned. The Puritan Visitors met with contempt, especially from Christ Church and All Souls, where there was 'most spiritual wickedness', as they expressed it.

We cannot here go in detail into the complexities of the situation within the university, merely note how it changed in accordance with the changes in power at the centre, responded to the intricate manoeuvres between the imprisoned king, Parliament and army. The army was more tolerant all through than the Presbyterian-dominated Parliament. It gave permission for Sheldon and Hammond to wait upon the king – they were his chaplains. The Dean of Christ Church, Samuel Fell, was imprisoned; Mrs Fell had to be forcibly turned out of the Deanery. Edward Reynolds, a mild Puritan, took the Dean's place, and was reviled by Cheynell for his 'detestable neutrality'. When Sheldon got back from attendance on the king, having refused to take the Covenant, he was expelled by an order from Prynne written on the spot. He had to be taken by force out of his lodgings and was escorted up the High by a sympathetic crowd – never before the twentieth century can a warden of All Souls have been so popular.

In the end a majority of heads of colleges were expelled, all the governing figures of Laudian Oxford – as was natural in the revolutionary circumstances of 1648–9: ten from the leading colleges outright, while six from lesser colleges and three halls submitted. Walker considered that altogether some four hundred persons were expelled; this is probably an over-estimate, though it includes

121

leading servants, butlers and manciples. In any case the number of Royalists expelled in 1648–9 was more than twice the number of the opposite parties replaced in 1659–60. We can see the changes in power at the centre interestingly reflected in the barometer of Oxford.

From 1648–52 the Parliamentary Visitors ruled. But the day of Cheynell and Prynne was brief; more moderate counsels prevailed, and it was an immense advantage to have the most admired of scholars, John Selden, in a position to press the university's case with Parliament, and not 'destroy, rather than reform, one of the most famous and learned companies of men that ever was visible in the Christian world'. The moderate Reynolds, Dean of Christ Church 1648–50, was characteristic of this period. Replaced by a Cromwellian in 1650, he devoted himself to numerous works on theology – he was very prolific in this nonsense field. But at the Restoration he had the sense to consent to be a bishop and ended up in the see of Norwich.

In May 1649 the two victorious Generals, Fairfax and Cromwell, both Cambridge men, paid an official visit to Oxford. They stayed at All Souls, where they were entertained by an intruded Fellow, a late colonel in their army, a person of no consequence. But Fairfax and Cromwell were members of the governing class, anxious to show that the Revolution was over; what both wanted was settled government and the settlement of a distracted country. They dined in hall at Magdalen, and played bowls in that bowling college; they sat in scarlet in Convocation and were created doctors of civil law. A number of their officers were made masters of arts; there were sermons at St Mary's, a banquet in the Bodleian. All passed off very well – so well, in fact, that next year Oliver Cromwell consented to become chancellor. This was after a decent show of hesitation, very becoming in a Cambridge man – Laud had not hesitated to assert his right as Metropolitan to visit Cambridge. (But Oliver was a gentleman, Laud a middle-class man who had risen up from the people – one sympathizes with him the more.)

With all the burdens upon him Cromwell put the chancellorship into commission, and brought in his own man, John Owen, to do the job as Dean of Christ Church and vice-chancellor. Owen was an excellent man; both the college and the university prospered under his rule. He had been at school in Oxford, and left Queen's rather than accept Laud's statutes; but he had been young then, and knew better now. He was no sour Presbyterian, but an independent; he even went in for physical exercise and flute-playing, and dressed like a dandy – all very unlike the Marginal Prynne. He was tolerant too, and took no notice of the well-attended Anglican services going on in Merton Street at his own backdoor. A good horseman, he was modern-minded enough to wish academic dress away; but here Oxford tradition was too much for him. Owen's only defect may be said to have been his prolific theologizing, in particular his polemic against Socinianism, i.e. common sense.

The royalist John Evelyn, visiting Oxford in July 1654, during Owen's vice-chancellorship (1652–8), noticed how little had changed in the traditional ways. He supped in Balliol hall, his old college, 'where they made me extraordinarily welcome – but I might have spent the evening as well'. Next day he went to the Schools, returned to their function of exercises and disputations, 'and in the afternoon tarried out the whole Act [i.e. degree ceremony] in St Mary's. The long speeches of the Proctors, the Vice-Chancellor's, the several professors', creation of Doctors by the cap, ring, kiss etc: those ceremonies not as yet wholly abolished, but retaining the ancient ceremonies and institution.' He was given 'a magnificent entertainment in Wadham hall, invited by my excellent and dear friend, Dr. Wilkins', the intruded warden. At All Souls 'we had music, voices and theorbos performed by some ingenious scholars; where after dinner I visited that miracle of a youth, Mr. Christopher Wren, nephew to the Bishop of Ely'. (Laud's co-adjutor was still in the Tower, refusing to recognize the usurping government in spite of all offers.) There were indeed scars of the late unpleasantness to be seen: 'the glass windows of the cathedral, famous in my time, I found much abused.' The chapel at Magdalen was, however, in proper order except that the altar was turned table-wise; even the organ was intact, 'which abominations – as now esteemed – were almost universally demolished'. They were to come back again, with the king.

When Oliver died things were in the melting pot again: complete instability reigned at the centre, with the great man's grip on power removed. Before his death he had handed over the chancellorship to his son Richard, who was quite incapable of filling his father's shoes and had none of his prestige. The Presbyterian Reynolds came back to Christ Church in place of Owen, but only for a few months; when Dean Fell returned at the Restoration, Reynolds, accommodating himself, was accommodated as warden of Merton on his way to being bishoped. John Conant took Owen's place as vice-chancellor. Of a good Devon family, he had been intruded into the rectorship of Exeter in 1649; the college had flourished under him. He was a conservative as to discipline, kept good order in the university and opposed Cromwell's scheme for a third university at Durham. All these people closed ranks to defend traditional university education against the fanatics jealous of it and the ideologues of the absurd Barebones Parliament, with the doctrinaire Rous as Speaker. No wonder Cromwell soon put a stop to their chatter. Conant was one of the moderates in favour of the Restoration as the only hope of stable government – as it was; but he jibbed at the subscription of 1662, then thought better of it in 1670 and became an archdeacon, when earlier he might have been a bishop.

We see how moderately things worked out in essence, so far as English society was concerned: no revolutionary upheaval, apart from the end of the monarchy – and Oliver Cromwell never wanted that: Charles I had brought it upon himself. We can see concretely how things were in such a case as that of Edward Pococke, the orientalist. An Oxford boy by birth, then at Magdalen Hall, he had been ordained by charming, convivial, Bishop Corbet, of 'Farewell, rewards and fairies', with its lament for former days:

> Lament, lament old abbeys,
>   The fairies lost command;
> They did but change priests' babies
>   But some have changed your land:
> And all your children stol'n from thence
>   Are now grown Puritans,
> Who live as changelings ever since
>   For love of your demesnes.

Bishop Corbet had a sense of humour, in itself heretical to Puritans: there is no evidence that they had any.

Pococke began early to put to good use the new collections in the Bodleian and discovered important Syriac versions of the New Testament. Laud, always on the look-out for talent, had given Pococke his backing as chaplain for five years at Aleppo, where he gained his mastery of Arabic. Laud gave him commissions to buy coins and manuscripts, and offered him the professorship in Arabic he had founded. He then aided him to make another journey, chiefly to Constantinople, where he was helped in his researches by Canopios, who came to reside in Oxford until driven out by the Parliamentary Visitors. Pococke visited Laud in the Tower, after he had safely sent his last consignment of manuscripts to the Bodleian.

The king had nominated this remarkable scholar to a canonry at Christ Church; the Visitors rejected him but allowed him to keep his oriental lectureship, largely owing to the pressure Selden brought to bear. Pococke had been presented to the Corpus living of Childrey outside Oxford; his odious parishioners agitated against his lack of 'unction' and cheated him of tithes, while quartering soldiers on him. They cited him, one of the most learned ministers in England, before the commission set up for ejecting 'ignorant, scandalous and insufficient ministers'. Good Dr Owen and others came to his defence; witnesses were called on both sides, wasting time: it took months to get Pococke off.

Meanwhile, in the revolutionary year 1649 he published his book on Arab history, the publication of which constituted an epoch in oriental studies. It was also the first book in Arabic type to come from the university press. This reminds us how many books of scholarly importance came from it at this time, while –

Mullinger informs us – owing to the ejections for royalist sympathies and the discouragements at Cambridge, the press there languished. This activity continued at Oxford and reached a new high level at the Restoration with the interest and energy of the younger Dean Fell, whose enthusiasm for good printing is commemorated still in 'Fell type' at the Clarendon Press.

At the outbreak of war a Cambridge follower of Laud, Brian Walton, after being imprisoned as a delinquent – like a number of the leading heads of houses there – took refuge at Oxford, as chaplain to the Duke of York, where he formed the project of a polyglot Bible. Three had appeared on the continent, but none as yet in England. With the advance of oriental studies, it was now possible to make progress with the project. The plan was backed by Archbishop Ussher and Selden; for over five years Pococke contributed his learning to it. It appeared in 1657 and was not superseded until the twentieth century. In addition to his works there was his collection of over four hundred manuscripts, which was purchased for the Bodleian in 1693. We may regard all this as a long-term fruit of Laud's foresight and care for scholarship, by which Oxford formed a leading centre of oriental studies from that time forward. Then too, Pococke brought back cones of the cedar of Lebanon, from which a magnificent specimen grew in his rectory garden, and others at Highclere; while his fig tree from Syria long flourished in the garden of the Hebrew professor, on the south side of Christ Church.

After these celebrities let us recall a simple pastoral type, whose life is no less eloquent of the time. Richard Sherlock was at Magdalen Hall – there could be no greater contrast with its most famous member, Thomas Hobbes – and then went to Trinity College, Dublin. Returning to England in 1643 he was captured at the siege of Nantwich; released, he took refuge at Oxford, where he was chaplain to the governor at the castle. Expelled in 1648, he moved out to Cassington, whence he was ejected in 1652. Thereafter he moved about the country in poverty, but not in despair: he answered George Fox's lunatic *The Great Mystery of the Great Whore Unfolded* with a reasonable reply, *The Quaker's Wild Questions objected against the Ministers of the Gospel.* At the Restoration he was appointed to the richest Lancashire living of Winwick – where the Presbyterian prolocutor of the Westminster assembly, Herle, had recently seen the light and co-operated with the royalist Earl of Derby in a premature move to restore Charles II. Unlike Herle, prancing about at Westminster, Sherlock resided at Winwick constantly for thirty years, living on a pittance to give away almost the whole of his stipend in charity; unmarried, he was able to make his rectory a training ground for the young clergy of the next generation.

Hardly less important than Owen in the government of the university during the Commonwealth was John Wilkins, but, as it turned out, immeasurably more significant intellectually. Wilkins was another Oxford schoolboy from Sylvester's school, his father a goldsmith of the town from whom the son inherited his mechanical bent. Wilkins graduated from Magdalen Hall to become chaplain to Lord Saye and Sele, through whom he met the Elector Charles Louis, Prince Rupert's brother – both of whom were mechanically minded. The Elector several times came down to Windsor to consort with Dean Wren, who was similarly interested in experimentation, as was his precocious son, Christopher.

So Wilkins became a man of the world: this was an element in his make-up and success in the world. He was a big man and as big-minded, broad-shouldered, lusty and masculine, an extrovert with an exceptional gift for getting on with people, attracting them and encouraging their work. In an ulcerated age, riven by fanaticism and foolishness, he was tolerant and ecumenical. The fanatics said that this was from want of conviction and attacked him as lacking in 'the power of godliness'; but they were mad. The truth was that he preferred to explore rational grounds for belief, inquiry into the created world of nature as a way to God; he did not find it necessary to separate science from religion, he constantly pointed out that men were as liable to err in one as in the other, with the inference that it was a mistake to claim a monopoly of truth – as both Puritans and Catholics did. We should today recognize this broadminded man as a Latitudinarian; and in fact it is from this moderate, middle-of-the-road grouping that the achievements of science at this time chiefly came. There was a broad spectrum all the way from Wren, with his royalist and High Church background, to Locke and Newton with their secret unitarianism. Wilkins refused squarely to engage in religious disputes, though quite firm in his own views. Thus he became the indispensable centre in whom the brilliant group that gathered round him at Oxford, with their different affiliations and backgrounds, could have confidence.

From about 1645, before the end of the war, there had been a small group in London around Wilkins and Jonathan Goddard discussing science and the new philosophy. But conditions in the capital were very unsettled, and Wilkins must have been glad when – making no bones about taking either Presbyterian Covenant or Independent Engagement (he saw such things in proper perspective) – he was made warden of Wadham. Here the men he drew around him had 'the satisfaction of breathing a freer air and of conversing in quiet one with another, without being engaged in the passions and madness of that dismal age'. The men whom Wilkins attracted were the most remarkable scientific intelligences of the age – except for Newton a little later, working away in his cell at Trinity, Cambridge, with his furnace in his garden, in intense concentration and almost complete isolation from other human beings. Wilkins was, above all, sociable and gregarious; he was the indispensable link that made his group the forerunners of the Royal Society.

Recovery: Commonwealth and Restoration

This was immediately upon the Restoration, when some of the group went to London; others remained on at Oxford, where the scientific work was of an even higher level than before. With Oliver Cromwell as Protector Wilkins was always *persona grata*; he made the position even more assured by marrying that unattractive morsel, Oliver's sister, the widow Robina, not out of any carnal desire but to protect his position and his good work. Goddard, yet another Magdalen Hall man, had been a doctor on Cromwell's campaigns; made warden of Merton in 1651, he also was a commissioner to execute the chancellorship. In 1655 he became professor of physic at Gresham College, which had a very close connection with Oxford, with professors going to and fro between them. Goddard was a full-time doctor, but, an original Fellow of the Royal Society, he contributed experiments and wrote on the texture and fibre of trees.

Lawrence Rooke was a Cambridge recruit of Wilkins', also a professor at Gresham (1652) going between London and Oxford – now quieter, when soldiers were quartered on Gresham College. Rooke's main interest was astronomy; he published his book on comets at Oxford in 1653. Others followed on the moon and the satellites of Jupiter, but Rooke was only forty when he died, or we should have heard much more of him. Two more Cambridge recruits had longer and fuller careers. Seth Ward had been one of the distinguished Cambridge men – like Barrow, Barwick and Gunning – to refuse the Covenant. He was one of the London group who retired to the congenial atmosphere of Oxford, where he became Savilian professor of astronomy. Wilkins gave him the big room over the gate at Wadham, to receive further renown from Wren's occupation. Here Ward made his chief contribution, working out his theory of planetary motion, based on Galileo and Kepler's discoveries; he too published his books on comets and trigonometry with the university press. At the Restoration Ward became a hard-working bishop at Exeter, with all the mess there was to clear up in the cathedral from its occupation by Presbyterians and Independents, who had built a brick wall across the middle not to hear each other's fooleries.

Still more important, with an immensely long career, was John Wallis (1616–1703). He covered a great deal of ground, for he was an exceptional linguist as well as a mathematician of genius. From his schooldays he had been devoted to mathematics, which 'at that time with us were scarce looked on as academical studies but rather mechanical – as the business of traders, merchants, seamen, carpenters, surveyors of lands, and the like'. There was no such prejudice in this group which formed the Royal Society – they were as interested in mechanical experimentation as in theoretical science. Wallis had been at Puritan Emmanuel, out of which came so many saints for saintly New England. In 1644 he became secretary to the tedious Westminster assembly of divines, and after Naseby accomplished a somewhat ambivalent job. He was a brilliant cryptographer, and

Robert Boyle, whose passionate interest in science, along with religion, helped to make the new natural philosophy fashionable.

unfortunately deciphered Charles I's incriminating correspondence captured at Naseby. He pleaded, afterwards, that he had been careful not to include anything too incriminating for persons still alive, and so made his peace at the Restoration.

In London Wallis had met Robert Boyle, whose passionate interest in science, along with religion, helped to make the new experimental philosophy – since he was both rich and an aristocrat – not only respectable but fashionable with the patronage of Charles II. In 1649 Wallis was recruited to Oxford – we must regard these men as recruits not 'intruders' – as Savilian professor of geometry; and in 1655 he published here his seminal *Arithmetica Infinitorum*, not only original in itself but decisive in its influence, for it suggested the binomial theorem to Newton. Indeed it contained the germs of the differential calculus – the incandescent fire of which we may appreciate from the old Oxford professor who told me that the thought of it warmed his feet when they were cold as stones in bed.

Wallis's *History of Algebra* did justice to his original predecessor, Thomas Hariot, as he was himself 'the greatest of Newton's English precursors'. In 1652 his *Grammatica Linguae Anglicanae* – another Oxford publication – showed his common interest with Wilkins in the philosophy of language and the problems of communication. Both Wallis and William Holder, Wren's brother-in-law, separately worked out a successful technique for teaching deaf and dumb people to speak. From 1669 to 1671 Wallis was publishing in three parts his *Mechanica*, 'the most comprehensive work on the subject then existing'. As prolific as he was original, Wallis published other mathematical works at Oxford, over one of which Thomas Hobbes fell foul of him. Hobbes was not a trained mathematician, but he was clever enough to catch out Wallis on one or two points of detail, while obstinately misunderstanding the specialist in the subject on the main issue. The controversy that ensued aroused tremendous interest – everything concerning Hobbes aroused controversy; but Wallis, besides being right, gave the great man as good as he got. He said that teaching the dumb to speak was 'as hard almost as to make Mr. Hobbes understand a demonstration'.

Hobbes was indeed an extraordinary intellectual phenomenon in the age; much older than any of these people – his premature birth due to the shock his mother received on the news of the Spanish Armada – in some ways he was more old-fashioned than this new generation, in others he was ahead of them. Obstinate and pig-headed over mathematics, for instance, he was more liberated, with regard to religion and politics. In person a humorous and crusty provincial Englishman, he had in fact lived far more of his life on the continent, in touch with the finest intellects of the age: Galileo, whom he reverenced; Mersenne and Gassendi, with whom he did agree; Descartes, with whom he did not.

Brought up at Magdalen Hall 1603–8 – it has not been noticed what a number of remarkable men that hall produced – Hobbes then became tutor to William Cavendish, later Earl of Devonshire, and his family, with whom he made three tours on the continent lasting some years. He also served Bacon, as an amanuensis, taking down his thoughts; he had a number of literary friends and made one of Falkland's circle. But Hobbes never felt that he owed much to Oxford, nor did he: like Bacon, he thought nothing of scholastic philosophy. He had worked out the lines his mature philosophy would take, materialism in psychology and natural philosophy, authoritarianism in politics based on his view of human nature, and had his *Elements of Law* circulating in manuscript before the Long Parliament met. When it did, he saw earlier than anyone what it portended and was sensible enough to leave the country that had taken leave of its senses.

He spent the next eleven years, 1640–51, abroad, mostly in Paris, mixing with the leading French intellectuals and, when Charles II was driven into exile, Hobbes taught him the elements of mathematics and, probably, of unbelief. When the royalist cause met final defeat on the battlefield at Worcester in 1651, Hobbes made his peace with the powers that were and published his *Leviathan*. The book was a bombshell and practically a battlefield in itself: the noise has gone on reverberating ever since. The book contained all that Hobbes thought, and implied a great deal more: intelligent critics, of whom there was a score – including Clarendon – were shrewd enough to see that the implications were more damaging to all they believed in than Hobbes spelt out in so many words. It was obvious that Hobbes had no belief in religion and not much in mankind: he thought that men in general were such mere animals, so little rational and so essentially aggressive, that absolute government was necessary to keep human society together: otherwise, left to itself – humans being what they are – it would fall apart. Who are we today to say that Hobbes was wrong? Communism, in agreement with

Thomas Hobbes, the philosopher, who had 'no belief in religion and not much in mankind'.

his views, acts on them, and their society holds together; ours, under liberal illusions and a fundamentally false view of human nature, falls apart.

Hobbes's drastically anti-liberal views had been entirely corroborated by the course of events: the attack on Charles I's mild and paternal government in the name of liberty led to a military dictatorship. Oliver Cromwell had no liberal illusions and so was able at least to save the social order when it was in danger of breaking down. Utter confusion and chaos would have ensued from the events of 1649 if the army had not kept its grip on power. But it was then obvious that only the naked fact of power was left to assert order and was all that stood between the nation and chaos. Oliver Cromwell, for all his prestige and genius as a politician, for all his efforts and twistings and turnings, and his humbug, could never disguise the fact or make his rule anything but a dictatorship, totally unconstitutional and almost totally unrepresentative of the country. There was left only power: the army.

But it was, as usual, improper to say so – it is always necessary to cover the naked facts of society with some humbug. Hobbes got a bad name for his incapacity for humbug and, worse, probably enjoyed it, for he was no respecter of persons. So 'Hobbist' became a term of abuse, like 'Menshevik' with Bolsheviks, or 'Bolshevik' in the 1920s, or 'Communist' in the 1950s, or 'atheist' with the Elizabethans. When Isaac Newton was off his head for a short time, the worst thing that he could think of to call his friend Locke was 'Hobbist', for which he apologized when sanity returned. We need not discuss Hobbes's epoch-making book here, for there was little of Oxford in his work – he was too individual, too radical – though plenty of Oxford men attacked one of the greatest intellects to come out of it. John Locke was directly influenced by Hobbes in his early unpublished work, though he never acknowledged it; and much of his later work was by way of reaction to the more original mind. Even the statistician, Sir William Petty, one of the founders of political arithmetic, was indebted to Hobbes.

Hobbes was quite radical about education: he thought that the concentration on the classics at the universities imbued students with republicanism and ideas of liberty (the idealization of Brutus and such) subversive of social order. His analysis of the causes of the Civil War in *Behemoth* was in keeping and much to the point: the 'democratical principles' of the universities had planted the seeds of rebellion. Though he had little following at the time, his influence went round the world. Not much of a saint, but a good materialist, he has been in our time promoted to the Marxist pantheon. In his own he was not promoted to the Royal Society, any more than the greatest of French novelists, Balzac, was to the French Academy. Hobbes was too scandalous, too controversial a figure; the Royal Society was bent on making science respectable. Both Locke and Newton kept their religious heterodoxy secret; Hobbes's genius was too clear in its candour and left him exposed.

In any case the emphasis of the Oxford group and the Royal Society was on experimental science. Before the war Wilkins had already begun popularizing science with his best-sellers in English, *The Discovery of a New World* and *A Discourse Concerning a New Planet*. There was a keen demand for scientific works in English besides those in esoteric, academic Latin; Wilkins was well aware of what he was doing and set himself to answer the demand, much as H. G. Wells did for a mass audience in our time. He went on with his campaign in *Mathematical Magic*, 1648, a work describing the principles of mechanics and their practical applications, since hitherto there were 'not any of them, that I know of, in our vulgar tongue'. The influence of Wilkins' writings was very considerable, not only in this country but on the continent, and they had long-term reverberations in literature, with Defoe and Dr Johnson's *Rasselas*, as well as more immediately in the satires of Samuel Butler and Swift.

Wilkins had the tide running with him in his rejection of traditional authority; he was able to put Copernicanism across to the public, so that even the almanac-makers adopted it at length. It is clear now that the simple prose style for which the Royal Society stood, and for which its historian, Bishop Sprat, has always been given credit, should really be attributed to Wilkins. Sprat was Wilkins' pupil at Wadham, and one of Wilkins' prime concerns was that of language and communication. He worked on the idea of gestures and motions of tongue and mouth by which to teach deaf-mutes to speak. In his garden Wilkins had a statue with pipes connected, which projected the voice a surprising distance.

Seth Ward and William Petty were working on a philosophical language in the 1650s. Wallis discussed linguistic questions with Archbishop Ussher and Langbaine of Queen's. The university became 'not only a scientific but a linguistic centre ... and also the centre of the efforts to create a universal character'. This was the subject of Wilkins' largest work, to which he devoted years: *An Essay towards a Real Character and a Philosophical Language*. He was convinced that this 'would not only facilitate scientific communication and international commerce but "prove the shortest and plainest way for the attainment of real knowledge that hath been yet offered to the world"'. We see what a forward-looking mind his was – something even more comprehensive and philosophically commanding than the Basic English of our time was in mind.

Wilkins was aided in his experiments in flying by a young Christ Church man of extraordinary inventive genius, Robert Hooke. They worked on models of a flying chariot with both springs and wings, one of which 'raised and sustained itself in the air' briefly. Wilkins forecast the possibility of space-travel in his book on the moon. 'The major difficulty was ascent from the earth, for which it was necessary to overcome the force of gravity ... This attractive quality varied with distance, and ceased altogether once one got beyond the sphere of the earth's attraction ... at that point travel would be rapid and easy.' He was no less convinced that a submarine was feasible. In his garden he constructed beehives of glass, to study the operations of the bees. The group was interested in improvements in planting – whatever increased the country's productivity, not in consuming its substance. The later seventeenth century saw a marked increase in real wealth, which enabled it to recover with remarkable speed from the losses of the Civil War – where today's society, bent on consuming the very seed-corn, has naturally been slow and laggard in recovering from the last war.

With so intelligent a group in control, moreover so well connected, the universities were easily able to beat off the attack on them by the doctrinaires of the Barebones Parliament, which considered 'suppressing universities and all schools of learning as heathenish and unnecessary'. Other fanatics attached more importance to spiritual illumination, which needed no human training or intellectual discipline (we have their counterparts today, but in the universities). Cromwell had no difficulty in sending such people packing. Not that Wilkins was taken in by his good brother-in-law: he did not hold with his 'enthusiasm' or his 'dissimulation' – but that only meant that Oliver was a first-class politician.

In the year after Cromwell's death a marked tribute from Cambridge came Wilkins' way: the Fellows of Trinity wanted him as master. He had only a few months in which to make his mark there, too, before the Restoration restored a Royalist. This freed Wilkins for London, where he drew up the charter of the Royal Society, continued his experiments and planned its policy of publication, for which he was well-equipped. He was lost to science when he became a bishop, but not to society: he pursued a policy of religious toleration and comprehension consistent with the latitudinarianism which was so propitious to the development of science.

Wilkins' departure did not injure science at Oxford: he had given so strong an impulse to it that an even richer harvest was to come. He had prevailed on Robert Boyle to settle here, who remained for fourteen years, making another centre for experiment from his house in the High (now occupied by the Shelley Memorial), where he built his laboratory. Here, largely with Hooke's assistance, he constructed the first practical air-pump and enunciated Boyle's Law, of a proportional relation between elasticity and pressure. Numerous experiments led to a stream of publications from Oxford during his residence: the most famous was the *Sceptical Chymist*, followed by *Experiments and Considerations touching Colours*, his *Origin of Forms and Qualities* and his *Hydrostatical Paradoxes*. Boyle's general services to science were more important than any particular discoveries. He was famous, from his rank in society no less than his high character: distinguished foreigners wanted to pay him their respects. His patronage not only elevated the status of science, but helped forward the work of younger people. His own work, carrying forward investigations in several fields, advanced 'the frontier of science all along the line'.

It was Boyle's lower-class assistant, Hooke, however, who had the genius – probably, considering how prolific he was of ideas and the range of his work, greater than any other of his time except Newton, with whom he was in complete contrast – and with whom he quarrelled. Where Newton worked with unparalleled intensity and concentration, and would not leave off until he had broken through the barrier with new laws of general application, Hooke's interests were so extensive that he was liable to move from one thing to another, not without results but often without making them conclusive.

The quarrel was about priority in the discovery of gravitation. Actually the idea was in the air, as with evolution in the nineteenth century. We have seen that Wilkins glimpsed it, and actually William Gilbert had been on the way to it with his concept of the earth as a great magnet. Hooke, Huygens and Newton were on to gravitation as a universal law at about the same time; but it was the mathematical genius of Newton that enabled him to prove it and state the law of its operation. Hooke left Oxford in 1662 to become curator of the Royal Society, where he proliferated in investigations and experiments, in regard to respiration, combustion, falling bodies, the barometer, the pendulum, the rotation of Jupiter and many astronomical observations. Since most of his work falls into his London years, we must not go into it here – he himself claimed 'a century of inventions', and his work has been summed up thus, 'his power of forecasting discovery was extraordinary, and he was the greatest mechanic.' Nor, though his grand buildings have disappeared, must we forget that, after Wren, he was the leading architect of the time.

Christopher Wren was nurtured in science; everyone paid tribute to his extraordinary talent and charm as a boy. He too was a *protégé* of Wilkins at Wadham, though even before this he had assisted Dr Scarburgh in anatomy. Scarburgh had been ejected from Cambridge, and come over to Merton to work with his friend Harvey on the generation of animals. For Willis' work on the anatomy of the brain the young Wren made the elaborate drawings: Hooke spoke of the perfect combination of 'such a mechanical hand and so philosophic a mind'. When he moved over to architecture this accomplishment stood him in good stead. So also did his brilliance as a geometer: he solved the problem Pascal had set, which defeated almost everyone, and himself set another which was left unanswered. He came to All Souls as Fellow 1653–7, where he left a memento of himself in a fine baroque sundial – all through these years he was engaged in the problems of making dials, making graphical constructions of solar and lunar eclipses. He made a geometrical determination of a comet's path, and even Newton, ever jealous of his own priority, allowed that Wren, Hooke and Halley had all arrived at the law of the inverse square in gravitation.

It is impossible to go into all Wren's contrivances and inventions: almost a page of the Wren *Parentalia* is given up to them. 'Ingenious' is the word that Evelyn and others used to describe him. He was constantly experimenting with barometers, to connect them with the weather, making contrivances for measuring rainfall; he invented an instrument 'to plant corn equally and without waste'. In 1657 he left Oxford to become professor of astronomy at Gresham College, but came back four years later as Savilian professor. As such he co-operated with Wallis on cycloids – Wallis published four of his tracts in his book – which preceded the publication of Newton's fluxions. Wren, unlike Newton, was a co-operator; one sees, even at this early individual stage, how much science advanced co-operatively. And also how characteristically it advanced on all fronts, as against the intense, and sometimes frustrating, specialization of today. Wren was the first to perform the experiment of injecting liquors or drugs into the veins of an animal. It was Dr Lower who carried this a stage further with blood transfusion. But in the early 1660s Wren was being called into service as an architect, both at Cambridge with Pembroke chapel and with the Sheldonian at Oxford. Then, with the Great Fire of London, Wren's fate was settled for him: no architect has ever had such an opportunity as Wren had. He took it: it filled to overflowing the rest of his long life.

We find the interest in medicine fairly widely distributed, with leading figures in the new approach to it at Merton, All Souls and Christ Church. Thomas Willis, whose father was killed during the siege of Oxford, came up to Christ Church and after the war practised in Merton Street; he worked with young Lower and Thomas Millington, another Cambridge refugee, in dissecting brains. In addition to his standard work on that subject, he published widely on fevers, muscular movement, hysteria and urinary troubles. In the last field he deserves to be remembered for isolating 'sugar diabetes', for which discovery he was of course attacked by those who hadn't discovered it. In 1660 he became Sedleian professor of natural philosophy; some of his medical works were published at Oxford.

William Petty concerned himself briefly with medicine while at Oxford. He had been educated chiefly abroad and in Paris was a friend of Hobbes. He had studied medicine at Leyden, and worked at anatomy at Oxford, of which he was briefly professor 1651–2. By far the leading figure in Restoration medicine was Thomas Sydenham. He came of a Parliamentarian family much torn by the war, in which he lost his mother and two of his brothers. He fought sternly all through the war, came up to Wadham in 1647, and in 1648 was rewarded by the Visitors with a Fellowship at All Souls, which he held for seven years.

135

Left: Sir Christopher Wren, eminent scientist as well as architect, Savilian professor of astronomy. *Right:* John Locke, the most influential of Oxford philosophers.

Sydenham was the most successful doctor in London and, more, is held one of the greatest clinicians in English medicine. He was exceptionally famous on the continent, his influence abroad being radiated from Leyden to Boerhave; there were numerous translations of his works. A rather testy man, he held that medicine was learned at the bedside rather than the university, from practice rather than books – so that we do not have to go into him in any detail. He was combatively anti-theoretical, though in fact he did not eschew sensible generalizations. 'It is necessary', he held, 'that all diseases be reduced to definite and certain species ... with the same care that we see exhibited by botanists.' Many diseases then described under a common nomenclature were actually different and required different treatment. He is regarded as 'the first among moderns to lead medicine back to the true Hippocratic road of observation and experience, with treatment *supporting* the patient's recuperation. He stressed the environment factors in epidemics.' Besides his practical success in treating patients, his influence spread widely towards studying outbreaks of disease in their habitats. Thus his influence spread to the American colonies, to Italy and Austria, finally to France and Germany. The Paris faculty remained hidebound through the eighteenth century, until Sydenham's influence prevailed with the French Revolution, when students began to be taught at the bedside.

At Oxford Sydenham's chief friend was John Locke, a fellow west countryman. Locke's contemporary at Christ Church was the Cornishman, Richard Lower: they both studied chemistry with Peter Stahl, whom Boyle brought to

Oxford. Lower also assisted Willis in his researches into the brain, hence the 'tubercle of Lower', named for him. His own vital contributions were in regard to heart and circulation. Lower's transfusion of blood into a dog in 1665 was intended to be followed by an experiment with men. This was performed two years later in Paris; it occasioned the kind of outcry there has been against heart transplanting in our time, and was prohibited and neglected for two centuries. Yet no one doubts today the beneficent result, sometimes the necessity, of blood transfusion. Lower went on from Oxford to become a leading doctor in London.

His junior, John Mayow, another Cornishman, was a recruit from Wadham to All Souls. At Oxford he published his tracts on respiration, rickets, etc, that on the first being his classic work. In that he described its mechanism, with ribs and diaphragm, in modern observational terms, making the capital discovery of the double articulation of the ribs with the spine. His view of the heart functioning as muscle was shortly corroborated by Lower, as his theory of combustion was ultimately developed by Lavoisier. Mayow dealt with a wide variety of subjects in his short life, from the recognition of different gases in combustion to the action of saltpetre in the soil upon plants. Only thirty-six when he died, 'he had the genius to perceive exactly the problems which must be solved before any great advance in chemistry or physiology could be made ... His premature death retarded the advent of modern chemistry for more than a century.'

John Locke turned to medicine in 1666 – hence his attendance upon and friendship with the Whig leader, Shaftesbury, which was decisive for Locke's career. Like Hobbes he had reacted against the schoolmen and their disputations, preferring experimental philosophy; he attended the lectures of Seth Ward and Wallis, and became a lifelong friend of Boyle. In an early essay on toleration he traced the discords in the state, like Hobbes, to the exaggerated claims of a priesthood and favoured the supremacy of the secular power. This became the standard Whig view, partly through his immense intellectual influence in the next century.

Locke was a good deal with Shaftesbury, and supervised the operation by which his internal ulcer was successfully drained through a silver tube. For the decisive Oxford Parliament of 1681 – when Charles II turned the tables on the Whigs and smashed them – Locke arranged for Shaftesbury to stay at Balliol, perhaps appropriately. He himself remained on at Christ Church, preparing his *Treatise on Government*, until James II ordered his expulsion in 1684. Dean Fell defended the most famous student of the House, saying that no anti-government expressions had been heard to fall from his lips, never was there 'such a master of taciturnity and passion'. Locke went into exile in Holland, to triumph with the Revolution of 1688, for which his political philosophy provided the intellectual defence. His influence indeed was prodigious: in philosophy with the *Essay Concerning Human Understanding*, on education with his *Thoughts* on the subject, on economics, particularly with regard to currency, where his advice was very successful, even in religion with his writings on toleration, and *The Reasonableness of Christianity*. All through the eighteenth century his influence expanded and flowered in all these fields. It can only be compared with that of his friend and opposite number at Cambridge: Isaac Newton.

The brilliance of the scientific movement must not blind us to the excellent work being accomplished in other directions. We have noticed the impetus given to oriental scholarship; no less remarkable was that in early and medieval English history, the study of antiquities – which had been endangered and so much damaged by war. When he saw it approaching Sir William Dugdale, the leading antiquarian of the time, made journeys into the country to record monuments and inscriptions in the churches liable to destruction. (Lincoln cathedral lost between one and two hundred brasses from the attentions of a Cromwellian colonel. And there must have been more than one Dowsing!) At Oxford with the king Dugdale was able to get forward with his masterpiece, the *Antiquities of Warwickshire*, which he published in 1656.

This work inspired others to do something similar for their counties, and it set a model for them to follow. Roger Dodsworth had been working for years making enormous collections on the history of the northern counties; but he was one of those unfortunates who can never bring their work to the point of publication. Dugdale could, and used some of Dodsworth's materials for his great *Monasticon*, his comprehensive survey of the English monasteries, their history and documentation. This 'excited the ire of many Puritans', who affected to think of it as preparing the way for a return to Catholicism. Dugdale's third great work was his *Baronage*. They all opened up new territories for scholarship.

We see how inspiring people found his *Warwickshire* from Anthony Wood's confession how his 'tender affections and insatiable desire of knowledge was ravished and melted down by the reading of that book'. Wood was inspired to do the same for Oxfordshire, with his history of the city, followed by the history and antiquities of the university. Wood was backed by the younger Dean Fell, who was a big man with schemes for the benefit of the university, in scholarship and publication no less than building. We must not linger over Wood's work, for it was essentially intramural, if not inbred; though his books were standard works and provided a foundation for all subsequent writings on Oxford, I do not know that they had any influence beyond the walls.

Collections of documents were piling up to enrich scholarship. Wood left his collection of broadsides, ballads and prints to the university. Dugdale bequeathed many manuscripts to Elias Ashmole, who also acquired the fascinating papers of Simon Forman and Richard Napier, through the latter's nephew, a Fellow of All

The portico of the Old Ashmolean, whose remarkable collection of early scientific instruments is an 'ocular reminder of this brilliant period in Oxford science'.

Souls. Ashmole had been a royal official, attending upon the Oxford Parliament, and had entered himself at Brasenose, but could not stay – government business called him away. But a wealthy marriage enabled him to become a benefactor. John Tradescant and his father had been notable gardeners, travellers and collectors of 'rarities'. The son bestowed his fascinating collections on Ashmole, who gave them to the university in 1677 on condition that a building was erected to house them. This was completed in 1682, and Dr Robert Plot became curator – author of the *Natural History of Oxfordshire*, and another of Staffordshire. We see the influence of Dugdale widening out into the counties.

Ashmole's manuscripts were later transferred to the Bodleian; of the collection of 'rarities' some of the pictures went to the Ashmolean Museum. The Restoration building, now known as the Old Ashmolean, gradually built up the most remarkable collection of early scientific instruments in the country – an ocular reminder of this brilliant period in Oxford science. The building itself is an enchanting small Renaissance palazzo, with splendid deep portico at the side – the whole harking back in style to earlier Caroline Oxford.

Beside it there had now come into existence the Sheldonian Theatre, magnificent in its Restoration opulence, the first big monument of Wren's architectural genius. It called into play his scientific expertise as well, for there was the problem of roofing the largest flat space yet to be covered, with an attic storey above. Anyone who has penetrated among the timbers up there will appreciate the

Tom Tower at Christ Church, built by Sir Christopher Wren. In 1680 the great bell from Osney Abbey was recast to hang in it.

Tom Quad at Christ Church, begun by Cardinal Wolsey, completed by Dean Fell.

practical geometer at work – as still more notably in the construction of the dome of St Paul's. When Evelyn was at Oxford in October 1664,

I went to visit Mr Boyle now here, whom I found with Dr Wallis and Dr Christopher Wren in the tower at the Schools, with an inverted tube or telescope, observing the discus of the sun for the passing of Mercury that day before the sun ... Thence to the new Theatre, building now at an exceeding and royal expense by the Lord Archbishop of Canterbury, to keep the Acts in for the future, till now being in St Mary's church: the foundation being but newly laid and the whole designed by that incomparable genius and my worthy friend, Dr Christopher Wren, who showed me the model, not disdaining my advice in some particulars. Thence to see the picture on the wall over the altar at All Souls, being the largest piece of fresco-painting – or rather in imitation of it, for 'tis in oil of turpentine – in England and not ill designed, by the hand of one Fuller. Yet I fear it will not hold long, and seems too full of nakeds for a chapel. Thence to New College, and the painting of Magdalen chapel, which is on blue cloth in chiaroscuro by one Greenbury, being a Cena Domini, and Judgment on the wall by Fuller.

All this painting in the chapels must have made the Puritans turn in their graves, or groan aloud if alive. But their day was over. The martyrdom of King Charles and Archbishop Laud had brought about the restoration of church and king. Wilkins had told the Protector in his last years that episcopacy was the only way to run the Church – as Sheldon had argued to the Parliamentary commissioners at Uxbridge. Now Sheldon was in the chair of St Augustine, Clarendon Chancellor of the University. Extraordinarily generous all through his life, Sheldon spared no expense to give the university a worthy auditorium for its ritual, a monument to all they had gone through in the last two decades. Wren said that it cost the man born to be archbishop £25,000. Two generations later Cambridge followed suit with a Senate House.

The projects that had been in mind before the war were now completed and others added to them. At Christ Church Wolsey's Great Quadrangle was at last completed by Dean Fell, with a north range. Wren was called in to finish the gateway with Tom Tower; the great bell from Osney was re-cast in 1680 to hang in it – thus bringing to Wolsey's college echoes from the old ruined abbey. In 1664 Ralph Bathurst, another of Wilkins' group, became president of Trinity. There was much to be done: he called upon Wren to design the ranges of the open Garden Quadrangle; a new kitchen wing followed, and at length the splendid chapel which was Newman's favourite building. A similar scheme of ranges opening to the garden was followed at New College; while a third storey was added to the big quadrangle, diminishing the proportions of chapel and hall, gate-tower and founder's tower. Neighbouring St Edmund Hall built a charming small chapel with library above (overshadowed in our time by buildings monstrously out of proportion and vulgar in themselves).

8
An Age of Security:
the Eighteenth Century

ARCHITECTURE is history made visible: we can see the society of Georgian England laid open to us in the buildings of eighteenth-century Oxford. There they stand solid and secure, well-proportioned and regular, entirely adjusted to the human scale, unlike modern architecture. The lines are plain for all to see, the horizontal properly related to the vertical, for theirs was an integrated society, its members articulated to function rationally; satisfactory and regular façades and fenestration, spaced columns or colonnades, restrained decoration emphasized rational order. Within its own terms, and all under control, there was variety, the rectangular and the rotund, sometimes stolid or heavy, occasionally dull like an eighteenth-century alderman or churchwarden, placid and well pleased with itself. It was a society that had reason to be pleased with itself; after the fanaticism, the conflicts and turmoil of the seventeenth century, the Revolution of 1688 achieved an accommodation, a constitutional balance, that was the admiration and envy of Europe. It enabled the small island-country to win an empire overseas.

At its best the buildings of the age achieved a summit of perfection and imagination – Gibbs's Radcliffe Camera, which gives Oxford its *clou*, or the splendid *palazzo* of Queen's, the interior of its library or the Codrington at All Souls – no less than in the achievements of the Oxford men of the time, Chatham and John Wesley, Blackstone and Dr Johnson, Gibbon, Adam Smith, Gilbert White of Selborne, Sir William Jones of India, greatest of orientalists. Nor was there wanting continuity with the past. Just as Oxford Jacobitism looked back sentimentally to the Stuart past, so the Gothic idiom was continued right up into the Augustan age: 'Oxford was not only the first home of the Royal Society but the last home of pre-revival Gothic.'

The society was stable without being static, and of course the 'torpor' of Georgian Oxford was greatly exaggerated by nineteenth-century reformers. Again criticisms of the university were apt to come from impatient young men of genius whose expectations were too high for *l'homme moyen sensuel*. Ordinary dons are ordinary people at all times – naturally they could not come up to the standards of an avid reader like the young Gibbon; but he was given access to the

Right: The staircase in the Radcliffe Camera (*c.* 1745).

library at Magdalen where he could read to his heart's content. So, too, with William Jones who spent whole days, and to some purpose, in the Bodleian. Charles James Fox worked so hard as an undergraduate – he never did again – that he had to be positively restrained; while the young Jeremy Bentham was scornful of Blackstone's lectures, which were models of their kind.

The fact was that the facilities for work and cultivation of the mind were there for anyone to make use of who wished – and remarkable men always learn more on their own than from dons, except for occasional tutors of exceptional gifts like Cyril Jackson or Jowett. And how could anyone describe as somnolent the Oxford that witnessed the fireworks of Atterbury – Dean Smallridge said that Atterbury raised a fire wherever he went and he, Smallridge, had to come along with a bucket of water to put it out – or the Letters of Phalaris controversy?* Or, a little later, the Oxford of John Wesley and Methodism, who said that he should regard himself no better than a highwayman if he didn't lecture every day of the week except Sunday? His brother Charles said that John was 'naturally and habitually a tutor', while he himself said, 'I propose to be busy as long as I live'. Or there is the Oxford of political excitements, the capital of Jacobitism, into which troops had to be drafted in 1715, or of the hotly contested county election of 1754, or of the enthusiastic reception of George III, who recruited to himself the loyalty that had gone to the Stuarts. It is true that Oxford was dominantly a clerical seminary, but no institution can sleep quietly where young men are in the majority.

That society had achieved a stable basis we might infer from there being no college founded during all this period. Worcester College was really a refoundation of the former Gloucester Hall; while the brief attempt to make a college of Hart Hall foundered, to await another day. Meanwhile, if some of the existing institutions flourished grandly, others languished – there was variety. The eighteenth century saw inequalities emphasized, but quality was recognized and pursued: the standards were set from the top, not from the bottom, hence the elegance and artistry of their achievements, visible in building. Nor were the poor excluded: one archbishop of Canterbury, Secker, had been a Dissenter and a local doctor practising midwifery; another, John Moore, was a Gloucestershire grazier's son; Sir Joseph Williamson, who had been a Poor Boy at Queen's, made a fortune as secretary of state and devoted some of it to the rebuilding of his college. It is possible that Victorian Oxford was more exclusive than Georgian Oxford – and this as in education generally.

But a selective society exemplifies the highest standards culturally, as a democratic society does not. Of this we have ocular demonstration in the buildings with which the eighteenth century equipped and completed the historic city

---

* This controversy over the authorship of certain Greek letters raised a *furore*, in which the wits of Christ Church were answered by the great Cambridge scholar, Bentley.

Right: An eighteenth-century print of the Clarendon building, the Sheldonian Theatre and the Bodleian Library.

within the walls and made it more beautiful than ever before. They were the work of a small group of connoisseurs who had taste, knew what they were about and worked hand in glove with the architects, especially Hawksmoor and the admirable dynasty of Oxford stone-masons, the Townsends. They collaborated with such happy results that sometimes it is not possible to disentangle their work – each contributed to or modified designs; but they all shared the distinguished standards of an age of taste. Both universities gained immeasurably from this, and their patronage of the arts enriched the nation.

The lead was taken by Aldrich, Dean of Christ Church, 1689–1710. A convivial bachelor – his only vice was his inveterate addiction to smoking – he was an enthusiastic lover of music and architecture. He himself designed Peckwater Quadrangle and All Saints Church in the High, with its impressive proportions and graceful spire. He gathered the collections which have made Christ Church library a treasure-house of early English music. Among his own compositions was the catch, 'Hark, the bonny Christ Church bells'. He greatly enjoyed life in a time when it was possible to make enjoyment the keynote of it (the country was

Left: The twin towers of All Souls College by Hawksmoor.
Below: The opening of the Radcliffe Library, now the Camera, built 1738–49.

going up in the world, instead of down). Later there came the no less splendid collection of Italian pictures and drawings from General Guise, to equip the House with a gallery, in addition to the noblest collection of portraits of any college in England.

Christopher Codrington, a rich commoner there, followed suit and, as a Fellow of All Souls, became a friend of the wits in London and a book-collector. Dying young, he left the college his library and a large sum of money for the splendid building that bears his name. He also founded Codrington College in Barbados (which All Souls helped to rebuild after a fire some years ago) – an early example of the influence of Oxford spreading ever wider in the English-speaking world. George Clarke of All Souls was a notable virtuoso, and his fifty-six-year tenure of his Fellowship gave him the opportunity to enrich the university with many gifts. He gave Brasenose a leaden statue-group of Cain and Abel, which made a *point d'appui* in the centre of the quadrangle until the Victorians swept it away. He was active in placing the royal statues in the niches at University College, gave portraits of the queens to Queen's College, numerous books and portraits to the Bodleian. At All Souls he took the lead in bringing in Hawksmoor to design the large quadrangle, with the new hall and library. He was responsible for the unique buttery, with its oval shape and elaborate coffered ceiling in stone. He built the house on the High which became the warden's lodgings, was the adviser in the restoration and enrichment of the chapel with Thorn-hill's fresco, which the Victorians destroyed. For Christ Church he designed the grand new library, which originally had an open piazza underneath, as had Queen's library and the Radcliffe Camera. Worcester College he largely made what it is, perhaps designing the central block of library, hall and chapel, certainly giving it most of his fortune. He left it his choicest books, drawings, manuscripts and papers, which have given the library its distinction; for it contains not only quartos of the Shakespearean drama and the famous 'Clarke Papers', from which we are informed of the army debates in the Civil War, but Inigo Jones's designs for the court masques at Whitehall before the catastrophe.

How much more rewarding was George Clarke's accomplishment than the acres of controversy that fill dull academic books!

There were other connoisseurs, too. Provost Lancaster of Queen's was one – hence we owe the rational articulation of the finest Georgian palace in Oxford. At All Souls the greatest of academic lawyers carried on Clarke's work; the ex-cellence of Blackstone's prose style was owing to his aesthetic taste. As a young man he wrote verse; on going to the bar, 'The Lawyer's Farewell to his Muse', is a charming poem, popular in its day. The eminent Shakespearean scholar, Malone, said that 'the notes which he gave me on Shakespeare show him to have been a man of excellent taste and accuracy, and a good critic'. Blackstone took much interest in reforming the university press and improving standards of printing, setting an admirable example with his own edition of *Magna Carta* in 1758. We owe to him the completion of the Codrington library, with its scheme of decora-tion, the ceiling, the busts and statue of Codrington by Sir Henry Cheere.

The noblest of all these works was accomplished in these years, the Radcliffe Camera, designed by James Gibbs and built 1738–49. The design was much in-fluenced by Wren's projected Mausoleum for Charles I at Windsor; but Gibbs had been a pupil of Carlo Fontana at Rome, and the building that emerged has something splendidly Roman about it. Having lived most of my working life under its shadow, I cannot but be grateful for the inspiration of this wonderful work of genius in all its moods: the honeyed colour of its stone lit up by the rose-flush of dawn or sunset, the leaden dome sifted with snow under moonlight, the lighted windows beaconing warmth and civilized culture on nights of storm, glimpses of the dome within reflecting the blue of sky without. It remains to say, what has been noted by Pevsner, that the placing and completion of the dome, at the navel of Oxford, gave the city a formal integration which Cambridge is without.

Paradoxically, considering Oxford's loyalty to and suffering for the Stuarts, it fell to the university to play a forward part in getting rid of them in the person of

James II. This was on account of his foolery in attacking the Church of England, the main support of the monarchy. His conversion to Catholicism – strictly against the last injunctions of his martyred father – was already sufficiently crazy in an heir to the crown of a fanatically Protestant country. As king he was supreme governor of the Church of England, but he was determined on a privileged position for Papists – after the terrible warning of the Popish Plot! Anxious to prise a foothold for his communion at Oxford, but mean about money, he tried to turn Magdalen – perhaps attracted by the name – into a Catholic seminary. He met with dogged resistance from the Fellows. They had statutorily elected Hough their president. The king tried to force upon them one Farmer, a Cambridge convert who was drunken and riotous, and statutorily ineligible. When his character alone necessitated his withdrawal, James ordered the Fellows to elect Parker, the Romanizing bishop of Oxford whom he had appointed. In September the king came down, attended by three troops of horse, to rate the Fellows in undignified language, thus putting himself in a hopeless posture with loyal Anglicans. The Fellows were called before James's Ecclesiastical Commission for their contumacy, and extruded from their Fellowships – their property and livelihood. Their places were taken by a number of intruded Jesuits and others. A year later, in September 1688, when even James felt the ground giving way beneath him, he ignominiously restored the rightful president and Fellows. Their restoration is still celebrated by a Gaudy at Magdalen.

On that unfortunate visit James at least had the consolations of his faith: vespers in the temporary chapel that old Obadiah Walker ('Old Obadiah, Sings Ave Maria'), the master, had rigged up at University College, and mass with Massey, the Catholic whom James had preferred to Aldrich as Dean of Christ Church rather than Aldrich. These nonsensical goings-on ended in loss of a throne. The militant Protestant Bishop Compton detached Princess Anne from the tottering fortunes of her father, and escorted her to Nottingham at the Revolution. There he collected recruits and marched at the head of his small army, with the Princess, under the standard, '*Nolumus leges Angliae mutari.*'

Thus was Oxford reconciled to the Revolution and the rule of William III, though it produced a small quota of non-jurors. Though these contained a number of distinguished men, like the scholarly Hickes and saintly Bishop Ken, the university got on very well without them and, in the reign of Queen Anne, positively rejoiced in the rule of a Stuart who was a good churchwoman, granddaughter of its chancellor and benefactor, Clarendon.

An historian of the university, Sir Charles Mallet, has said that Oxford was 'the capital of the Jacobite reaction as naturally as half a century before she had become the capital of the Cavaliers'. But it is doubtful if this was really important. Oxford's Jacobitism under the first two Hanoverians was sentimental rather than

148

Right: Magdalen College: cloister with gargoyles.

wholly serious – a reaction to the German charmlessness of George I and George II. More to the point, these two monarchs were in the hands of the Whigs; Tories were for two generations out in the wilderness, without loaves and fishes. The Church was Tory, and all worthwhile preferment went to Whigs: this was a sufficient cause of grievance. The moment a young king came to the throne, who spoke English like an Englishman and was no Whig puppet, Oxford returned to loyalist sentiment: George III had no more loyal support than from the university.

The transition may be seen in the career of its leading Jacobite, Dr William King, principal of St Mary Hall. He was a distinguished man, a friend of Swift and admired by Dr Johnson, an amusing writer and good orator. At the opening ceremony of the Radcliffe Library he introduced into his speech the phrase '*Redeat!*' ('May he return', i.e. the Pretender) three times, each time pausing for thunderous applause. It was the kind of silliness that dons delight in. Then Dr King met the Pretender on a visit incognito to England, saw what a fool he was, and was completely disenchanted. It was simply distance that had lent enchantment to the view. On George III's marriage Dr King was one of the deputation sent up to present an address of congratulation to the charming youth. The aberration was over.

While it lasted, it was a source of irritation to Cambridge Whigs like Horace Walpole who thought, in 1751, that the relics of Charles I 'should be given to that nursery of nonsense and bigotry', Oxford. But, apart from politics, the creator of Strawberry Hill had a perfect *tendresse* for the Gothic city. To Charles Lyttelton in 1736: 'I have been at Oxford – how could you possibly leave it? After seeing that charming place I can hardly ask you to come to Cambridge. Magdalen Walks

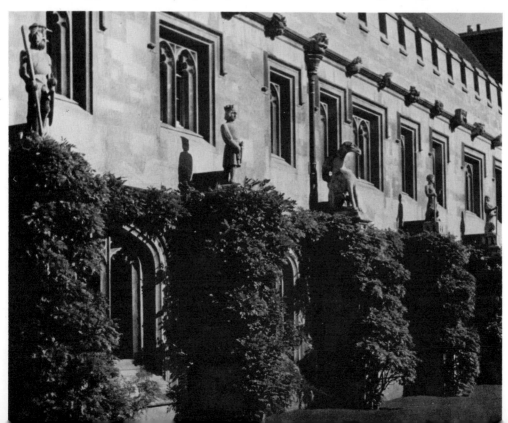

please me most; I felt a pensive joy in 'em occasioned by thinking two Lytteltons had been drowned in the adjoining stream, and another had so often walked there.' He enclosed a poem: 'Oxford inspired me; Magdalen Walks gave me the hint, and friendship dictated.' In the autumn of 1753:

the whole air of the town charms me, and what remains of the true Gothic un-Gibbsed, and the profusion of painted glass, were entertainment enough to me. As soon as it was dark I ventured out, and the moon rose as I was wandering among the colleges and gave me a charming venerable Gothic scene, which was not lessened by the monkish appearance of the old Fellows stealing to their pleasures.

In July 1760:

You know my rage for Oxford; if King's College would not take it ill, I don't know but I should retire thither and profess Jacobitism, that I might enjoy some venerable set of chambers. I ferreted from morning to night ... and I believe saw more antique holes and corners than Tom Hearne did in three score years.

In the buttery at Christ Church Horace discovered what he thought 'two glorious portraits by Holbein. I took them down, washed them myself and fetched out a thousand beauties.' In 1783, when he was an old man of seventy-seven, staying at Nuneham, it is still:

I went to my passion, Oxford, and saw Sir Joshua's Nativity [i.e. in New College chapel]. To see the window tolerably I was forced to climb into the organ loft by such a pair of stairs that, not having broken my neck, I can almost believe that I could dance a minuet on a horse galloping full speed.

So much for the background, now for the work of the university.

Within its walls it was dominantly, almost exclusively, clerical: practically all Fellows had to be in holy orders. Altogether, in mid-eighteenth century there were about two thousand, Fellows and students. Every society needs its myth to keep order in the nursery, and Church of England doctrine provided a sufficient working ideology for Georgian England, its ethical practice a good deal more satisfactory and worthy of respect than its metaphysics. The dominant philosophical influence of Locke raised awkward questions for the religious, for its implications were sceptical. In 1703 the heads of houses tried to stop his *Essay on Human Understanding* being read with pupils, but in vain. The Deist controversy raged for the next two or three decades, and Oxford made interesting contributions to the heterodox side. Far more influential was 'the greatest theological work of the time and one of the most original of all time', Butler's *The Analogy of Religion*.

Locke's philosophical views were attacked by Cambridge Calvinists as Socinian, a term of abuse for reason and common sense. (Cambridge was quite as clerical and orthodox: Newton had been terrified of his real beliefs becoming known, and his successor Whiston lost his professorship for his heretical views in 1710.) Joseph Butler had been brought up as a Dissenter but, being of an inquiring mind, realized the relativism of religious belief. Coming up to Oriel, he gradually worked out a psychological approach to religion, which went altogether deeper than fantasy-dogmas. It took the phenomena of conscience as its basis, argued that these revealed the true nature of man and indicated a moral government of the universe.

Butler was far more effective than any ordinary theologian – his influence went on powerfully into the next century with Gladstone, Newman, Matthew Arnold. Newman said that the study of Butler made 'an era in his religious opinions' and, with a similarly sceptical side to his intellect, he was impressed by Butler's characteristic conclusion that 'probability is the guide to life'. I love him for his realism without illusions: 'Things and actions are what they are, and the consequences of them will be what they will be: why then should we desire to be deceived?' Why indeed? It is one of the most salutary pieces of wisdom ever to come out of Oxford, particularly in a time when demotic society is reducing itself to anarchy.

Butler could have been primate if he had wished; but Horace Walpole said that he had been 'wafted to his see in a cloud of metaphysics and remained absorbed in it', i.e. he took no interest in politics. The nearest he came to it was to suggest a plan for providing the American colonies with bishops – about which the revolting colonists made so much insincere fuss. In fact there could be no better archbishop than William Wake (1716–37), a Christ Church man of immense industry and learning, who effectively answered the arrogant Bossuet's *Variations des Eglises Protestantes*. As archbishop, Wake was in touch with Gallicans in revolt against the ultramontane claims of the Bull *Unigenitus*. A truly ecumenical spirit, he was tolerant of Nonconformists at home and conducted an enormous correspondence abroad, in good relations with the Greek Orthodox Church as well as French Gallicans. He bequeathed his large library and papers to Christ Church.

Edmund Gibson of Queen's should have succeeded him. He came up as a 'poor serving child', and proceeded to make himself one of the leading Anglo-Saxon scholars, alongside Hickes; he produced editions of the *Anglo-Saxon Chronicle*, of Camden and Spelman. A better scholar than the brilliant, fire-eating Atterbury, Gibson demolished his case for the independence of Convocations, and compiled the definitive account of English church law. The ecclesiastical affairs of the colonies came within his jurisdiction as Bishop of London, and he became Sir Robert Walpole's adviser on church matters and appointments: 'Walpole's Pope, and a very good Pope he is.' He was immensely energetic and active. Oddly enough on the one subject on which he opposed Walpole Gibson was wrong; so he lost the primacy: a second-rater was appointed. Still, most of these Georgian prelates were worthy of the places they occupied.

What on earth would have happened if John Wesley had become Archbishop of Canterbury?

Three generations of that remarkably gifted family were Oxford men: the original John Wesley at New Inn Hall, his son Samuel at Exeter, then three grandsons, Samuel the younger, John and Charles at Christ Church. The original John was an Independent – there was a strong nonconforming streak in the family, one way and another. Samuel Wesley the younger had both Bishop Sprat and Atterbury as patrons; as an undermaster at Westminster he promoted the Westminster Hospital and helped the new-founded colony of Georgia. This was something of an Oxford enterprise, since the founder, Oglethorpe, was a Corpus man; John and Charles Wesley and George Whitefield all went out to help. The younger Samuel generously aided his brothers' education, but disapproved their 'Methodism'.

This nickname referred to the strict rules of study and religious observance, including weekly communion, on the part of the 'holy club' whose natural leader and inspiration was John, the genius of the group. While at Oxford they were few in number, and fewer when the autocratic John was away. He was a good classical scholar and an even better dialectician – no one could get the better of him in the exchanges his evangelizing involved him in. The group carried their inner devotion into regular visiting of prisoners in the castle, preaching and holding services there, feeding and clothing the poor, themselves leading exemplary lives. Meanwhile John faithfully taught and lectured his pupils – coming up to Christ Church at sixteen in 1720, in 1726 his father was able to write proudly, 'My Jack is Fellow of Lincoln.' The rector had used his influence to get him elected, to become the world-famous son of that college; while Bishop Potter of Oxford, who got the primacy instead of Gibson, was friendly and encouraging to these young men.

Bishop Butler, however, disapproved of the hysterical phenomena that attended John Wesley's early preaching in the open, as 'a horrid thing, a very horrid thing'. As for Wesley, he found the *Analogy* too profound for him. His genius was all for practical action – direct personal appeal in preaching, followed up by the organization and administration of societies; immense energy as propagandist, popularizer, educator – he found himself in a decade or two, to his surprise, a rich man. All went into the society he founded. The energy of the little man, throughout a long life, was Napoleonic; all under strict discipline, without being ascetic. In the end, from those small beginnings at Oxford, he created a world-wide Church.

The Oxford collaborators were few, but in his brother Charles the movement

John Wesley, the genius of the Methodist movement. As founder of a world-church, 'no Oxford man has ever accomplished more'.

had a hymn-writer of genius – though John's must not be underestimated. Both of them were exceptional preachers and each peregrinated all over the country, John going further afield to Scotland, Ireland and America. In the early days the movement was looked at askance, with its irregular itinerant preaching – like the medieval friars; but when it became clear that its implications, so far from being subversive of society, were highly conservative – Wesley greatly disapproved of the American Revolution – the authorities, the bishops and even Dr Johnson became friendly and respectful.

Throughout his career John Wesley never ceased to be the Oxford don, tutor, mentor, leader of his disciples; in the end, he made himself a bishop, by undertaking to ordain his itinerant preachers. And why not? Of the original Oxford group one or two attained to an independent name. James Hervey's writings, especially his lugubrious *Meditations among the Tombs*, were vastly popular: they appealed to the religious side of Gothic sentiment as Horace Walpole's to the secular. George Whitefield, the most powerful preacher of the lot, with his voice of vast compass and his histrionic tricks, was a later recruit to the group, of which he took the lead when the Wesleys left Oxford. He, too, journeyed all over England, Ireland and America, but found his most permanent ground of support in Wales. He dared to deviate from Wesley's high Arminian line over Predestination, and thus became the prophet of the Welsh Calvinist brand of Methodism. To be the inspirer of a church is something, however absurd its doctrines; but to be the founder of a world-church as John Wesley was – no Oxford man has ever accomplished more, and perhaps only Newman anything comparable.

153

More interesting intellectually are the unbelievers, for they carried the future with them. One understands sociologically the opposition they aroused: it was not a question of 'truth' on either side so much as the fact that their calling in question the current ideology was subversive of social order – as with Communist countries today. Of course, simple people believe in the 'truth' of the prevailing myths, and it is not socially desirable that their faith should be disturbed. A clear-sighted Oxford man, Mark Pattison, realized that 'the greater part of mankind have no mind'. It is, however, the vocation and the duty of the elect – a small number in any society – to discover what is true, as far as possible. Thus the younger Pitt's permission for Godwin's radical *Political Justice* to circulate at the time of the French Revolution was much to the point – the book was so highly priced that it would do no damage among the common people.

The first of English deists, and perhaps the first of our modern metaphysicians, was an Oxford man, Lord Herbert of Cherbury (1583–1648). He is popularly known for his interesting autobiography, with its engagingly Celtic vein of vanity. He was a close acquaintance of Donne, with his Catholic background, who agonized over religious issues and controversies. This must have opened Herbert's eyes to their futility regarded as 'truth' – claimed as such by each side. When Herbert published his original work, *De Veritate*, in Paris in 1624, he rejected so-called Revelation as the artifice of priests. This was in keeping with Hobbes, and aroused similar hostility all round. Herbert was a very independent mind, out on a limb of his own; he put forward his own theory of perception and of innate ideas, which Locke rejected while sympathizing with his anti-theological views. Disregarded in England, for the excruciating delights of the Civil War, Herbert was regarded with respect on the continent, by both Gassendi and Descartes – to be attacked later at home, when they got round to him, by such Puritan lights as Culverwell and Baxter.

Toland (1670–1722) was not an Oxford man, but he read in the libraries and wrote his book here, *Christianity Not Mysterious* (1696). An Irish Catholic, he was converted to Protestantism, so he was in a position to see through both sides. He was a close disciple of Locke, who had to disavow Toland's indiscretion when his book raised a storm. It emphasized the importance of historical inquiry into the origin of creeds. He had the critical perception to see that *Eikon Basilike*, supposedly written by Charles I, which had such immense influence in spreading the cult of the martyr, was really the work of John Gauden. And this piece of mystagoguery made all the more understandable the supposititious accounts incorporated in the New Testament. This insight was very dreadful; fortunately Toland was impoverished and in want, and did not survive to be old or do any more damage.

Matthew Tindal (d. 1733), as a Fellow of All Souls, was not starved; but he cheated by being a water drinker, so that he could always score in argument with all the other Fellows, except the poet Young, who would come up with something unexpected of his own. Tindal too had been a Catholic for a time, persuaded that there was no logical defence for the Anglican schism from the 'universal' Church. When he went into the question with his *The Rights of the Christian Church asserted against the Romish and all other Priests*, he found that there was no rational justification for their claims either. The book provoked a score of answers, and was ordered to be burned by that rational assembly, the House of Commons. Years later he returned to the attack with his notorious *Christianity as Old as the Creation*. Under the guise of accepting it as 'a most holy religion', he showed that the idea of Revelation was superfluous, and a rational religion of nature more cogent. This proved the culmination of the deist controversy and provoked some thirty replies. When Tindal answered them in a second volume, good Bishop Gibson prevented its publication. It is curious that so much of this controversy should have been connected with Oxford, though Cambridge produced its distinguished freethinker in Anthony Collins. It enables us to see in perspective the unbelief of Hume and Gibbon, and throws light on the background of Swift's *Tale of a Tub* and the obscure question of what he really believed. (He was only an Oxford man by virtue of taking his degree from Hart Hall, though he had friends at Christ Church, of which he would have liked to be dean.)

The leading scientist in England in the second half of Newton's life, when he had given up scientific work, was Edmond Halley (1656–1742). Like Hooke, Halley was in marked contrast to the Cambridge prophet: where Newton was intensive, mathematical, introvert, they were extensive, discursive, extrovert. Halley had an immensely long career of varied activity and discovery; he made 'notable contributions to astronomy and physics; he was an accomplished mathematician, a pioneer in geophysics and in demography, a learned Arabist and an intrepid navigator'. He gave years of work to the Royal Society, and performed a crucial service in bringing Newton's *Principia* to birth, prevailing upon him to publish it, editing it and paying for its publication. Halley finally shattered the idea of a solid celestial sphere 'by establishing the independent motions of certain stars in space'. He spent his last twenty years as Astronomer Royal determining their exact position.

As an undergraduate at Queen's he published three papers on the orbits of the planets, sunspot and the occultation of Mars. The glaring lacuna in astronomy was in knowledge of the stars of the southern hemisphere; in 1676 Halley left for St Helena: 'the deficiency was now to be made good by an Oxford undergraduate only just entering upon manhood.' In spite of the cloudy atmosphere he managed to determine the places of 341 stars: these were added to the star catalogues, and the young man gained for himself the title of 'the southern Tycho' (Tycho Brahe having been the greatest observational astronomer of the north).

Halley should have been elected Savilian professor of astronomy in 1691, but his views were suspect and the cautious Newton recommended David Gregory, an enthusiastic Scotch promoter of the great man. In 1703 Wallis died, 'one of the greatest mathematicians of the age, a pioneer in the use of the techniques that were developing into the calculus'. In the sixteenth century significant progress had been made in algebra, and Wallis fully recognized the genius of Hariot here. Wallis's *Algebra* of 1685 was not only the best textbook of the subject, but contained a valuable account of its historical development, when hitherto geometry had held the field. Halley succeeded Wallis and to his house in New College Lane, where an observatory was built for him on the roof, where one can still inspect the simple equipment with which he made his epoch-making observations.

His prime contributions were in cometary astronomy. He correctly predicted the return of the comet named after him, in 1758, 1835 and 1910 – when popular wisdom associated it with the death of Edward VII. He also did an enormous amount of work in other fields, establishing the mathematical law connecting barometric pressure with height above sea-level, which he developed on the basis of Boyle's Law; on rainbows, solar heat, physics of the earth and its atmosphere; thermometry; meteors and eclipses; the transits of Venus. A happy extrovert, he went on Atlantic voyages to observe trade winds and the phenomena of monsoons, the variation of the compass, charting the seas. He explored diving and underwater activity, and turned his mathematical knowledge to the practical theory of annuities and life insurance. What a prodigious life his was, prolonged to eighty-six! The keynote of it was the excellent principle of empiricism: 'all that we can hope to do is to leave behind us observations that may be confided in, and to propose hypotheses which after-ages may examine, amend or confute.'

Is one to consider Gilbert White (1720–93) an Oxford scientist? He was all his life a Fellow of Oriel, though it was at Selborne in Hampshire, where he served a cure, that he made the observations and wrote the book which made him the first of English naturalists. His work offers a prime example of empirical method: 'a prince among observers, nearly always observing the right thing in the right way, and placing before us in a few words the living being he observed', he made daily observation, investigation, exact note-taking the rule of his life. Nothing in natural history escaped him – birds, beasts, insects, plants, trees, weather, seasons. Some of his separate monographs were among the earliest in zoological literature. A born naturalist, all his life he was working towards his classic book, *The Natural History and Antiquities of Selborne*; but it was not until 1789, four years before his death that he brought it out.

It was the book of a lifetime – and has lasted better than the French Revolution.

A Rowlandson cartoon, 'a varsity trick, smuggling in'.

No one who has ever read it, however little given to the subject, has been able to resist its spell, and no one has ever been able to define its secret. It is a completely satisfying work of literature as well as of science; perhaps Lowell came nearest when he spoke of its 'natural magic . . . open the book where you will, it takes you out of doors'. But the book also reveals a life of the utmost charm and goodness, unselfish and unself-conscious, in the most natural manner in the world – and he was an Oxford cleric of the eighteenth century. So the age had its charm. It is true that it was the first book of its kind to appear, but it has never been surpassed; it has a kind of perfection, like the novels of Jane Austen. It not only appeals, to naturalists like Darwin, who much admired it, but has been an inspiration all over the world.

What did Oxford stand for in the literature of the age?

In the first two decades of the century Addison succeeded to the ascendancy of Dryden, and for a quarter of a century he retained his connection with the university, as undergraduate and Fellow of Magdalen – we remember him there still in Addison's Walk. He was a person of exceptional charm and cultivation; this allied to his literary gifts brought him popularity – everything that he touched turned to success. His poem 'The Campaign', written to celebrate Marlborough's victory of Blenheim, with its famous line describing how the hero

> Rides in the whirlwind and directs the storm

won the author an under-secretaryship of state, in a society that set a high value on literature. And we are reminded that Marlborough's reward, the park at Woodstock and the building of Blenheim Palace by a grateful nation, came to have historic importance for Oxford, politically and socially, for the next two or three centuries.

Addison's play, *Cato*, had similar *réclame*, but even wider influence and impact. Approved on the continent for adhering to classical principles (Addison was a cultivated linguist in French and Italian, as well as a good classical scholar) *Cato* was translated all over Europe. George Washington is known to have modelled his persona on the Republican hero, and Addison's are the only literary works, I noticed, in Washington's library in the Boston Athenaeum.

Most important were the model Addison set, and the standards he inculcated, with his famous essays in the *Tatler*, *Spectator* and *Guardian*. These were something new, urbane, cultivated, humorous; it was not only that Addison created a lasting character in Sir Roger de Coverley, but he propagated more refined standards of taste, conduct, manners after the fanaticism and brutality of the seventeenth century. Swift had a far more powerful genius, but Addison exerted a greater influence on society. It is difficult for us to appreciate it, though the Victorians did – in some ways he was a pre-Victorian: conventional, pious, kind – his work was an extrapolation of his delightful personality.

He came of an Oxford family, of the Cumbrian stock connected with Queen's. His father had been a Queen's man, befriended by Joseph Williamson. Lancelot Addison was a Royalist, who, while chaplain at Tangier, wrote an excellent book on Morocco, which was printed at the Clarendon Press, of which Williamson was a curator. Addison followed up with an interesting account of the Jews in that unfamiliar territory – both books dedicated to Williamson. When Addison's son, Joseph, came up in turn to Queen's, Provost Lancaster – who had a discerning eye not only for architecture – observed that the boy had promise and got him a demy-ship at Magdalen. We see how beneficently these territorial college associations and patronage worked with persons of taste and discernment.

Addison's leading disciples, Tickell and Steele, were both Oxford men; Tickell indeed another Cumbrian at Queen's, of which he was undergraduate and Fellow from 1701 until he married in 1726. That dispensation of property – celibate tenure of a Fellowship – enabled him to make a useful contribution to the literature of the time. He began with a poem, 'Oxford' and, a better scholar but worse poet, dared to translate Homer in competition with Pope. This led to a typical literary squabble, in which vanity and envy were to the fore. Tickell wrote other Oxford pieces, on the rebuilding of Henry v's supposed lodgings at Queen's, and lectured on poetry. He addressed verses to Addison on his opera *Rosamund*, inspired by the folklore of Woodstock and Godstow. In the end Tickell was engrossed by politics and office, but remained, as everybody owned, a good man.

Steele had a more original spark than Tickell, but dissipated it by his way of life – they all drank too much, except of course Swift, who had other troubles. Steele was at Oxford from 1690 to 1694, where he made the acquaintance of Addison. Steele left without taking a degree, for the army and the theatre, but later published a 'Prologue' to the university. His was the original idea of the *Tatler* and of the Coverley Club, but Addison had more application and wrote the larger number of the papers. Steele rather lost his talents in political pamphleteering, though one pamphlet, *The Crisis*, supporting the Hanoverian succession, made history.

Edward Young occupied a high place in the literary life and esteem of the century, and on the continent his *Night Thoughts* made him the most admired of contemporary English poets. He is, of all poets, the most difficult for us to appreciate – a fascinating literary enigma; for one thing he exemplified to the extreme the eighteenth-century conception of what poetry should be: generalizing, moralistic, sententious, to which we are unsympathetic. On the other hand he undoubtedly had genius, a strange, somewhat morbid imagination which has recommended him to the surrealists in our time. (It recommends him to us that he should have been attacked by the portentous, and pretentious, George Eliot.) Young was a Wykehamist, a son of the Church – his father was Dean of Salisbury. He came up in 1702; in 1708 Archbishop Tenison pushed him into a law Fellowship at All Souls, where he remained until he got the college living of Welwyn in 1730.

Young never intended the Church; a properly ambitious Fellow of All Souls, he intended literature and politics, like Addison, to whose circle he was a recruit. But he failed to find a footing in politics, through the ill-luck of having the unreliable rake, Wharton, as his patron. (He prevailed on Wharton to subscribe to the building of the wing next to the Codrington, where I have lived and worked for many years.) Young began with an attempt on the theatre, with tragedies I have not read, *Busiris* and *The Revenge*. Unsuccessful, he wrote a series of satires, *The Universal Passion*, which he took to be the love of fame (of which he can hardly have disapproved, since he shared it). These made him a small fortune; it disappeared in the South Sea. Pope said that Young had more genius than common sense.

He fell back on the Church and became an exemplary parson, regular in his attendance to his duties, not only in church and parish, but as local justice, virtually a squarson. He built himself a fine house, being a man of taste; he went in for gardening and Gothic arches like Pope; he built a steeple to his church, founded a charity school, and was open-handed in good works and philanthropy. But he never received any preferment or recognition to speak of from the powers that be. This neglect of one of the most famous writers in England, a distinguished orna-

Left: Edward Young, poet, 'a fascinating literary enigma'. Portrait by Joseph Highmore.
Right: Dr Johnson, by Sir Joshua Reynolds.

ment to the country, was disgraceful, an open scandal. But it was also fortunate: it left him free to concentrate on his real vocation, writing, by which he became famous and, in the end, rich.

When his earlier play, *The Brothers*, was at length produced with applause, he was able to give the profits to the Society for the Propagation of the Gospel. But *Night Thoughts on Life, Death and Immortality* won him European fame. Enormously admired by Klopstock, who addressed a poem to him, other German writers, with characteristic bad judgement, considered him superior to Milton. In France he was eulogized by Diderot and Madame de Staël; Robespierre kept the book under his pillow to solace sleepless nights during the Revolution. The French even forgave Young's terse summing-up of Voltaire on meeting him:

> Thou art so witty, profligate, and thin,
> At once we think thee Milton, Death, and Sin.

The French Romantics continued the cult of him, and he is still read in France, though not in England: his college since the war has had to lend his fine, somewhat satyr-like, portrait by Highmore to the exhibition of surrealism in Paris. Perhaps he is due for a revival? But there is something mysterious about him. Though his letters have recently been collected and published by the university press, Young on his death-bed had all his private papers destroyed: we cannot get back behind him to the man he really was.

He wrote other works well known in their day: *Resignation*, to offer consolation to Fanny Boscawen for the death of her Admiral; a curious prose-work, *The*

Centaur not Fabulous. But few people realize how much of Young has entered into the language, that they are quoting him when they say, 'Procrastination is the thief of time', or 'A fool at forty is a fool indeed', or 'All men think all men mortal, but themselves'. When he wrote a satire on the theme, 'Men talk only to conceal the mind', was he thinking of himself? One would think so to read his correspondence, what remains of it. We do not need his letters to duchesses to realize his distinction in the life of the time; his friendship with that man of feeling, the novelist Richardson, brings him closer to us.

A Wykehamist who had the future more with him as a poet was Collins, who was up from 1740–3, when he was a friend of Joseph Warton and Gilbert White. Collins was precocious and of brilliant promise; besides being a classical scholar, he had a wide knowledge of French, Italian and Spanish literature. No poem has ever more completely achieved the ideal of unrhymed classical poetry than his 'Ode to Evening':

> If aught of oaten stop, or pastoral song,
> May hope, chaste Eve, to soothe thy modest ear ...

While the way the poem goes on,

> Now air is hushed, save where the weak-eyed bat,
> With short shrill shriek, flits by on leathern wing.
>   Or where the beetle winds
>   His small but sullen horn ...

pointed as clearly to the new path the Romantics would take as does Gray's 'Elegy in a Country Churchyard'. The Cambridge poet was as supercilious in his judgement of his Oxford contemporaries as A. E. Housman was of his colleagues. Though Gray had the Horatian good fortune to be recited by Wolfe before the capture of Quebec, Collins expressed with equal force and sincerity the patriotic feelings of that age of glory in achievement:

> How sleep the brave, who sink to rest,
> By all their country's wishes blest! ...
> By fairy hands their knell is rung,
> By forms unseen their dirge is sung;
> There Honour comes, a pilgrim grey,
> To bless the turf that wraps their clay,
> And Freedom shall awhile repair,
> To dwell a weeping hermit there!

The ground was prepared for the Romantic movement by the admirable criticism of Joseph and Thomas Warton. Their father was professor of poetry, and as a schoolmaster had Gilbert White for pupil. Joseph Warton was a friend of Collins at Winchester, and came up to Oriel in 1740. His first volume of verse avowed his unalloyed love of nature and eschewed moral didacticism. He preferred the Elizabethan poets to the Augustan standards of Pope and Young, and took his stand against them in a celebrated *Essay on the Genius and Writings of Pope*. His critical insights into Shakespeare, his essays on various *genres* of poetry, pastoral and epic, all helped to generate a new literary sensibility.

The younger Thomas Warton carried this much further, and from Oxford – where he spent forty-six years as undergraduate, then Fellow, of Trinity (1744–90) – exerted a significant literary influence. Warton first won a reputation with an heroic poem on Oxford, *The Triumph of Isis*, which celebrated some of its historic alumni along with its Gothic architecture. This was in reply to Mason's *Isis*, which cast aspersions on the university's Jacobite leanings. Warton shared Walpole's enthusiasm for everything Gothic but, a much better scholar and archaeologist, always provoked Horace's Cambridge Whiggery. Warton was a loyal Oxford man, who encouraged all kinds of literary activity within the walls. He edited a celebrated anthology, *The Oxford Sausage*, full of amusing parodies and skits, which was often reprinted and was the ancestor of the light verse of the late Victorian *Oxford Magazine*. Works of *pietas* were his biographies of the founder of Trinity, Sir Thomas Pope, and its president, Ralph Bathurst.

In 1754 came his *Observations on the 'Faery Queen' of Spenser*, a work of exceptional perception and sympathy, all the more remarkable from a Georgian. Though Dr Johnson was critically on the other side, he recognized its quality: 'You have shown to all who shall hereafter attempt the study of our ancient authors the way to success by directing them to the perusal of the books those authors have read'. There was more to it than this: anyone who has read Warton's book will recognize its inner sympathy with the spirit of medieval romance. Johnson's generosity led to a warm friendship between the two; Warton's status as critic was established, he became professor of poetry and embarked on his *magnum opus*, the *History of English Poetry*.

Pope had thought of doing it, Gray intended it but got no further than a preliminary sketch. Warton tackled the immense task, and produced three volumes carrying the story down to the end of the Elizabethan age. He did not live to finish with a fourth volume, bringing it down to Pope, but he did produce the best critical edition of Milton's shorter poems, with explanatory notes. Thus

Warton's name is a landmark in the history of English literature. His great history exerted a signal influence on its contemporary currents. Together with Percy's *Reliques* it helped to awaken an interest in medieval and Elizabethan poetry. By familiarizing his contemporaries with the imaginative temper and romantic subject-matter of the poetry that was anterior to the eighteenth century, Warton's work helped to divert the stream of English verse from the formal and classical channels to which the prestige of Pope had for many years consigned it.

As a work of scholarship 'no literary history discloses more comprehensive learning in classical and foreign literature, as well as in that of Great Britain'. It was, of course, criticized by people inferior to it and him, but appreciated by a superior intelligence, of classical sympathies, in Gibbon, who considered that the work showed 'the taste of a poet and the minute diligence of an antiquarian'.

Warton was a good archaeologist and antiquarian; so was Thomas Percy, who opened up new territory with his long studies in ballads and folk-poetry. He was at Christ Church from 1746 to 1753, but, obtaining a college living in North-amptonshire, he pursued his researches for the next thirty years, and brought out his various works, from there. Of these by far the most influential was his *Reliques of Ancient English Poetry*, which appeared in 1765 in three volumes. This opened the eyes of the educated Georgian world, with its confined classical standards, to the wealth of poetry in the old ballads. This was something new; it set going the movement for the collection of folk-poetry, not only in Britain – notably with Scott's Border ballads – but in Germany, a generation later, with the brothers Grimm. Besides this, it communicated a vital electric spark to the next generation of poets: without Percy's *Reliques* Scott and Wordsworth, Southey and Coleridge would never have written their ballads. It has been held, too, that without the backward-looking, medieval inspiration of Walter Scott the Oxford Movement would not have taken the form it did.

One way and another the Gothic city, with its lingering medieval enchantments, gave direct impulse to the new movement in literature, the Romantics who were to dominate the nineteenth century.

Meanwhile, the Great Cham of literature, Ursa Major, and the rest of it, whose word was law, Dr Johnson, remained firmly with his huge bulk, his benevolent dictatorship, in the classical persuasion. He had come up to Pembroke in 1728, a sullen, silent youth, who suddenly astonished the dons by quoting Macrobius (he had the advantage that his father was a bookseller). He was poor and no less proud, and could stay only a couple of years. But he had some good times sliding on the ice in Christ Church Meadows, instead of attending lectures, and he afterwards recalled that Pembroke was in those days a nest of 'singing birds' with Shenstone, Richard Jago, Richard Graves, author of the admired *Spiritual Quixote*. Failing to return Lobo's *Abyssinia* to the college library, Johnson went up to eat the bread of poverty for twenty years in Grub Street – the long-term inspiration of the book appeared in his *Rasselas*, with which he at last won popularity.

Meanwhile, he had been carrying through, practically single-handed, the heroic undertaking of his English *Dictionary* – impossible to exaggerate the importance of this, for it set the standards and laid down the law for the language during the next century. Its immense intellectual vitality, good scholarship, and inspired common sense still keep it alive and give it a continued authority. In 1754, the year before its publication, Johnson returned to Oxford to acquire an M.A., so that it might appear on the title-page. His kind friends, Tom Warton and Wise, Radcliffe's librarian, had procured it for him. When Johnson came back at forty-five, he was pleased that the college servants remembered him, disappointed that the master did not order a copy of the *Dictionary*. But the lexicographer and the attendant Boswell walked three or four times up to Elsfield, where Wise had created a charming garden with its view out over Otmoor. (In my time John Buchan preserved Wise's antiquities there and carried on the eighteenth-century tradition of generous and kindly hospitality – and is now buried in the little churchyard along the village street from that house with its memories.)

Johnson went about the place nostalgically, reviving his recollections. He went to Osney Abbey, of which considerable ruins remained: 'I viewed them with indignation' (he thought of the Reformers as Whigs, which in a way they were). In Pembroke hall the fire was always in the middle, 'till the Whigs moved it to one side'. He inquired for 'poor dear Collins. I knew him a few years ago full of hopes, and full of projects; versed in many languages, high in fancy, and strong in retention.' (Collins was languishing in imbecility and was only thirty-eight when he died.) Johnson did not share Warton's enthusiasm for Spenser, but was big enough to encourage the work: 'I would not have it delayed. Three hours a day stolen from sleep and amusement will produce it. Let a servitor transcribe the quotations and interleave them with references to save time.' Next year, it was: 'Where hangs the new volume? Càn I help? Let not the past labour be lost for want of a little more; but snatch what time you can from the hall, and the pupils, and the coffee-house, and the parks, and complete your design.'

Dr Johnson, like most first-rate men, was an encourager of other people's work. Tom Warton was gregarious, and had an endearing habit of going down to the river to smoke a pipe with the bargees, and listen to their low language. After the publication of the *Dictionary* and his public recognition, Johnson loved coming down to Oxford, and came frequently. He was recognized everywhere and had acquaintance all round, but he liked best staying at his old college or with Warton at Trinity, where he enjoyed reading in the Gothic room of the library – and sent them a Baskerville's *Virgil*. Asked whether modern libraries were not more commodious: 'Sir, if a man has a mind to *prance*, he must study at Christ Church and All Souls.' 'All my mornings are my own', then there were meals with friends and tea-drinking. Pembroke Senior Common Room still has the vast tea pot which kept his bulk replenished. Going to stop with Warton in Kettel Hall, 'I wish your brother could meet us, that we might go and drink tea with Mr. Wise in a body. I hope he will be at Oxford or at his nest of British and Saxon

Walton Street showing the Clarendon Press. Dr Johnson complained: 'Why books printed at Oxford should be particularly dear I am unable to find.'

antiquities. I shall expect to see *Spenser* finished.' It was.

Dr Johnson fancied himself as a businessman, and enjoyed taking a hand in Thrale's brewery. Mrs Thrale was a lady of old Welsh family, who had married a middle-class brewer; she said, however, that 'his education at Oxford gave him the habits of a gentleman'. In the 1770s the Clarendon family gave a bequest to establish a riding school. Johnson was deputed to go down to investigate, and found that the funds were inadequate. They were allowed to accumulate till the 1850s, when they were used to establish the Clarendon Laboratory, which was to achieve great things in this century under the impulse of Lindemann.

Like Blackstone, Johnson addressed himself to the problems of the university press. 'Why books printed at Oxford should be particularly dear I am unable to find. We pay no rent; we inherit many of our instruments and materials; lodging and victuals are cheaper than at London.' Then, why? In conversation with George III in the royal library, the king, who was a devoted book collector, asked what was doing at Oxford. Dr Johnson 'could not much commend their diligence, but in some respects they were mended, for they had put their Press under better regulations and were at that time printing Polybius'. Johnson later wrote to encourage Warren Hastings, who contemplated an institution to study Persian at Oxford – we have observed that oriental studies were never entirely neglected there, after the impulse Laud had given them.

Boswell noticed that Johnson seemed to feel himself elevated as he approached Oxford: 'one of the first universities of the world', he called it, modestly. He always enjoyed his visits, talking about how to write biography with Tom Warton, dining at University College on their St Cuthbert's day Gaudy, though he had been invited to Christ Church. Or there was drinking tea with President Horne of Magdalen – with whom young Gibbon expressed disappointment, for he had gone expecting literary conversation, as if ordinary dons had the intellectual interests of a Gibbon! Silly people were afraid of talking in Johnson's presence, as they were in Swift's. The doctor had no sympathy with such a person: 'he need not have been afraid, if he had anything rational to say. If he had not, it was better he did not talk.'

In the spring of 1776, while trouble thundered in America, Johnson rattled down in the Oxford coach, talking all the way. He went to University College to visit Scott, the lawyer who became eminent as Lord Stowell. Next morning Johnson called on the master to discuss the press; the master suggested that Johnson should write them a work on the British constitution. The thought of work put the doctor off: 'Why should *I* be always writing?' So Johnson lumbered off to the new master of Pembroke, whom he much approved of, for he had written an able answer to Hume's *Essay on Miracles*. Some colleges were now excluding students from their common room. At Oriel gentlemen-commoners were allowed its use after dinner; but they seldom availed themselves of it, except on Gilbert White's visits: he always filled the room when he was there, 'such was his happy manner of telling a story'. The doctor was in favour of excluding them: 'a man who has a character does not choose to stake it in their presence'.

There were the pleasures of walking 'in the venerable walks of Merton', or visiting out of Oxford, to dine at Wheatley with Mickle, the translator of the *Lusiad*, afterwards calling on an old friend, Sackville Parker, the bookseller, of that family that carried on their business right up to this century. Parker had married his maid; Johnson approved: they had lived together many years and had 'mingled minds'. One spring Johnson went on a delightful day out in a postchaise to Blenheim Park, where Capability Brown 'had collected a magnificent body of water and drowned the epigram' (on Duchess Sarah's charity being as exiguous as the trickle of the little Glyme). Or the master of his old college would take him in his coach to dine with the principal of St Mary Hall in his 'beautiful villa at Iffley' (now ruined by the thundering traffic over Donington Bridge).

Johnson's last visit took place only a few months before his death in 1784. He had been very ill, but cheered up as usual on approaching the place he had so much at heart. He talked away in the coach before two unknown American ladies, the husband of one of whom had been a member of the American Congress: Boswell warned her not to let on. The doctor's openness with people whom he did not know, at a first interview, was remarkable; but why not? He had no fear, and there was no time to lose. When they arrived at the master's lodgings at Pembroke, the famous old man surprised everybody with unexpected views. He never knew a non-juror who could reason; he would be a Papist if he could, 'but an obstinate rationality prevents me'. The doctor was very gallant to Miss Adams, who made his coffee in her pot, 'the only thing she could call her own'. 'Don't say so, my dear; I hope you don't reckon my heart as nothing.' The old Tory, who remembered Queen Anne as a lady in a black hood sparkling with diamonds, and had had Jacobite sympathies, surprised them over the political crisis of 1784: 'I am for the King as against Fox; but I am for Fox against Pitt.' Why ever? 'I do not know Pitt, and Fox is my friend.' He could not but admire Fox that he could divide the nation with the king, so that there was a doubt 'whether it should be ruled by the sceptre of George III or the tongue of Fox'.

We are brought up short by the independence of mind of a truly great man, who was attacked as a pensioner of George III; but perhaps we may take into account that Charles James Fox was a descendant of the Stuarts, and an Oxford man. It is probable that that did not go for nothing in the loyal mind of Dr Johnson.

Blackstone's *Commentaries on the Laws of England*, based on his lectures at All Souls, came out in four volumes in 1765–9. It was one of the most successful books of the age, and one of the most influential of any age. It long remained the best general history of English law, in either England or America, where it was equally influential; for a century it provided the best basis of a legal education in both countries. In addition it described the state of the law to date with classic clearness and conciseness; as such, it kept its authority well into the next century, with frequent editions and annotations to bring it up to date. Blackstone was no philosopher of law (who wants that?), but exemplified the Oxford spirit, historical and descriptive, practical and to the point. Of course he was complacent, as he had reason to be, about the institutions of his country – then the most successful society in the world. He preferred a practical working system to theoretical perfectionism which does not work, and considered that 'by the law, the people had as large a portion of real liberty as is consistent with a state of society'. We have the worst reason to appreciate the force of that today, when, without direction or discipline, 'progressive' society is breaking down around us.

It is obvious that a society's laws need change and adaptation in accordance with new needs and developments. A lasting impulse in this direction was given by Jeremy Bentham. He was at Queen's for no less than seven years, though, in the manner of supercilious clever men, he did not appreciate his luck. Also in the manner of young men he was rude about Blackstone's lectures, when he stepped up the High to hear them. His mind was at the opposite pole from the complacent professor; nothing like such a stylist or man of taste, Bentham carried a more powerful analytical apparatus, had more genius and saw the weaknesses of the Georgian legal system. His life's work in probing them and suggesting reforms operated like a time bomb: it took practically a century – much longer in regard to the laws about sexual offences (his rational opinion of homosexuality has been given legislative effect only quite recently) – to carry out Bentham's far-reaching proposals for reform, in accordance with his utilitarian test of what best provided for the happiness of the greatest number. It fell to an All Souls jurist to describe the influence of it all, in Dicey's *Law and Opinion in the Nineteenth Century*.

Bentham indicated his programme and provided a basis for it in his early book, the *Fragment on Government*, 1776, which was really an acute and destructive criticism of the received opinions given authority by Blackstone. From there Bentham went on to survey the whole field of law: its philosophy, principles, practical legislation, penal reform, institutions. His ultimate influence was prodigious, at first on the continent of Europe before it took effect in England; it is probable that no legal figure in our history has exerted so much influence. It is ironical to think that its original impulse came by way of reaction to the dominant authority of the previous generation; but such is the way things happen.

A singularly fascinating figure is the Welsh orientalist and jurist, Sir William Jones (1746–94). His father came from a small Anglesey farm to become an eminent mathematician, who lived with the astronomically minded Lord Macclesfield out at Shirburn Castle. Jones had been a friend of Halley and editor of Newton: hence the invaluable library of scientific books and papers still there. The son was a prodigy of languages even as a boy at Harrow; his verse translations from Persian were admired all over Europe, and he received a tribute to his genius in *The Decline and Fall of the Roman Empire* – like having one's name inscribed in the dome of St Paul's, once upon a time.

Young Jones had his base at University College for the best part of twenty years, 1764–83; he brought a Syrian to Oxford, from whom to improve his Arabic. The brightest jewel in the crown of Oxford orientalism, he was able not only to answer supercilious French strictures on its scholarship but to put them in their place by his own astonishing gifts and attainments. His ardent desire was to get to India; but as a Whig sympathizer with the American Revolution, his appointment to a judgeship at Calcutta was held up for five years by the reactionary Lord Chancellor Thurlow. When Jones got to India he had only ten years of life in which to accomplish his historic work.

The opportunity India afforded to such men as Warren Hastings and William Jones was inspiring in itself – but they were inspired. Jones was the first westerner to win the confidence of the Brahmins and to be allowed to penetrate their arcana; thus he was the first to master Sanskrit, realize its root-affinity with the classical

Left: Sir William Blackstone by Bacon, at All Souls. His *Commentaries on the Laws of England* was one of the most influential of all Oxford books. *Right:* Jeremy Bentham, the Utilitarian, whose reforming influence was felt throughout Europe.

European languages, and so to inspire the immense development of comparative philology that flowed from it. Among his translations was the Sakúntala, the famous drama of Kalidása, which opened the riches of ancient Indian literature to the West. In his spare time he laid the foundations of Indian botany.

A brilliant jurist, who had made an original contribution to English law, he formed the project of making a complete digest of both Moslem and Hindu law. With the intellectual ambition and intuitive sympathy of a true Celt, he 'purposed to be the Justinian of India', and won the confidence of both pundits and native lawyers to this end. Before he died he had practically accomplished it. The difficulties were immense, the consequences colossal. It was easier to cope with Moslem law, because it had prevailed with the Moghul empire. But Hindu law, custom, folklore, anthropology had been pushed down among the people; the ancient intellectual sources in Sanskrit were occult, esoteric, partly forgotten and hard to come at. In revivifying them, reconstructing and bringing them back into the light of day, the Welshman performed an historic service for the submerged Indian people. In this way he may be regarded as an original creator of Indian nationalism; it is appropriate that this should have come from one of the oldest and half-submerged peoples of the British Isles, a sympathizer with American independence.

It is to be hoped that his inspiration is remembered in India, for it is forgotten in England. He loved India. He was a wonderful man, only forty-six when he died, after accomplishing so much! He has a fine Flaxman monument in University College chapel, and a lesser one in St Mary's.

Adam Smith is a figure of prose indeed, after this (he was notably prosy in conversation). It is curious that romantic Oxford should have had such a large part, with Sir William Petty and Adam Smith, in creating the dismal sciences, economics and statistics. Smith was at Balliol for six years, 1740–6, and – though he had no high opinion of the tuition – he made himself a good Greek scholar there, and read widely in English and French literature. So qualified for a professorship at Glasgow, he there produced his *Theory of the Moral Sentiments*, an important book and subject of much appeal to Scots. His life's work, *The Wealth of Nations*, came out in the *annus mirabilis* 1776. It began to be immediately acted upon; Lord North easily took some hints from it for further taxation, though their fellow-Oxonian, Fox, claimed that he had never read the book and could never understand it. He had no head for figures, as his own finances showed; this did not prevent him from aiming at the Treasury (where he might qualify today: an egregious spendthrift, he bankrupted himself and would have done the country). The younger Pitt, a Cambridge man, venerated the book and applied

The Flaxman monument in University College chapel to Sir William Jones, 'an original creator of Indian nationalism'.

HE FORMED A DIGEST OF HINDU AND MOHAMMEDAN LAWS

it consistently; Buckle called it 'in its ultimate results, probably the most important that had ever been written'. But he was a somewhat bleak historian of
civilization.

However, Smith serves to remind us of the important part an education at
Oxford played in the formation of public figures, numerous prime ministers,
lord chancellors and chancellors of the exchequer galore, administrators, pro-
consuls, prelates, one-half of the clergy and of the country's educators. One sees
their portraits on the walls and in the halls of every college, especially at Christ
Church, that picture gallery of the Georgian governing class. (They are well
portrayed, too, by Kneller, Reynolds, Gainsborough, Lawrence, Romney,
Hoppner.)

Cyril Jackson, dean of Christ Church 1783–1809, was a grand figure, an inspired tutor who thought it much more important to train the young men who
were to rule the country than to decline, or recline, upon a bishopric, and he
refused several. He was actually, at the end of the century, a reformer; 'he had a
wonderful tact in managing that most unmanageable class of undergraduates,
noblemen'. He made them work; he inspired them by the expectations he had of
them and followed their careers attentively. He chose the best possible tutors,
Gaisford for example, and believed in examinations. 'It was an absolute monarchy of the most ultra-Oriental character', wrote Bishop Heber; but it worked.
The dean was looked up to, in London as well as at Oxford – he even took a part
in toppling the inadequate Addington.

Jackson sensibly took special care of pupils of brilliant promise, like Canning
and Peel, the latter the first man to take a double first in the new Honour Schools.
To Peel in his early years in Parliament: 'Work very hard and unremittingly ...
Don't be afraid of killing yourself ... Be assured that I shall pursue you, as long as
I live, with a jealous and watchful eye. Woe be to you if you fail me.' It is just like
Jowett, with the later Victorians from Balliol; no wonder Peel became, as Gladstone said, the last statesman who was familiar with the working of every department of state. These were golden days for Christ Church. Most of the Georgian
prime ministers, apart from other officers of state, came from that one college: the
two Grenvilles, Shelburne, Portland, Lord Liverpool, Canning, Peel and so on
to the Victorians, Derby, Gladstone, Salisbury, Rosebery. Henry Pelham was at
Hart Hall; Chatham and Lord North at Trinity; Addington at Brasenose.

But politicians we have always with us: they occupy too much space in the
public prints, and even in history books.

We are more interested in cultural history.

9
The Nineteenth Century

OUR aim once more, as throughout this book, is to tell not so much the internal story of the university as its effect upon the nation and the world outside. It is all the more important to keep this in view as it becomes more difficult; for the nineteenth century was a period of continued changes and new developments within the walls, in response to the country's astonishing expansion and growth in prosperity. The Victorian age saw Britain the leading power in the world, proliferating in industry and invention, hard work and creativeness in every respect, particularly in science and literature. The difference in inflection between Cambridge and Oxford becomes more marked: where Newton's university makes an unparalleled contribution in this century to mathematics and the natural sciences, the university of Hobbes and Clarendon and Locke makes an equally marked contribution in the humanities and the social sciences, takes the lead in politics and law, administration and the empire.

Oxford was beginning to stir itself out of its Georgian complacency already by 1800, becoming aware that more must be done to make the youths work. We have seen Dean Jackson at Christ Church already at it; two other heads of houses were already in harness, Provost Eveleigh at Oriel, and Parsons, master of Balliol from 1798. A new examination statute was pushed through in 1800 and an honour school set up; competition began to have its usual beneficial effects: young men of promise like Peel and the Cannings, Gladstone and Henry Hallam and Manning were anxious to do well. Oriel threw its Fellowships open to the whole university: this had an extraordinary effect, which can be read in the history of England. Competition was a sharp spur: an Oriel Fellowship became the blue ribbon of an Oxford career. One needs only to cite a few names to see what they meant to England: Keble and Newman to the Church; the dynasty of Arnolds to education and literature; the Froudes to history and science; Whately to logic and economics, the Wilberforces to the churches, Anglican and Roman, Clough and Hartley Coleridge to poetry. Oriel gained an intellectual ascendancy in Oxford which lasted almost up to Newman's defection.

The moment Oxford began to reform itself with an honour school based on

Right: John Henry Newman, the leading member of the Oxford Movement, 'a church movement rather than a university movement'.

the classics, to which mathematics was added, with stricter scholarship and more attention to tutoring, as exemplified at Oriel, the university was attacked – as the manner often is – by its own members out in the world. These were notably the Edinburgh Reviewers, Francis Jeffrey and Sydney Smith. They were brilliant young men who wanted everything reformed in accordance with Bentham's utility principle, to which they had become converted. Newman used to refer to them as the 'useful knowledge people'. Actually, utilitarianism provided a rough and ready yardstick by which to test a hoary old system, rotten with dead wood and much in need of bringing up to new requirements. The Reviewers were effectively tackled by Copleston and John Davison, two of the Oriel 'Noetics', who had no difficulty in showing the insufficiency of a mechanical utility as a principle for university education. Many years later, when Newman wrote *The Idea of a University*, the classic statement of what Oxford stood for, he simply developed the Oriel argument that whatever was good was in itself useful, and that to restrict a university simply to utilitarian sciences was contrary to the generalizing purpose, in regard to the intellectual faculties, that was of the very nature of university education.

The story of the Oxford Movement is so appealing, and it left such a mark on the Anglican Church and in literature, that any Oxford man of sensibility is bound to respond to it, and even have a certain affection for it. But that must not blind us to the qualities, the more relevant contribution to the time, of its opponents, the Oxford liberals and reformers. That was equally well represented at Oriel by Whately, who did a full man's job in difficult Ireland, as Protestant Archbishop of Dublin, or by Dr Arnold. Everybody knows that Arnold's work at Rugby set a model for the reform of the public schools – very badly needed – throughout the country. That was just what the Provost said Arnold would do: if he were appointed, 'he would change the face of education all through the public schools of England'.

But this was not all that he did in his brief life of forty-seven years. He was a man of tempestuous energy, always a controversial figure, of such outspoken liberal views that he was nearly dismissed from his post. Eight years at Oxford, 1811–18, made him a good classical scholar, but of much wider reading than usual: he was the first to import the new critical standards of Niebuhr in Roman history into England. Dean Stanley, his disciple, once said what a difference it might have made to the Church of England if only Newman had known German. In the end it was Arnold's followers, not Newman's, who prevailed in the university, the schools, the Church and the country – even in the army. Hodson of Hodson's Horse, a Victorian hero, wrote home from India of Arnold's early death as 'a national misfortune. The influence which he did produce has been most lasting and striking in its effects. It is felt even in India; I cannot say more than that.' Dean Stanley, who wrote Arnold's biography, became the most appealing of Victorian churchmen, creator of the present tradition of Westminster Abbey, among many other things; Arnold's successors at Rugby, Tait and Temple, became Archbishops of Canterbury. New public schools were created to meet the expanding needs of the prospering upper classes, others were re-made, practically re-created, following the model of Rugby.

But few people are aware that Arnold's son, Matthew, did an even bigger job for national education than his father, who got so much more *réclame* for it. All his life as a school-inspector, by his classic reports on higher education in Germany and France, by his continuous stream of articles and books, Matthew Arnold made the propaganda for a nationwide system of secondary education, in which England was lamentably behind. Fourteen years after his death in 1888, the Education Act of 1902 brought into being a national system of secondary schools, modelled on Arnold's ideas, only one remove from his father's and Rugby brought up to date. We cannot go in detail into these ideas here, or the Oxford standards they set; but the Act was shaped by one of the most creative minds in the civil service, the Wykehamist Sir Robert Morant – an impoverished scholar at New College, who knew where the shoe pinched. He was the creator of a real ministry of education, as later of the ministry of health; he was a prime instrument, with Beveridge, in the development of social insurance and the welfare state. Morant's Act of 1902, and his volcanic energy in pushing forward the creation of secondary schools in every county in England, constituted the grandest constructive achievement for society in this century. I was in time to witness the idealism it inspired in such a backward area as Cornwall, in the life's-work for education of a liberal like Q. (Quiller-Couch), himself as an early Cliftonian only the second generation on from Arnold's Rugby. Those were the ideals that inspired them: they came from nineteenth-century Oxford.

Today, their good work for secondary education is all being unscrambled, educational standards lost, in the interests of a lower comprehensive social equality. Since men's mental are far more unequal than their physical outfits, the very idea of educational equality is a contradiction in terms; equal opportunity makes sense, but education should obviously be related to human beings' very different aptitudes and capacities.

By his marriage to a highly intelligent Cornishwoman, Mary Penrose, Dr Arnold begat a line that made remarkable contributions to English life. His eldest son, Thomas, followed his father into education and, in and out of the Catholic Church, was for a time a professor of literature under Newman in Dublin. Matthew Arnold, the poet, was more like his mother, but followed his father's profession ('So he became his father'). Edward Penrose Arnold was also a school-inspector; another brother, William Delafield Arnold, had a career in the army and in education in India, and wrote *Oakfield*, a critical comment on the life there. In the next generation, a grandson, Arnold-Forster, was a cabinet minister and reformer of the war office. Another grandson, William Thomas Arnold, won the Arnold Prize at Oxford, and combined Roman history with writing for the liberal *Manchester Guardian*. A granddaughter was the prolific novelist, Mrs Humphry Ward, author of *Robert Elsmere* so much admired by Gladstone, and founder of a London settlement for the poor. Her daughter was Janet Penrose Trevelyan, with whom the family penetrated Cambridge; and her daughter again, Mary Trevelyan (Mrs Moorman), author of the standard biography of Wordsworth.

The celibate Newman, with his cult of virginity – he was very feminine – begat no one; but his spiritual children are all over the world.

Because the Oxford, or Tractarian, Movement was defeated within the university we must not overlook its eventual victory in the Anglican Church and in its communion in the outside world – one can *see* its influence wherever one goes, in the churches of the United States or South Africa or Australia as well as in Britain. The historian J. A. Froude, brother of one of its inspirers, Hurrell Froude, pointed out that Newman despaired of his own church too soon: Arnold's term for Clough, 'too quick despairer', might have been applied to Newman. After he had left for Rome, his impulse largely won in the Church of England. But the number of eminent men who left the Church for Rome revivified and changed the face of the Roman communion in England too. This became obvious when its leadership fell to two Oxford cardinals: the intellectual to Newman, the practical to Manning.

The truth is that the movement was essentially a church movement rather than a university one, as Mark Pattison, who was at first affected by it, perceived. 'Religion was evidently to Newman, in 1830, not only the first but the sole object of all teachings.' It was essentially clerical, the last kick of the old clerical monopoly: its leaders were specifically reacting against the reform movement of the 1830s, which was beginning under the utilitarian impulse to remake the face of English society. This small group at Oxford hated and feared it: they reacted with a defence of the privileged claims of the national Church – Keble's sermon of 1833, which sparked it off, was summarily on 'national apostasy'. There could be no better base, or sounding-board, for the reaction than Oxford; sermons, correspondence, hymns, articles, tracts, arguments: a vast literature poured out of it and thrilled through the Church along the clerical lines of communication, reaching such people as Robert Stephen Hawker, son of a celebrated Evangelical, in his remote vicarage of Morwenstow on the cliffs of north Cornwall.

Of course it set going the rejuvenation of the Church, itself badly in need of

Robinson.
Sidney Pusey.
Dr. Pusey
Alice Herbert. Edith Pusey.
Rev. J. Brine.
Mrs. Brine.
Clara Pusey.

A sketch of the Pusey family and friends by Clara Pusey in 1856.

reform, with its rich bishoprics, and deans and chapters, and often a starveling clergy. It would have been well if its impulse had continued on those lines. But the literary command fell to a man of genius in Newman, who was essentially a party man: he always took up a position, on emotional or subconscious grounds – the process is betrayed in all his works from *The Development of Christian Doctrine* to *The Grammar of Assent* – and then used his subtle and casuistical logic in order to defend the position he had taken up. He was a good logician – he had learnt it from Whately (someone said that the Oriel common room 'stank of logic') – but it was not a rational process. Newman's mind was a combination of scepticism and extraordinary credulity; his brother Frank said that he never had had any sense of truth. In the event he misled the movement into the swamps of dogma, sheer sillinesses of belief, the untruths of the *Lives of the Saints*, which opened the eyes of J. A. Froude and shocked others into sense.

What Newman was looking for was some rock of security, and of course he found it in Rome. On the whole those who followed him were those who suffered from similar insecurity – very obvious in the case of a poet of genius, Gerard Hopkins (another feminine type). Those who had an independent strength of mind ultimately came through: both Pattison and Jowett came near to following Newman but managed to sheer off. J. A. Froude lost his faith (and, more important, his Fellowship), a process described in his Oxford novel, *The Nemesis of Faith*. Other stalwarts remained within the Church to carry forward the original impulse, but no longer claiming monopoly: Keble and Pusey among the original leaders, while Dean Liddon, an admired Victorian preacher, carried on its message from the pulpit of St Paul's. Dean Church, a more appealing figure, carried it into literature; his *History of the Oxford Movement* is the classic account of it, Newman's *Apologia pro sua vita* its abiding literary monument. The inspiration – and it proved a permanent one – went forward into lay life and secular society, with such leaders as Gladstone, Lord Salisbury and the Halifaxes.

We should pause to note the comparable influence of Evangelicalism in the lifelong devotion to philanthropy and good works of the seventh Earl of Shaftesbury – such a contrast to his ancestor, the reptilian first earl. The good earl was a Christ Church man, who devoted his life to social reform: factory legislation; protection of coal miners, lunatics, chimney-sweeps; ragged schools for the poor, better housing and sanitation, work for juvenile offenders. A boring list of subjects, but an inspired life – very curious to observe an aristocrat from the House so obviously gone to the good! Some others went to the bad. Charles Stewart, no less curiously a scion of the house of Blenheim, was another Evangelical who devoted his later years to mission-work; he went to Canada, and ended as Bishop of Quebec. Bishop Heber – somewhat improbably saintly for a Fellow of All Souls – carried the influence of Oxford churchmanship all over India; for his diocese of Calcutta included most of the sub-continent, and he travelled in all parts of it. He had literary gifts, and was a household word as a hymn-writer:

> From Greenland's icy mountains,
> From India's coral strand ...

> The Son of God goes forth to war,
> A kingly crown to gain ...

> Holy, Holy, Holy! Lord God Almighty!
> Early in the morning our song shall rise to Thee ...

How many would recognize these lines today, or indeed the source of

> Though every prospect pleases,
> And only man is vile.

His brother Richard Heber was even more interesting: a brilliant classical scholar, one of the founders of the Athenaeum, he was a prince of book collectors and built up a marvellous library. For a simple difference in sexual tastes he had to leave the country, and he – and his library – were lost to it.

The Oxford Movement touched only a minority within; with all its dynamic effect eventually outside, its defeat and the withdrawal of Newman were a release from a spell and opened the way to radical reform. Mark Pattison regarded Newman's defection later as 'a deliverance from the nightmare which had oppressed Oxford for fifteen years. For so long we had been given over to discussions unprofitable in themselves, and which had entirely diverted our thoughts from the true business of the place.' He dated the regeneration of the university from 1845. 'Science was placed under a ban by the theologians, who instinctively felt that it was fatal to their speculations. Newman had laid it down that revealed truth was absolute, while all other truth was relative – a proposition which will not stand analysis, but which sufficiently conveys the feeling of the theologians towards science.' Pattison knew the movement from the inside and, later, recognized it for the obscurantism it was. 'Hence the flood of reform, which broke over Oxford in the next few years following 1845, which did not spend itself till it had produced two government commissions, until we had ourselves enlarged and remodelled all our institutions.'

In 1850 a commission was proposed, with the internal aim of strengthening the university *vis à vis* the colleges, and the external one of opening its gates to the poorer class; in the upshot the first was more successfully attained than the second. Though the commission's report was largely written by Tait, the Bill that carried it into effect in 1854 was drafted by Gladstone. The changes introduced were decisive. A redistribution of endowments suppressed some scores of Fellowships to found university professorships, and many Fellowships were thrown open. In place of the oligarchy of heads of houses a representative council, balancing interests, became the governing body of the university. A school of natural science was established, professors recruited, new professorships founded.

A monument shortly arose in the Parks as an incarnation of the new spirit: the University Museum. It elicited much enthusiasm: many eminent people contributed pillars and marble shafts to this temple of a new age – as symptomatic for Oxford as the Crystal Palace was for the country at large. Dr Acland of All Souls took the lead in planning the large edifice: it was intended to exemplify every branch of natural science, a demonstration of what the future held. In time to come the area was to contain a litter of science departments, the progeny of the original museum. Subscribers were recruited from all over the country, from the Duke of Argyll to William Froude down in Devon. Acland was a friend of Ruskin: the temple of science revived the purer medieval Gothic of Venice; while the workmen, in that spirit, were allowed to carve their own capitals – 'such capitals as we will have!' wrote Ruskin; and even the new Oxford movement, the Pre-Raphaelites, were called on to design birds and beasts and flowers. A new spirit was abroad indeed.

Something of its effect may be glimpsed in the work of the leading geologist of the century, Sir Charles Lyell. His predecessor, Professor Buckland, had been content to accept the Old Testament nonsense of primitive Jews about a universal flood. How to account for the fossils? Keble was simple enough to think that the Almighty had put them there for a special purpose. Lyell overthrew all this and reduced it to sense; though one would scarcely credit the obstruction, the obtuseness, the obscurantism he met with. Holy scripture, being literally inspired, had interposed its barrier, for centuries, to sense. The keynote of Lyell's life-work was his observation, from geological evidences from all areas and of all kinds, that the processes of past change were continuous with the present. His classic *Principles of Geology* overthrew the Mosaic cosmogony, the flood and catastrophe school of geologists and, even more important, pointed to the analogy of the changes in organic life on the planet. All this opened the way to Darwin, the origin of species by natural selection, the descent of man, and the theory of evolution, general and specific.

One of the foremost of Cambridge men paid tribute to what he owed to this Oxford man of science: Darwin said, 'the science of geology is enormously indebted to Lyell – more so, as I believe, than to any other man who ever lived.' When Darwin's epoch-making *The Origin of Species* came out in 1859, Lyell's support was invaluable in all the shindy it caused. Next year, in the celebrated confrontation at the British Association in the Museum at Oxford, its bishop – 'Soapy Sam' Wilberforce, who occupied a large space in Victorian life – expected to score on this issue, but was unexpectedly made to look a fool by T. H. Huxley.

Fresh winds were blowing some – not all – of the cobwebs away in the ancient halls and common rooms, new academic interests stirring. As early as 1847 a generous bequest started the Taylorian for the study of modern languages. This was housed, along with new galleries to show the Arundel (1677) and Pomfret (1755) marbles, along with the rich collections of Italian paintings and drawings beginning to accumulate – the acquisitions of high Victorian culture – in the last and most splendid of our classical buildings, by Cockerell: the Ashmolean Museum.

The Union Society was started as early as 1823 with debates at Christ Church: it proved an invaluable training ground for aspiring politicians, and not only those, for Manning was as much to the fore as Gladstone. By mid-century it was so important in undergraduate life that it was able to set up buildings of its own, a Gothic debating hall to be decorated by the frescoes of the young Pre-Raphaelites. Its first half century was dominated by House men, the next century more by Balliol, with the rise of that college to intellectual primacy. A whole succession of prime ministers and cabinet ministers got their apprenticeship in public speaking and debating within those walls. But not only those, Archbishop

Left above: The University Museum. Built in the 1850s, it was intended to 'exemplify every branch of natural science'.
Below: The interior of the Museum, *c.* 1870, with ornamental ironwork.

Three eminent Victorians: *Left to right* Dr Acland, Regius Professor of Medicine; Dr Jowett, Master of Balliol; Woods, President of Trinity.

Lang was as prominent there later as Cardinal Manning earlier in the century, and figures as diverse as Hilaire Belloc, Philip Guedalla and Father Ronald Knox.

Already, under the beneficent impulse of British rule in India, Indian students were beginning to arrive. In 1868 a delegacy was set up to provide for students who could not get a place in a college: the non-collegiate students body, from which in our time grew the largest of new colleges, St Catherine's.

Dr Acland, active in so many good ways, revivified the moribund medical school. He succeeded, where others had failed, in introducing biology and chemistry into the curriculum, and transformed it from almost medieval teaching into a flourishing medical faculty. Clinical studies and practice he thought better pursued in the metropolis, with its hospitals. He exerted immense influence on the nation at large, as a propagandist of the state taking a lead in medicine. He served on the Royal Commission of 1869 on sanitary laws, inundating the country with pamphlets on drainage, propaganda for sewers etc. '*Sanitas sanitatum*, all is sanitation', said the cynical Disraeli. But how much Victorian England needed it; while Acland combined his enthusiasm with his lifelong friendship for Ruskin and the arts – a more cultivated man, when all is said, than Dizzy.

In 1853 William Morris and Burne-Jones came up to Exeter, and set going a movement in art and literature that has not ceased to reverberate still. They were inspired by medieval Oxford: years later, Morris said, 'the memory of its grey streets as they then were has been an abiding influence and pleasure in my life.' It was, he wrote, 'a vision of grey-roofed houses and a long winding street, and the sound of many bells'. As Burne-Jones remembered it, 'the city came to an end abruptly as if a wall had been about it, and you came suddenly upon the meadows. There was little brick in the city; it was either grey with stone, or yellow with the wash of the pebble-cast in the poorer streets, where there were still many old houses with wood carving, and a little sculpture here and there.' These young men, with the residual Celtic strain in each, inspired each other; they learned from the place, rather than the dons. Merton chapel was a favourite haunt; they copied illuminated manuscripts in the Bodleian; Burne-Jones drew foliage in Bagley Wood; they went about the countryside studying brasses. Ecclesiological interests were much to the fore, not only with them; there was Pugin to point the way, and Parker's at hand to publish admirable handbooks to Gothic architecture, set standards of good printing.

The young men formed a fancy for a brotherhood of religious artists, which bore fruit in the *Oxford and Cambridge Magazine* and ultimately in the firm of Morris and Co, with its widespread influence in interior decoration, furniture, wallpapers, tapestries, hangings, china, book-production, printing – every form of decorative craftsmanship. The results of inspiration began early to appear: Morris served his poetic apprenticeship here, and wrote his best early poems – inspired by their revival of the Middle Ages, to them an age of chivalry and romance – like 'Riding Together', the finest poems in *The Defence of Guenevere* (1858). Meanwhile, Thomas Combe, director of the Clarendon Press, introduced them to Rossetti and his circle in London, and thus full-fledged Pre-Raphaelitism was born. Combe turned out a discerning patron; he had already given Millais a commission to paint 'The Return of the Dove to the Ark'. A good man of business, Combe was as generous as he was percipient: he built the chapel of the Radcliffe Infirmary, and the Italianate church of St Barnabas (Hardy's 'ritualistic church of St Silas' in *Jude the Obscure*). Combe bequeathed his Pre-Raphaelite paintings to the Ashmolean, where they hang as brilliant and jewelled as the day they were painted.

The 1850s was a time of much artistic activity. The Oxford Movement was making progress in the Church. G. E. Street became the Tractarian architect *par excellence* (later succeeded by Butterfield); Street had his office in Beaumont Street 1852–6, was busy restoring churches all over the county, and built a prime example of a Tractarian church in St Philip and St James. The model caught on, provision for ritual and ceremony the first object – the ritualistic movement spread outwards from Oxford, still its home. Morris apprenticed himself to Street, whose senior clerk was Philip Webb, succeeded by Norman Shaw, their work is written in the history of nineteenth-century architecture, on the face of London and in the country. Morris was no architect – he spent all his spare time carving, modelling clay, working with his hands – and gave up his apprenticeship.

But he stayed on an extra year at Oxford. Benjamin Woodward was designing not only the museum but the debating hall of the Union. It was proposed to decorate the upper walls with frescoes; the young men recruited Rossetti and Hughes to paint feverishly their medieval fantasies upon the fresh masonry. The frescoes began at once to fade; attempts have been made to restore them, and they still glimmer like wraiths their fragmentary vision upon the faded scene below. Acland was a good friend of the painters and introduced them to Ruskin, whose influence in the art world was prodigious; they made the acquaintance of diminutive Swinburne at Balliol. In 1859 Morris married, in St Michael's church, the Oxford girl whose looks became famous as the Pre-Raphaelite ideal of feminine beauty – but as an inspiration to Rossetti rather than her husband. It was the end of the Brotherhood idea.

But it was not the end of either Morris's or Burne-Jones's associations with the place. In 1875 Morris came back to redecorate the roof at the Union. Two years later people wanted him to succeed Matthew Arnold as professor of poetry; but he was more interested in writing poetry than in lecturing about it. In 1883 he returned to give his historic lecture on 'Democracy and Art', which – now a convert to socialism – he turned into socialist propaganda, and there was a protest. Morris's influence in this last phase was not upon the people, about whom he had middle-class illusions, but upon other middle-class intellectuals, like G.D.H. Cole, who was 'converted' to socialism by reading Morris. This, of course, was when he was young; Morris himself, with his naif idealism, totally misconceived the nature of the people and their artistic potential, even their capacity for appreciation. If he had had the privilege of living in a mass-civilization he would have learned that it does not rise above the lower forms of television.

His were the fancies of a generous artist, the dream in which he lived. (He was not very effective even in marriage; Jane Morris came to prefer the more sensual, Italian Rossetti.) Fancies and dreams of the ideal are the seed-bed of poetry and art, not politics; the legacy of the Pre-Raphaelites is to be seen in the work they did, not in nonsense about art and socialism. (Communist art in Soviet Russia, the 'art of the people', would be an eye-opener for them!) Curiously enough there is more work of these Oxford men, and on a larger scale, at Cambridge, notably at Peterhouse and in the chapel of Jesus. At Oxford there are the splendid east window, with its ruddy wine colours, in the Latin chapel at the cathedral and the paler, less forceful, late Burne-Jones glass elsewhere there, besides the attractive common room at Keble with its Morris wallpaper.

The cobwebs of theology had not, however, been wholly blown away. In 1860 there was an unholy rumpus about the publication of *Essays and Reviews*, to which three of the most eminent liberals had contributed – each of them a figure distinguished in his own right and symptomatic of the time: Temple, who was to become Archbishop of Canterbury, Jowett and Mark Pattison. They were modernists, who sought to apply the canons of textual and historical criticism, which they had learned from classical scholarship, to the books of the Bible like any other classics. This was anathema to Victorian humbugs; even Tait condemned them: he was not a humbug but, Arnold's immediate successor, he was now Bishop of London on his way to Canterbury, an ecclesiastical statesman. He

The Adoration of the Magi – a tapestry by Burne-Jones and William Morris (1890) in Exeter College chapel.

was a very fine one – his Broad Church statesmanship carried on by his son-in-law, Davidson, into our time.

Jowett's critical work on St Paul's Epistles had already alarmed the faithful adherents of the literal inspiration of scripture and Jowett was shockingly prosecuted in the chancellor's court. Even his exiguous salary as Regius professor of Greek was meanly withheld from him; for years he was looked at askance as a heretic. They effectively shut him up on these subjects; he turned his attention to his popular translation of Plato, which long held the field, his work as the most effective tutor in Oxford and for the extension of university education outside. The rise of Balliol to be the foremost college, intellectually speaking, with a prodigious influence in public affairs, in politics, government, education, derived from Jowett more than any other man. He had an infallible eye for spotting talent and promise, and encouraging it.

The leaven of Jowett may be seen in the good work of his pupils in many fields, and even by reaction in that of those who were antipathetic. Walter Pater was a pure aesthete, the inspirer of the aesthetic movement in its later form, carrying on from the Pre-Raphaelites to Oscar Wilde, Lionel Johnson, Arthur Symons and the decadent poetry and art of the 1890s. Jowett was a moralist, no aesthete, and could not be expected to approve of this. All the same, he spotted Pater's exceptional quality, and foretold that his 'mind would come to great eminence'. In Jowett's direct line, however, were such social idealists as T.H. Green and Arnold Toynbee – the philosophical and practical inspiration of university extension, the education of the working class, settlements like Toynbee Hall to do good work in the slums of London. Wider afield, we may regard the Workers' Educational Association, the familiar old WEA, as a product of Balliol: churchmen like Bishop Gore and Archbishop Lang took a leading part in its early days, as R.H. Tawney and G.D.H. Cole in its prime. Today its idealism has evaporated, the need for it gone; but the damage to society from the loss of that generation's idealism, with the breakdown of standards and values in a mass-civilization, may be easily seen in the widespread increase of delinquency and the reversion to natural violence among the undisciplined young.

The more worldly, and probably more valuable, because realist, side to Jowett's influence may be read in the life's work of those who rose to power in state or church, civil service or university: such men as Asquith, Edward Grey, Lansdowne, Curzon, Lord Milner, Archbishop Lang, Sir William Anson. This last was the re-creator of All Souls, which in his day was dominated by Balliol men, many of whom rose to eminence; Anson himself was a leader in the university and combined this with service at the Board of Education. Asquith could not have come to Oxford but for the aid of scholarships, as he told Parliament in recommending the report of the last university commission. The same was true

An early Oxford summer extension school, taken on the steps of Balliol College. Dr Jowett appears seated next to the ladies with Dr Acland.

of Milner, a grand servant of the state, in Egypt, South Africa, and in Lloyd George's war cabinet. He was almost as responsible for the disastrous Boer war as Kruger, both obstinate men; but the German strain in Milner and in his early training made him more inflexible than the English are apt to be. However, his reconstruction of South Africa after the war, a magnificent job, enabled him to call in a younger generation of Oxford men to take part in it – Milner's 'Kindergarten': Amery, Lionel Curtis, Robinson (better known as Dawson, editor of *The Times*), John Dove. These formed the subsequent *Round Table* group who carried forward Milner's ideas into empire affairs in general, particularly in their high ideal of trusteeship of native races – all now gone with the wind.

Curzon was one of the Balliol men who came to All Souls as a prize-fellow, and he had already won the Arnold history prize. Through all his varied political career he retained his passion for archaeology, ancient buildings and monuments. Britain, no less than India, owes him an immense debt for the historic treasures he saved and preserved. One cannot go into his insufficiently appreciated achievements here, except to say that at Lausanne (1923) he won a surprising diplomatic victory out of the defeat Lloyd George had brought down by his support of Greek expansion against the Turks. Curzon always maintained a close association with the university through All Souls and his chancellorship, 1907–25. His heart was broken by the preference awarded to Baldwin for the succession as prime minister; though far less popular, he could hardly have been more fatal to his country in the event.

Grey was a special case: he scarcely woke up intellectually until his Balliol days were over. As foreign secretary he carried forward the policy which Lansdowne re-shaped in time to meet the mortal menace of militarist Germany to Britain and European civilization. If one wants a personal glimpse of how Jowett's inspiration worked with these men one can see it in the case of Lansdowne, who succeeded to a great position and vast estates when only twenty-one. Jowett:

I hope that you will not give up the resolution of finishing the *Ethics* before you return to Oxford. One owes it to oneself as a matter of honour and conscience to carry out resolutions ... The object of reading for the Schools is not chiefly to attain a First Class, but to elevate and strengthen the character for life. I would say the means was, first, hard work; secondly, a real regard for the truth, and independence of mind and opinion; thirdly, a consciousness that we are put here in different positions of life to carry out the will of God ... I think you would find an advantage also in getting more hold on politics and literature, and getting to know all manner of persons who are worthy of being known.

There is Jowett in a nutshell. A more emotional touch comes in a letter in which the master describes passing by the walls of Lansdowne House one night, the young Marquis absent, and thinking of the large responsibilities descending upon him so young. (The great house is now destroyed, the wonderful Adam dining room removed to the Metropolitan, where one can reflect ruefully on the talk at that table between Shelburne, the first Marquis, and his following of philosophic radicals, Bentham, Joseph Priestley, James Mill.) On the young man's marriage, the master offers excellent advice on the management of his estates – Jowett had a good business head – and what might be accomplished in the next fifty years 'for the agriculture, for the houses and, above all, for the people'. He was a forward-looking man: we owe to him the preservation of the University Parks and the land around and beyond. If only there had been more men of his vision the university would not be so hemmed in today. There was, too, his valuable cultural influence as a literary and social figure: Tennyson, Browning, Swinburne were frequent visitors to the master's lodgings at Balliol (today not occupied by the master: an alibi occupies the heart of the college).

Jowett's concern for his pupils reminds one of Dean Jackson's at Christ Church. From mid-century the House was reformed and revivified by Dean Liddell

Right: The Sheldonian Theatre, 1815, by J. Buckler.
Overleaf: Oxford from Holywell by Michelangelo Rooker.

(1855–91). He too had been a member of the commission that transformed the university. The House proceeded on its stately way, the most aristocratic of colleges, somewhat apart from the university. The dean was almost as successful as Jowett in making his young aristocrats work, or at least in taking their future service to the state seriously. After all, the world was their oyster. The college not only continued to add to its long roll of prime ministers but produced an almost equally long one of viceroys of India, Dalhousie, Canning, Elgin, Northbrook, Dufferin, in our time Halifax. In the Church the roll includes in modern times, we learn, five Archbishops of Canterbury and nine of York: it is like the Middle Ages. Some of us may prefer to some of them two contributions of genius to literature, in Ruskin and Lewis Carroll.

Nevertheless the prime contribution in public affairs was very noticeable at the turn of the century, with twelve Oxford men in Salisbury's cabinet, the prime minister himself chancellor of the university. An odd man out on a limb was Cecil Rhodes, who was already beginning to make history and a colossal fortune in South Africa when he 'sent himself' to Oriel belatedly in 1873, and in 1876–7. He spent the long vacations in South Africa building up his empire in diamonds and gold. Taking to politics he aimed at the federation of South Africa on the basis of equality between Boers and British – owing to the Boer War it came out differently – and the extension of British power into central Africa in the vast dominion called by his name. He was a man in a hurry – he was dead before fifty – but he bore the stigmata of genius. His will was of historic importance, founding a trust to bring 150 Rhodes Scholars a year to Oxford from the British Commonwealth and the United States, with even a contingent from Germany.

Within its walls the university was expanding to meet the late Victorian needs. We have seen that both Magdalen Hall and Hart Hall had had a remarkable number of distinguished alumni; however, owning no property, they had no security, but a chequered and discontinuous existence. We cannot go into the complicated story, but their remains and memories were brought together in the new foundation of Hertford college, by a bequest of Thomas Baring and an Act of Parliament of 1874. Shortly the new body recruited a group of eminent Fellows, Inge, Hastings Rashdall, Lord Hugh Cecil. John Keble died in 1866, and within a couple of years a new college was founded in memory of the inspirer of the Oxford Movement. The college was planned in noble proportions by Butterfield; by 1876 there arose the splendid Tractarian chapel, to tower like a cathedral out over the Parks and Mesopotamia.

The first warden of Keble, Edward Talbot, a High Church liberal, was a good friend to university education for women – which met with opposition from ordinary dons as absurd as it was discreditable. But the idea had distinguished friends in T. H. Green and Mark Pattison, as well as a number of forceful dragons,

193

Emily Penrose, Principal of
Somerville College.

The 'splendid Tractarian chapel' of
Keble College, erected in the 1870s
in memory of John Keble, inspirer
of the Oxford Movement.

like the humourless Mrs Humphry Ward, the alarming Mrs Creighton and bleak Bertha Johnson (whom I remember). In 1879 Lady Margaret Hall came into existence, with Miss Wordsworth as principal, a name famous enough to guarantee respectability. The college had twelve students. Somerville started the same year with nine; in 1886 St Hugh's was founded, in 1893 St Hilda's. There was no resisting the women. Among the early students at Somerville was Emily Penrose – to become Oxford's first Dame, 'the greatest of the college's past principals', says Vera Brittain in her informative book, *The Women at Oxford*. A Penrose on one side, of the family associated with the Arnolds, on the other a collateral descendant of Archbishop Cranmer, what could be more reassuring? 'Not a word was wasted, not a charm nor a wile exercised' – but indeed she had none: hers was a masculine personality – almost one of the whiskered academic ladies, with a marked gift for administration and finance. She made her college the first of women's colleges in her day, and was accorded the status, among the men, of an honorary man. However, the day of the women was yet to come, in this century, with a wonderful flowering of talent.

Newman had not been allowed by the Papacy to return, as a Catholic, to teach at Oxford: it is fascinating to think how many innocents he would have caught in his net if he had. When he was safely dead Catholics began to set up their small teaching institutions, to be recognized in time as permanent private halls, after the medieval model. In 1896 the Jesuits returned – shades of Robert Parsons of Balliol and Edmund Campion of St John's! – to start Campion Hall; next year the Benedictines followed with St Benet's, and in 1910 the Greyfriars to revive those long-dead memories of Roger Bacon and the famous Oxford Franciscans. The Anglicans had already set the model with their special halls to train clergy of different brands of churchmanship: St Stephen's House (1876), High Church; Wycliffe Hall (1877), Low Church; Ripon Hall (1897), Broad Church, inclining to Modernist. These were followed by the Nonconformists: Mansfield (1885), Congregational; Manchester (1891), Unitarian; to be followed in our time by the Baptists with Regent's Park College (1940).

Evidently Oxford continued to exert an irresistible attraction. We cannot go into the separate history of these bodies – each of them put forward and sustained distinguished men: the Jesuits, for instance, Martin d'Arcy; among the Nonconformists, Dr Selbie and L. P. Jacks. These bodies are also evidence of the breakdown of the old Anglican monopoly, and the shivering of religion into varied fragments.

Nor can we go into the remarkable expansion of the Bodleian – now, with the unfortunate interference of the state with the British Museum, the first library in

Britain. The good fortune of the Bodleian has gone far beyond what Sir Thomas Bodley or Archbishop Laud could have dreamed: it would do their hearts good to see it. Rich bequests continued to come to it in the eighteenth century: more oriental manuscripts from Archbishop Marsh, the splendid collections of Bishop Tanner, the papers of Clarendon, Sancroft, Carte, indispensable for the Civil War. In 1756 came the Rawlinson bequest, the largest to date, five thousand manuscripts, over two thousand rare books. So much for the supposedly 'torpid' eighteenth century! In the nineteenth century came a magnificent donation from a Cambridge man, Gough's spreading topographical collections; Malone's invaluable Shakespearean and Elizabethan library, and Douce's treasures, who had been a keeper at the British Museum. We can go no further; the expansion necessitated large new building in our time, with results less lovely than they would have been in the eighteenth century.

The diversification of studies was a feature of the later nineteenth century; the impulse gathered strength from 1874 when the supremacy of the school of literae humaniores (classics) was ended by other subjects being made alternatives to it. It retained its primacy, however, right up to the Second German War, and still has a special place in a true Oxford man's heart. However, from the classics flowered other studies with a brilliant future, notably archaeology and anthropology. Much of the best work in medieval and modern history, law, philology and English literature was shaped from that background: one can observe the transition from that best of trainings, best because exact and precise. The splendid enterprise of the *Oxford English Dictionary* had the standards of classical scholarship behind it. Ironically enough for the successor to Dr Johnson its editor was a Scot, James Murray. 'The greatest lexicographical achievement of the age' would never have been accomplished but for the support of the university press. This, and a no less historic undertaking, the *Dictionary of National Biography*, have made its grandest contributions to scholarship and national culture in the past century.

Diversification was the keynote of this period, as the proliferation of the sciences is of ours. Natural science had not been entirely neglected in the eighteenth century, but it was taught in the colleges. Dr Lee had founded his lectureship in anatomy in 1750, and Christ Church erected a laboratory for its study along with some chemistry. Now in 1872 the Clarendon Laboratory was built, one of the oldest physical laboratories in Europe, to be rebuilt under the aegis of Lindemann by 1940. In 1875 the University Observatory was established; in 1880 the Indian Institute, with its oriental treasures; in 1885 the Pitt-Rivers Museum with its important ethnological and archaeological collections. The university had already acquired the invaluable maps and manuscripts of the self-taught 'Father of English Geology', William Smith (1769–1839), sprig of a long line of Oxfordshire farmers.

We can track something of the gathering momentum of this in the work of our scientists in the world. William Froude (1810–79), of that remarkable family, became one of the leading engineers of the time. At Oriel under his brother, 1828–32, he devoted his spare time to chemistry and mechanics. He assisted Brunel in building the Great Western Railway, but found his true genius as a naval architect. I am incapable of doing justice to his inventions in reducing the roll of ships, the effects of bilge-keels, his researches into steam-screws and propellers, 'of immense importance to the Royal Navy and to the mercantile marine'. He became a leading designer of marine engines, and one of the engineering laws he propounded carries on his name. (It is a far cry from the Oxford Movement, and his brother Hurrell – and an altogether more useful career.)

George Rolleston (1829–81), Linacre professor, was the leading anatomist of his time, foremost in accumulating evidence for the evolution of species by natural selection from the study of skull-types, which he first introduced. From cerebral anatomy and classification he moved into archaeology and became a prime influence in the formulation of scientific anthropology. The master of this new discipline, Tylor, whose classic *Primitive Culture* appeared in 1871, became keeper of the University Museum and, as professor, created the Oxford school of anthropology. 'Tylor's genius, which is to say his power of divination, was shown by his power to grasp the true scope and method of anthropology from the outset ... As regards method, he realised from the first that the inward springs of human behaviour rather than its outward conditions afford the best clue to its history.' In explanation, and in style, 'dealing as he does with the thoughts and actions of primitive people, he eschews in his interpretations the language of the learned, deeming it more appropriate to describe such simple-mindedness, as it were, in terms of itself'. Which is, of course, the right strategy: it is a quality of genius to be able to render the complex simple.

Ray Lankester (1847–1929) attended Rolleston's lectures and experiments in zoology at the new University Museum. Later on, as professor, he reorganized its zoological exhibits, before moving to the wider world of London, to be recognized as the leading zoologist of his time.

He had a great love for the wonders and beauties of nature, a knowledge ranging over the whole field of biology. A keen observer, a skilful manipulator, he was also a great teacher and master of exposition. He was a quick worker and prolific writer. Some two hundred scientific papers stand to his credit; his researches extended over almost every group of the animal kingdom; but it was as a morphologist that he gained most distinction ... Lankester was among the first, in 1871, to describe protozoan parasites in the blood of vertebrates.

We can see how fundamental this was in the development of bacteriology, the advance of knowledge in the cause and prevention of disease.

Unmarried, Lankester allowed nothing and nobody to come between him and his work. As conscientious in research as he was prolific in communicating its results, he too, like Tylor, had a gift for simple, popular exposition. He thus made enemies among the envious third-rate, about whom he minced no words; but his was a household name in his time, while his contributions to knowledge remain to testify for him.

In music Oxford meant chiefly Stainer (Sir John) to the late Victorians. Always popular from boyhood – his beautiful voice was lifted up at Wellington's funeral – he was closely associated for years with Oxford and is buried here. Matriculating at Christ Church, he became organist of Magdalen but lived for some years in St Edmund Hall, whence he conducted his fruitful researches into the early music in the Bodleian. While here he married the daughter of a city alderman, and founded the Oxford Philharmonic Society; thence in 1872 to St Paul's and a career of astonishing energy and output in London. He came back as professor 1889–99, and so was able to complete his chief works of scholarship, *Dufay and his Contemporaries* and *Early Bodleian Music*. Immensely popular as the composer of his 'Crucifixion', forty anthems, a hundred and fifty hymn-tunes and a seven-fold Amen that reverberated all over the world, his scholarship has lasted better than his music. He did good work in the revival of plain-song, and for the appreciation of Bach: it was a pity that his music did not follow those models instead of Mendelssohn and the sentimental Spohr. His manuals of composition and his text-books were very popular, and he made a unique collection of old song-books, mainly of the eighteenth century: what has become of it?

He encouraged Hubert Parry, his successor in Oxford music and as a professor; when an undergraduate he was instrumental in founding the University Musical Club, still going strong: the eighteenth-century Music Room in Holywell, where they meet, is one of the oldest in Europe. Parry was as prolific as Stainer; a number of his compositions were written for Oxford: the instrumental music for various comedies of Aristophanes, for example. His work, too, for the Bach Choir meant that they kept vocal works of his, singable as they are, like 'Blest Pair of Sirens', faithfully performed. Such works are, however, not to be compared with a work of genius, such as Elgar's inspired by Newman's text, 'The Dream of Gerontius'.

What were the names Oxford stood for, in the national culture, to the late Victorians? They were principally literary figures: Ruskin and Matthew Arnold, and some of the historians, notably Froude and John Richard Green, both best-sellers.

John Ruskin (1819–90) exercised an extraordinary ascendancy in the Victorian art world. He was at Christ Church 1836–40 and in 1842, and describes his undergraduate life in his autobiography. *Praeterita*: like the vast majority, he was left untouched by the Oxford Movement of those years. He always loved the university and was responsive to 'the ineffable charm of the place'. He published the first volumes of his masterpiece, *Modern Painters*, as by 'an Oxford graduate'. Later, as we have seen, he was as enthusiastic as his friend Acland over the University Museum and wrote the book about it with him; ocular evidence tells one that he must have influenced his old college to choose a similar Venetian Gothic for the Meadow Buildings. William Morris responded gallantly to Ruskin's idealism about medieval craftsmen, and put it in practice with the arts of handicraft and printing, the works of the Kelmscot Press. In 1871 Morris bought the untouched Elizabethan manor house of Kelmscot – now owned by the university – out among the water-meadows of the Upper Thames. There he spent his last twenty-five years and is buried in the churchyard; there too his daughter May Morris lived right up to our time, keeping going the tradition, amid the flapping tapestries, the creaking boards and panelling, the wood fires and old-world draughts.

Ruskin returned as Slade professor of art, 1870–9, a decade crowded with lectures and good works. He was even more prolific than most eminent Victorians; his lectures on art, on drawing and sculpture, *The Elements of Drawing*, *Val d'Arno*, etc, were published as books; he produced handbooks on botany, geology, what not; as art preacher to the nation, he turned aesthetics into ethics, in a guise to which Victorians could respond better. (Not so well to the 'art for art's sake' of the next generation of Pater and his disciples: this thought raised a doubt in the Victorian mind, gave them a *frisson*: was it not, quite possibly, immoral? With John Addington Symonds it was, and he lost his Fellowship at moral Magdalen, which proceeded to recruit Oscar Wilde as an undergraduate.)

Ruskin was extraordinarily generous; he had already given Turners to both Oxford and Cambridge, he now founded the Ruskin Drawing School, presenting it with many works of art, and attracting pupils from the crowds who attended his lectures. (How avid the Victorians were for culture!) Keen on the moral effect of manual work, for middle-class people if not for the workers, he attracted recruits from his classes to dig up and repair the Hinksey road. The work was very ill done, *qua* road-making, but the idealistic Arnold Toynbee was one of the diggers. (It seems to have done his health, which was bad, no good: he died at thirty.) After a breakdown Ruskin was back as professor again, 1883–4; his lectures were more crowded than ever, the performances of the professor more and more eccentric. One who was present at the last, Sir Charles Oman, told me that in the course of it the professor took off his boots to demonstrate. After this, the prophet retired to the Lake District in quasi-insanity; his property there, Brantwood, was later willed to, but refused by, the university.

In a satirical Oxford book of the period, Mallock's *The New Republic* (1877),

Right: John Ruskin, who published the first volumes of his *Modern Painters*, by 'an Oxford Graduate'. Portrait by Millais.

Matthew Arnold, who wrote the 'finest poems ever written about the countryside round Oxford'. He was Professor of Poetry for ten years.

Ruskin is portrayed favourably as Mr Herbert, Jowett unfavourably. But, then, Jowett thought little of young Mr Mallock at Balliol as a dilettante; the latter, who was a nephew of Froude and inherited the family gift for writing, responded by portraying Jowett, Matthew Arnold and Pater all caught in the awkward posture of holding dogmatic views without any positive beliefs. The book hit the mark; though Mallock never achieved an equal success, the dilettante wrote hard all his life, and ended, like several of the Froude family, in the arms of the Catholic Church.

To many people, especially those who loved poetry, Oxford meant chiefly Matthew Arnold. He had the advantage of that famous name, and he was closely connected during three decades, 1841–67, as undergraduate at Balliol, Fellow of Oriel, and professor of poetry. From that chair he laid down his principles of literary criticism, of translating Homer, etc, taken by many as authoritative. But criticism is far less important than the poetry it is commenting on, and Arnold's criticism has lasted less well than his verse. It fell to him to write the finest poems ever written about the countryside round Oxford, some of it now eaten up in desolation, some still recognizable. A Celt on his mother's side, whom he took after, his lectures on the study of Celtic literature inspired the founding of the chair of Celtic. A daughter married in the United States; so his grandson, Arnold Whitridge, carried on the family tradition in education and literature at Yale.

'The Scholar-Gipsy' was inspired by a story from 'Glanvill's book', *The Vanity of Dogmatising*. Joseph Glanvill had been at Oxford during the 1650s, and became an idiosyncratic figure in literature, both credulous and sceptical, interested alike in witchcraft and science. His affinities are with Sir Thomas Browne and the Cambridge Platonists; he was a precursor of psychical research, an anticipator of telepathy and telegraphy: 'to confer at the distance of the Indies by sympathetic contrivances may be as natural to future times as to us is a literary correspondence'. Glanvill's was the book Arnold had with him that summer day in the half-reaped harvest-field on the hills above the city:

> Where I am laid
> And bower me from the August sun with shade;
> And the eye travels down to Oxford's towers.

All the loved countryside is recalled, Cumnor Hurst in spring, the stripling Thames at Bablock-hythe, the hunters at the ferry returning home on summer nights, the Fyfield elm in May, the gipsies camping on the skirts of Bagley wood, Hinksey ridge in winter from which one sees

> The line of festal light in Christ Church hall.

The sequel to this was 'Thyrsis', in memory of the poet Arthur Hugh Clough. By the time Arnold came back to celebrate Clough's death change was beginning to lay its hand on the countryside they had roamed together in their young days:

> In the two Hinkseys nothing keeps the same;
> The village street its haunted mansion lacks,
> And from the sign is gone Sibylla's name,
> And from the roofs the twisted chimney-stacks.

Yet Oxford remains the same as he looks down from the familiar hills:

> And that sweet city with her dreaming spires,
> She needs not June for beauty's heightening,
> Lovely at all times she lies, lovely tonight!

The girl had gone who used to unmoor their skiff at the boatman's door above the locks, and

> Where are the mowers, who, as the tiny swell
> Of our boat passing heaved the river-grass,
> Stood with suspended scythe to see us pass? –
> They are all gone, and thou art gone as well.

Yet, there was still the Fyfield elm they had taken years before for a signal:

> Backed by the sunset, which doth glorify
> The orange and pale violet evening-sky,
> Bare on its lonely ridge, the Tree! the Tree!

The personality of Clough has always aroused more interest than his work is able to satisfy: he died young, his promise unfulfilled – though he will always be remembered for the famous lines from 'Say not the struggle naught availeth', with which Franklin Roosevelt encouraged Churchill at the worst moment of the last war:

> And not by eastern windows only,
> When daylight comes, comes in the light,
> In front the sun climbs slow, how slowly,
> But westward, look, the land is bright.

At Rugby Clough was a favourite with Dr Arnold – and he was a fellow-Celt with Matt at Oriel. He was one of those, like Pattison and Froude, whom Newman's intellectual gyrations reduced to scepticism. Giving up his faith and his Fellowship and Oxford, Clough wandered abroad, into sympathy with the revolutionaries of 1848; he died before he found himself or his true vocation. Thus he had a symptomatic, rather than a poetic, importance for his generation; though he left a novelistic poem, in classical hexameters, very redolent of Oxford, *The Bothie of Tober-na-Vuolich: a Long Vacation Pastoral*. If he had lived he might have become a novelist; his death inspired Arnold to a finer poem than anything Clough ever wrote.

There was no more Oxonian book than *Alice's Adventures in Wonderland* (1865); its author, the Rev C. L. Dodgson, mathematical tutor at Christ Church, where he lived all his life: his rooms, cupboards, closets crammed with everything to entice and amuse little girls. (It was fortunate for him that he lived before Freud, or he would never have got his children's books written.) *Alice* indeed began as tales he told the children, particularly Alice Liddell, the dean's little daughter, on boating excursions in the afternoons up the river. It had a sequel in 1871: *Through the Looking Glass, and What Alice Found There*. These books became classics the world over; not so *Sylvie and Bruno*, with its academic background of wardens and professors, though we can all appreciate today the cry, 'Less Bread! More Taxes!!' Dodgson was an inveterate pamphleteer on university and college issues, which he turned into nonsense, he found them so ridiculous. The contest between Gladstone and Hardy for a university seat he described in 'The Dynamics of a Particle'; the contraption of a wooden box into which Christ Church bells were moved from the unsafe cathedral spire, and the fuss over it, are caricatured, with illustrations, as 'The Meat Safe'.

The Reverend C.L.Dodgson, of Christ Church, better known as Lewis Carroll, author of *Alice's Adventures in Wonderland*, also a fine amateur photographer, as this self-portrait reveals.

There was an element of mathematical logic, or illogic, that ran all through his nonsense. He was a distinguished, if somewhat off-centre, mathematician who wrote original books on his subject: *Euclid and his Modern Rivals*, works on plane algebraical geometry, trigonometry, a treatise on determinants. These were not taken as seriously as they deserved, for the nonsense would come breaking into the discourse. His last, abstruse book on *Symbolic Logic* begins, for example: '(1) Begin at the *beginning*, and do not allow yourself to gratify a mere idle curiosity by dipping into the book, here and there.' There follows an exordium on the disutilities of dipping. And all the examples given are fantastic:

(1) Babies are illogical;
(2) Nobody is despised who can manage a crocodile;
(3) Illogical persons are despised.

Univ. 'persons'; a = able to manage a crocodile;
b = babies; c = despised; d = logical.

The answer given at the end of the book is: 'Babies cannot manage crocodiles.' Lewis Carroll would have made a wonderful subject for psychoanalysis; but, then, he would have ceased to be able to write his books.

Oxford also meant other brilliant, sexually odd, men – men of genius because abnormal: John Addington Symonds, Swinburne, Walter Pater, Oscar Wilde, all associated with the later phase of the aesthetic movement. (Somehow Victorians were queerer than the Georgians had been, and this must have something to do with the repressiveness of Victorian morality, and the obvious reaction from it.) John Addington Symonds' homosexuality is now well known; he was an ardent propagandist for it, wrote on the subject and left a candid autobiography now open to publication. (A granddaughter was a principal of Somerville recently.) This aspect of his career has perhaps been made too much of, and may now be taken for granted; it has obscured his distinction as a cultural historian with his masterpiece, *The Renaissance in Italy*, the only English parallel to Burckhardt.

Walter Pater (1839–94) lived most of his life in Oxford, though withdrawn, something of a recluse, a familiar figure in the landscape, becoming steadily more famous. His background was odd: Dutch-American (indeed he was rather like an expatriate character out of Henry James), a family in which the sons were brought up Catholic, the daughters Anglican. Walter ended up with no religious faith, except art: art was his religion, and a very good one too. He was somewhat overwhelmed by Ruskin, became friendly with the Pre-Raphaelites, and intimate with Swinburne. He gradually accumulated his *Studies in the History of the Renaissance* (1873), which has remained influential ever since. All his books were Oxford products: *Marius the Epicurean* putting forward his philosophy of life and art – that the pursuit of beauty in the world in every form, the world of nature and of art, is a sufficient end in itself, gives meaning to life and redeems it from the mud. This gospel was preached in successive essays and books, collected together as *Imaginary Portraits* and *Greek Studies*, all written in the finest prose to come out of Oxford. It is worthy of note that the best prose-stylists of the age had that classical background: Newman, Ruskin, Froude, Pater, and the philosopher Bradley. Pater's *Plato and Platonism*, one of his most original books, led to a *rapprochement* with Jowett, never happy with pure aesthetics without ethics.

Jowett was always good to Swinburne, young rebel as he was when at Balliol, 1856–9: from old Catholic stock like Shelley – anything to be out of step. While here he made the acquaintance of Ruskin and the Pre-Raphaelites; after going down he always kept in touch with Jowett. He spent the autumn of 1864 with him in Cornwall, at Tintagel, Kynance Cove and St Michael's Mount; ten years later they spent the January of 1874 together at Land's End. Out of these visits came *Tristram of Lyonnesse*. Next year Swinburne was stopping at West Malvern with Jowett, writing 'Erechtheus'; the poet stayed now and again at the Lodgings, submitting his compositions to the master, who usually recommended shortening – rightly again.

Oscar O'Flahertie Wills Wilde, the child of very odd parents, came from

The tower of Magdalen College from the Botanical or Physic Garden in winter, *c.* 1880.

Dublin to Magdalen, 1874–8. A brilliant scholar and wit, he not only enlivened the literary life of the university but took part in Ruskin's stone-breaking at Hinksey which was supposed to have such good moral effects. The poet Lionel Johnson ('By the Statue of King Charles at Charing Cross'), who wrote the best early book on *The Art of Thomas Hardy*, was a Wykehamist at New College 1885–90. Also a good classical scholar, Johnson introduced to Wilde young Lord Alfred Douglas, who followed him at Magdalen in the 1890s. The most charitable explanation of Lord Alfred's career – he was mad, bad, and dangerous to know – is that he was psychotic. He was the ruin of Wilde, whom he introduced to low

207

J. A. Froude, 'the one modern Oxford historian to rival Macaulay in brilliance of writing'.

company; though it was Wilde's vulgar Irish exhibitionism that brought the crash upon himself – and by consequence upon scores of thousands of others who shared his tastes; such is the cruelty and absurdity of men's behaviour to each other in society.

More respectable, and more widely influential, were the historians. Henry Hallam, a high and dry Whig – a somewhat odd specimen to come out of the Christ Church stable – died in the same year as Macaulay (1859). Though less brilliant, he was richer and did not have to boom like Macaulay for a living. As a constitutional historian he exerted hardly less impact: in this field his word was taken for law, his authority held for the best part of a century. This refers to his classic work, *The Constitutional History of England from the Accession of Henry VII to the Death of George II*. He wrote two other standard works based on immense reading: *A View of the State of Europe during the Middle Ages* and his Survey of European Literature during the fifteenth, sixteenth and seventeenth centuries. Leslie Stephen considered Hallam one of the founders of the English historical school, his training in the law having given him particular strength as a constitutional interpreter, to which he added a conscientious study of original sources.

The one modern Oxford historian to rival Macaulay in brilliance of writing, breadth of scholarship, command of unpublished material, and popular appeal was Froude – as people realized when his *History of England from the Fall of Wolsey to the Defeat of the Spanish Armada* began to roll out its length, to reach twelve volumes, 1856–70. It was Froude's sixteenth century as against Macaulay's unfinished seventeenth. But Oxford was never kind to Froude as Cambridge was to Macaulay, where they made a veritable cult of him. In fact Oxford treated Froude badly. He was at Oriel from 1835, the youngest brother of Hurrell and brought up in the bosom of the Oxford Movement. But he revolted against its credulousness, the retrogressive cult of the saints, etc, and lapsed into scepticism. When he expressed this in *The Nemesis of Faith* (1849), the book was burned in the hall of Exeter by the sub-rector; Froude resigned his Fellowship and left Oxford, without any means. From this he was rescued by marriage to Kingsley's sister, a Cornish Grenfell; from his scepticism he was rescued by Carlyle, with a strong injection of an undoctrinal Calvinism: the remedy was worse than the disease. There always remained in Froude these two tendencies at war with each other: his own latent scepticism, and the over-insistent Protestant moralism he got from Carlyle, which was more in keeping with and encouraged by the age. It was the second that brought him his success and made him an eminent Victorian. But tension is a characteristic of genius, a condition of creativeness.

There is no question that Froude had genius. He touched the age at many points, both in writing and practice. He was for long the influential editor of *Fraser's Magazine*, to which he contributed many of his scintillating *Short Studies on Great Subjects*. Very much interested in the origins of Britain's sea-empire in the Elizabethan age, he took a hand in politics to advance imperial expansion in South Africa, the West Indies, Australasia, accompanying this with books like *English Seamen of the Sixteenth Century*, *The English in the West Indies* and *Oceana*. His big book on *The English in Ireland* let loose a flood of controversy; but the most bitter of all was over his biography of Carlyle, which occupied the last decade of his life. It is now recognized as, on the whole, the greatest of English biographies.

Every book Froude published was the subject of controversy – a tribute to its vitality, and perhaps to the creative tensions within the author. For, like the independent spirit he essentially was – independent even of Carlyle – he fell between, or among, all stools. The child of the Oxford Movement, he lost his faith, then became the defender of the Protestant Reformation. A liberal in the critical 1840s, he developed into an exponent of empire; an imperialist and a genuine Englishman, who knew the origins of empire in the Elizabethan voyages, he could not admire the rhodomontade of Disraeli. So he got the brickbats from all sides, and the more people fumed the more his books circulated.

Above all, the academics were furious; for he wrote like an angel and, a handsome man, was a social success, a distinguished figure in London life. Moreover, he was a rapid worker and very prolific. His great history actually contained more unpublished material, both from English and Spanish archives, than any other –

far more than Macaulay's, of whose history he made criticisms very much to the point. Froude's gifts, and his success, aroused a venomous Oxford enemy in the Regius professor, Freeman, a regular Saturday Reviewer who lay in wait for every volume to appear, in order to attack it. Froude hardly bothered to reply (Freeman got his come-uppance later from J. H. Round) – he was much too busy; but he was a sensitive man, who had had this kind of thing to put up with from the second-rate all along. The corrosive envy to which he was unceasingly exposed from the Regius professor was recognizably a merely talented man's envy of a man of genius. At the end of it all, when Freeman wished for a reconciliation, Froude wrote an unpublished letter, quoted to me by Sir William Holdsworth: 'Mr Freeman is a person with whom I desire to have no relations, not even those of controversy.'

Bishop Stubbs, who was a friend of Freeman but had a touch of magnanimity about him, summed it up: 'Froude is a man of genius, and he has been treated abominably.'

Freeman died suddenly in 1892, and then Froude made his mistake. He was already older than Freeman, but he accepted his chair: it killed him. 'The temptation of going back to Oxford in a respectable way was too much for me,' he wrote; 'I must just do the best I can, and trust that I shall not be haunted by Freeman's ghost.' He had written beautifully about the place, in an essay 'Words about Oxford', describing a visit nearly thirty years after he had left; and he has given us a most perceptive account of Newman, his own brother Hurrell and their Movement in an essay, 'The Oxford Counter-Reformation' – for that was what it was. Now, in 1892, as a man of seventy-four he came back: the lectures of this famous, enigmatic, controversial figure drew crowds; Sir Charles Oman, who was a disciple of Freeman, described it as 'the golden age of Oxford history lecturing'. It lasted only three years, but each course made a memorable book: *The Life and Letters of Erasmus*, *English Seamen of the Sixteenth Century*, and *The Council of Trent*. Then, exhausted, Froude went home to Devon to die: he lies in the cemetery at Salcombe, within sound of the sea he wrote about so vividly.

The one Oxford historian to compare with him was not, of course, Freeman but J. R. Green, who had a similar gift of bringing the past to life. An Oxford schoolboy, he gathered inspiration from the grey streets and ancient byways, was fascinated by old customs, and was awestruck by a glimpse of old Dr Routh who had seen Dr Johnson in the city. Green's forte was social history, in which he was something of an initiator; hence, in part, the astonishing success of his *Short History of the English People*. Green was still young when he died, but his spirit – eager, sympathetic, and fresh – completely expressed itself in that book and he, like Macaulay and Froude, got his message across to the wide public of the nation, and beyond.

Stubbs (1825–1901) never did, though, of all the pure academics, he was the grandest spirit. In spite of all discouragements he created the Oxford history school: to become the largest and most formative in the country, supplying those who created history schools in younger universities such as Manchester, University College, London, Reading. A mere servitor at snobbish Christ Church, he could never become a Student (i.e. Fellow); he was rejected again and again for professorships. When he at length got one in 1866, he proceeded to accomplish a mountain of work; as rapid as he was accurate, and with no one attending his lectures, he was able to pour forth a dozen volumes of medieval chronicles in the Rolls Series, and cap it with his big *Constitutional History of England*. This became a standard work, and Stubb's *Charters* the indispensable *vade-mecum* of the history school to this day.

Though Stubbs had breadth and justice, even objectivity, of mind, by no means all of his interpretations have endured, any more than Froude's. His disciple Tout tells us that where 'his conclusions least meet the views of modern scholars are those in which he looked into the facts with the eyes of his German guides', notably Maurer and Waitz. Who remembers them now? This reminds us of the immensely exaggerated influence of German thought and scholarship upon English (and American) universities in the later nineteenth century. In so far as more exact textual standards prevailed with classical and Biblical scholars, closer attention to original sources with historians, this was all to the good. But German thought is weakest in judgement and sense of proportion – as the upshot in the twentieth century has revealed disastrously to the world. The influence of Hegel, and of German philosophical 'idealism' has been, as Santayana shows in his *Egotism and German Philosophy*, little short of a disaster in itself, unless mediated through the sceptical mind of a philosophic Bradley. Its outgrowth in the historical writings of a Treitschke were merely monstrous – an enemy of European civilization.

Stubbs, Freeman, Green, even Froude, through the deleterious influence of Carlyle, all belonged to the Teutonic school:

> See ladling butter from alternate tubs,
> Stubbs butters Freeman, Freeman butters Stubbs!

Freeman was not negligible as an historian, and he had gifts, particularly in the realization of place as the scene of events. The notice of him in the *Dictionary of National Biography* informs us that 'his historical work is distinguished by critical ability, precision and accuracy of statement . . . His judgement was rarely swayed by feeling, and as a rule his estimates of character are masterly.' This summing up is almost exactly the opposite of the truth. Freeman was vehement and irascible, a party-man, a Gladstonian liberal. In his heavy *History of the Norman Conquest*

everything Anglo-Saxon was idealized and seen through rose-coloured spec-
tacles, everything Norman was denigrated; the old Teutonizer could not get over
the Norman Conquest of England – though it made the country what it was –
and it is well known that Earl Godwin was portrayed with the lineaments of Mr
Gladstone.

What is more extraordinary was Freeman's refusal to consult anything other
than printed sources – where Froude had brought to light masses of new material
from the archives. However, Freeman did good work, his best being his histories
of towns and cathedrals: he had a *penchant* for architecture.

Mandell Creighton was a scintillating intelligence, to become a high ecclesiastic, intended for Canterbury; it used to be said of him that, though it was
doubtful if he believed in God, he certainly believed in the apostolic succession.
At Merton for thirteen years, 1862–75, he had Lord Randolph Churchill as a
pupil, and must have had some share in forming that precocious and brilliant
mind. (The Churchills were an Oxford family; it was a grief to his son, Winston,
that he did not come up to the university.) Creighton was a good deal of a
politique, with the instincts of a statesman. There could be no more appropriate
historian of the Papacy during the Reformation – unfortunately, becoming a
bishop, he never finished it. But his portrait of Elizabeth I is the most politically
perceptive we have and immensely superior to Froude's, who was as shockingly
unfair to her as he was far too laudatory (again under Carlyle's influence) of
Henry VIII: the two chief blots on his grand book.

Creighton went over to teach history at Cambridge, as the first professor of
ecclesiastical history, 1884–91. While there he became the first editor of *The
English Historical Review*, which came out of this devoted group, and set its
standards. Alas that, like Stubbs, he was lost to history for a seat on the bench of
bishops! – but such was the Victorian age.

The greatest single achievement in academic history was S.R. Gardiner's
History of England, from the accession of James I to (almost) the death of Cromwell, in sixteen volumes. Gardiner was no bishop, but an Irvingite; a solitary
student, who therefore had an inner sympathy with the sects that proliferated in
that age and devoted his whole life to research, teaching and writing, without the
distractions of public life and pomposity. Nor did his descent from Oliver
Cromwell detract from his justified admiration for that heroic figure. Though
as unlike Froude as a man could be, Gardiner followed him into the archives, at
Simancas as well as elsewhere; but when *his* first volumes came out, they had to
be remaindered as waste paper. He never appealed widely; a Christ Church man,
1847–51, he could not hope for a studentship any more than Stubbs, in Gardiner's
case for theological reasons. In later life All Souls and Merton supported his
researches, and they were richly fulfilled. No genius as a writer, Gardiner was the

most scrupulously conscientious, painstaking and accurate of historians, with an over-riding desire to be just to all parties. He had natural good judgement, but this gave him a clarity of insight all his own. As his pupil Firth says, Gardiner was 'content with the distinction of being the most trustworthy of nineteenth-century historians'; he has reaped the reward that, of all its monuments of historical writing, his stands least in need of revision or re-interpretation.

Considered together – and we have considered only the peaks – what a wonderful body of work was achieved by Oxford historians in the nineteenth century! Today there are ten times the number of professors, but their books are not to be compared with those of the eminent Victorians. It is difficult to estimate their effect upon the national life and culture – a whole subject in itself. It must have been an important element in educating the mind of the governing classes, particularly the middle classes rising in strength and prominence, for political responsibility at Britain's apogee as a world-power. It must have made them not only proud of the most remarkable achievement of any European state, and that a small island-country, in the modern period since the Reformation, but it must have helped to mature them in making them aware of the past, its mistakes and cruelties, and in that rendering them more civilized, humane, and tolerant. As, on the whole, the Victorian age was: a lucid interval in the human record of folly, barbarism and insanity – as Gibbon saw it, and Swift before him: a record in which the twentieth century is well to the fore.

A most striking Oxford figure to make a name in the Victorian world was Charles Reade, the novelist. He came from an old Elizabethan family out at Ipsden, and as a boy was educated by a clergyman at Iffley. Coming up to Magdalen in 1831, he was elected to a Fellowship and was careful to retain it for life by not marrying. Though he went through the regular course of college offices, including vice-president in 1851, he lived mostly in London. For he was immensely stage-struck and wrote a large number of plays, mostly melodramas, on which he made (and lost) money. He also met his fate in the shape of an actress, whom he never married but lived with all his life. Tall and athletic, he found it a satisfactory arrangement to keep on his fine set of rooms in the New Buildings, which he panelled with glass to bring the greenery of the Grove, and the deer, within. He also used to bring down from London the theatrical ladies of his acquaintance.

This reminds us that, so long as Fellows had to remain unmarried, a number of them kept their women, or surreptitious wives, away from Oxford. No wonder that the theme of illegitimacy occupied a large part of Reade's best-known book, *The Cloister and the Hearth*, which the Victorians regarded as their finest historical novel. Charles Reade owed to his mistress the suggestion that he turn novelist, and this he did to much effect. A prolific writer, his novels are his best work. He probably owed to his academic training his method of writing them: he did an immense amount of research before embarking on one; the subject was usually some social hardship or scandal of the time which his tender heart, like Dickens, ached to put right. Such were the themes of novels like *Hard Cash*, *Griffith Gaunt*, and *It Is Never Too Late To Mend*. One novel dealt with the insanitary condition of a hamlet on his brother's estate at Ipsden. The Reades had several Anglo-Indians in the family; as a mark of esteem for their services, two philanthropic maharajahs sank a couple of deep wells through the Chiltern chalk to bring water to the poor villagers. Such were the charming exchanges of those days.

A nephew of Charles was Winwood Reade, a Magdalen Hall man, whose posthumous fame belongs to the twentieth century rather than his own. For his heretical unbelieving survey of man's history and fate, *The Martyrdom of Man*, became a classic only in our time. Too strong meat for the Victorians, it was highly regarded by people like H. G. Wells, who thought of the book as a forerunner of his *Outline of History*. Winwood Reade was a remarkable traveller, deeply interested in the descent of man; in pursuit of his subject he penetrated into hardly accessible parts of Africa, one of the first to track down our cousin, the gorilla. Worn out with tropical fever, he died quite young. His not wholly conformist uncle thought that if he had lived longer he might have retracted his opinions, so disagreeable to Victorian orthodoxy.

Various works of fiction portrayed different aspects of Oxford life for the world outside. The first was *The Adventures of Mr Verdant Green, an Oxford Freshman*, by 'Cuthbert Bede', 1853–6. The author, a clergyman named Edward Bradley, was not an Oxford man, but was possibly all the more observant for that. He resided here for a year, an outsider; his book had such success – people must have been interested by the subject – that it was extended to three parts, with a further sequel. Though Bradley wrote a lot, he never had such another success. The book is really sub-Pickwick, with its vulgar bouncing humour: I must say, Victorians were easily amused.

What a contrast with Froude's disquieting *Nemesis of Faith* (1849), or Newman's revealing novel, *Loss and Gain* (1848). In this last Newman's intellectual procedure is revealed as clearly, if unintentionally, as in his *Grammar of Assent*. In the novel the hero's emotional sympathies are from the earliest with Charles the martyr-king and the Cavaliers; he then rigs up an intellectual position to justify his *parti pris* – just what Newman always did.

There is more than one might suppose of an affiliation with Henry Kingsley, brother of Newman's puzzled opponent, who wondered just what Dr Newman meant. The answer was the *Apologia pro Vita Sua*, most moving of Oxford autobiographies. Henry Kingsley was up at Worcester, 1850–3. There was a strong strain of feeling in him for youthful male beauty (as in Gerard Manley Hopkins), which we can recognize now for what it was. Kingsley and Edwin Arnold, of *The Light of Asia*, were close friends, and Kingsley a fine athlete and sportsman. The background of Worcester, as St Paul's College, and the theme of platonic love between men, appear again and again in Henry Kingsley's novels and stories, in *Ravenshoe, Stretton, Silcotes, Jackson of Paul's*. Was this why he was looked at askance by the rest of the family, particularly the dragon, Mrs Charles Kingsley?

Another muscular Christian was Charles Kingsley's companion, Tom Hughes, an Oriel man in the 1840s, friend of Matt Arnold and Clough. Twenty years later he wrote *Tom Brown at Oxford* (1861): it had the disadvantage of being a sequel to his best-seller, *Tom Brown's Schooldays*, with its unforgettable portrait of Rugby and Dr Arnold. The sequel was authentic enough, but never had a comparable success. Tom Hughes was a grand fellow, a Christian socialist, who poured out money like water on the Working Men's College he largely founded in Great Ormond Street. He had reason to be disillusioned, but wasn't. He wrote an essay on 'The Manliness of Christ': there is all the Victorian age in the title – the twentieth century offers another alternative.

The grandest or, at least, the most presuming, fictional portrait is that by George Eliot, otherwise Mrs Cross (John Cross tried to jump out of a window after marrying her). George Eliot was an intimate of the rather egregious Mrs Mark Pattison, afterwards Lady Dilke, and an observant visitor at the rector's lodgings at Lincoln, that strange and strained interior. There is little doubt that the character of Mr Casaubon in *Middlemarch* was sparked off by that of Mark Pattison. Mr Casaubon in the novel never could get round to finishing his *magnum opus*, any more than the rector could his on Scaliger; he did manage, however, to publish a biography of Casaubon.

We can go no further with these contributions to literature, any more than with the other poets and imaginative writers who passed through the portals of the colleges, like other undergraduates to make or mar in the world: Southey and Lockhart from Balliol; De Quincey from Worcester; Beddoes from Pembroke. Walter Savage Landor, another rebel, was sent down from Trinity; but he exemplified in verse and prose, especially the marmoreal *Imaginary Conversations*, the classical spirit which Matthew Arnold propounded.

In the bewildering diversity and varied richness of the epoch we turn back to Arnold, in the poem he dedicated to the memory of his father, for the values Oxford stood for and upheld. First, for the ordinary mass of people, who recur:

> What is the course of the life
> Of mortal men on the earth? –

Most men eddy about
Here and there – eat and drink,
Chatter and love and hate,
Gather and squander, are raised
Aloft, are hurled in the dust,
Striving blindly, achieving
Nothing; and then they die –
Perish! and no one asks
Who or what they have been ...

Then there are the few, the elect:

And there are some, whom a thirst
Ardent, unquenchable, fires,
Not with the crowd to be spent –
Not without aim to go round
In an eddy of purposeless dust,
Effort unmeaning and vain.
Ah yes, some of us strive
Not without action to die
Fruitless, but something to snatch
From dull oblivion, nor all
Glut the devouring grave!
We, we have chosen our path –
Path to a clear-purposed goal,
The path of advance.

Right: Watercolour of St Aldate's showing Tom Tower by J. M. W. Turner.
Overleaf: Christ Church from the Meadows by J. M. W. Turner.

10
The Twentieth Century

THE dominant feature of twentieth-century Oxford is the immense pro-liferation of science, witnessed by the way the science departments – spawned from the original Museum – are eating up the Parks. At the beginning of the century Britain in general, and Oxford in particular, had fallen behind: scientific researchers had to go to Germany for training. The tragedy of the century has been that Germany's scientific and technological development went along with a recessive militarist system, politically irrespon-sible, which directed its immense power on an aggressive course towards *Welt-macht* at all costs and led to the two world wars which wrecked this century.

It is now clear – recognized at last even by German historians, at least by the most eminent of them, Fischer – that the two wars were but the crests of one long wave of aggression. The most admired of Oxford historians, Sir Lewis Namier, with his eastern European background, understood what was happening better than any. An Oxford statesman, with a central European background, L. S. Amery, appreciated it better than insular English politicians between the wars: his judgement of the situation was completely borne out. He said to me, 'Germany so nearly brought it off the first time that it was to be expected that she would have a second try.'

German arrogance and brutality did not go unobserved by the scientists who went there to learn their technique. Sherrington, first among modern physio-logists, 'achieved for the nervous system what William Harvey achieved for the circulation'. He 'never forgot the arrogance of German militarism' which he witnessed in conquered Strasbourg in 1884–5. He had the intuition and compas-sion of a poet; he grieved for the young men of 1914–18 'giving their lives un-questioningly for the mental blindness of others'. It was all to do again in 1939–45, with less excuse, for we had been warned. In his poems this noble scientist paid tribute to

> The young folk, splashed with death in the trenched loam.

Professor Lindemann, too, knew Germany intimately: he was born there, of mixed Alsatian-American-English stock; he received his research training in

Robert Bridges – 'through three decades the dominating figure in the landscape' – who returned to Oxford in 1907 and lived there until 1930.

Berlin. During the Second War he was the strongest advocate of the bombing of Germany with maximum precision and force. Some people thought that Lindemann hated Germany; if so, he was quite justified. These men *knew*.

Of course, Germany paid a heavy price for her insane barbarism towards the Jews and others; Oxford profited by the brilliant men of science saved from the Nazi regression to type. Lindemann brought to the Clarendon laboratory the finest low-temperature physicist in the world, in Franz, later Sir Francis, Simon. The team around the Jewish Chain who helped Florey with the fundamental work on penicillin were refugees from Germany.

These are lurid instances of a significant general tendency: the recruitment to science from all parts, other universities, other countries – the increasingly cosmopolitan character of scientific research (like theology in the Middle Ages). Some of the foremost figures came from Cambridge: Sherrington himself, Hardy the mathematician, Tansley, the leading botanist and plant ecologist. Others came from overseas: just as the biggest man in Cambridge, Rutherford, came from New Zealand, so Florey, a Rhodes scholar, came from Australia. So did Hugh Cairns, another Rhodes scholar, foremost of brain surgeons.

A number of eminent scientists have been Oxford men *e gremio*:★ Soddy and Sidgwick among chemists, Tizard, a pupil of Sidgwick, Hinshelwood and E.J. Bowen; Titchmarsh among mathematicians; Florey among Sherrington's pupils; J.B.S.Haldane, and E.B.Ford among geneticists. Julian Huxley carried on his grandfather's rôle as popularizer and propagandist of science.

If Rutherford and the Cavendish laboratory have the chief credit for splitting the atom and initiating the nuclear world, with its terrifying consequences for mankind, it is some consolation that the discovery of penicillin at Oxford, in-

★Or, so to say, from the beginning.

augurating the science of antibiotics, has also produced its revolution: the greatest step in history towards man's conquest of disease.

Up to 1914 there was little change at Oxford: life continued along nineteenth-century lines, socially selective and, in patches, elect. The university acted still, in part, as training ground or privileged nursery for the upper classes, with an admixture of scholars, intending clergy and civil servants. It was dominated by the public schools and classical culture; this is reflected not only directly in the university, its leading figures and studies within, but in the larger world of literature without. We may take Max Beerbohm's *Zuleika Dobson* as a classic of the inside world, the privileged few with their gaiety and irresponsibility, their addiction to practical jokes and fleeting their time carelessly, if stylishly – for the world was their oyster. For those for whom the world was not their oyster, who stood outside and remained outside, Hardy's *Jude the Obscure* is their book – with its letter of rejection to an inquiring youth by the master of the college (thought to be Balliol). Compton Mackenzie was an in-man; his early success, *Guy and Pauline* (now a 'World's Classic' with the university press), floats upon the Oxford air, but *Sinister Street* describes the undergraduate life of the place with ambivalent undertones of Magdalen aestheticism – sub-Wilde.

More important is the poetry Oxford gave rise to. Robert Bridges came back to live on Boar's Hill from 1907 to 1930. Through three decades he was the dominating literary figure in the landscape – underestimated by his inferiors today. He took an influential, if lofty, part in the cultural concerns of the place, musical as well as literary. He began by writing *Demeter: A Mask*, for the ladies of Somerville to act at the inauguration of their new building in 1904. He was interested in fine printing and co-operated with Daniel of Worcester College, who did exquisite work on his private press. Bridges joined with Henry Bradley of the Oxford English Dictionary, Walter Raleigh and Pearsall Smith to found the Society for Pure English. Ardent always for the best, Bridges lectured to the working men of Swindon.

Again in 1907 Bridges wrote the Invitation to the memorable Oxford pageant of that year. The city in the vale inspired his verse, for he usually saw it from Boar's Hill:

> The lovely city, thronging tower and spire,
> The mind of the wide landscape, dreaming deep,
> Grey-silvery in the vale; a shrine where keep
> Memorial hopes their pale celestial fire . . .

Or there are poems with a seventeenth-century touch, like that 'To the President of Magdalen College', the literary Herbert Warren. In the last decade of his life the old poet was writing his *Testament of Beauty*. Written in a new measure of his own devising (he had made many experiments in classical prosody), it was a complete assertion of his belief that only the pursuit of beauty redeemed man's life. During the war, in 1916, he brought forth his *Spirit of Man*, an anthology which the sense of Aristotle and the idealism of Shelley dominated, 'designed to bring fortitude and peace of mind to his countrymen in wartime'.

The Testament of Beauty recorded his earlier friendship with Gerard Manley Hopkins; they had been undergraduates together 1863–7. For years Hopkins sent Bridges his strangely original poems and they corresponded about their mutual interest in prosody. At last, when the war was over, Bridges launched his friend's poetry upon an unreceptive world, giving it careful and scholarly editing. At the time it was too original for people to take; after a decade it appeared that a new star had been added to the firmament out of the vanished Victorian world. Hopkins, who had followed Newman into the Roman Church, was inspired by Oxford like him and Arnold and Bridges; but with a difference: for him it was Duns Scotus' Oxford:

> Towery city and branchy between towers;
> Cuckoo-echoing, bell-swarmèd, lark-charmèd,
>   rook-racked, river-rounded ...
>
> Thou hast a base and brickish skirt there, sours
> That neighbour-nature thy grey beauty is grounded
> Best in; graceless growth, thou hast confounded
> Rural rural keeping-folk, flocks, and flowers.
>
> Yet ah! this air I gather and I release
> He lived on; these weeds and waters, these walls are what
> He haunted who of all men most sways my spirits to peace ...

A strange choice for a Victorian – Duns Scotus! However, it is nice to note the Oxford loyalty going back over half a millennium. The 'base and brickish skirt' refers to the growth of north Oxford, the substantial villas going up to house the families of now married dons, with back streets for their serving families. An area which has given inspiration in our degenerate time to a subsequent poet-laureate with his passion for Rawlinson Road, and Chadlington Road, the pink hawthorn of Maytime, and Linton Road with 'St C. S. Lewis's church'.

Theirs was a cosy world, in which the Basil Blackwells, the Salters and the T. E. Lawrences were born. Little can they have imagined the wrath to come: civilization has never had it so good again.

Of the classical scholars of their time two were of European stature, A. E. Housman and Gilbert Murray; both St John's men, they afford a pointed contrast. Housman (1859–1936), a brilliant Latinist already working at Propertius, perversely refused to take Greats seriously or to do any work for it. He was ploughed – an extraordinary case. Banished to the Patent Office in London, he proceeded to make himself the finest Latin scholar in Europe and 'one of the best Grecians'. With his English poems he became also one of the first poets of his time. Everything about him was pure α – except his character: a repressed homosexual who had reason to fear the barbarism of opinion and the cruelty of average human fools, he responded with savagery and gave them quite as good as he got. His sarcasms at their expense have the quality of art, for he was a perfectionist. He had no superior as a classical scholar in his time; his contempt for inferior scholars was scathing, especially for the heavy pedantry of the Germans, though he admired the scholarship of Wilamowitz-Moellendorf. On his visits to the continent he always shunned Germany and, after his early humiliation, like the scholar-gipsy, he 'came to Oxford and his friends no more'. He took his scholarship to Cambridge, where he became a famous, enigmatic and solitary figure, as much feared as he was respected.

Gilbert Murray (1866–1957) came from Australia, of Celtic stock on both sides. He was an astonishingly rounded human being, with brilliant gifts of mind, essentially happy and well-adjusted. A complete rationalist, without any religious sense, he was a standing refutation of C. S. Lewis's perverse position that it is too difficult to be a good man without religious belief – Gilbert Murray was a secular saint. Though the foremost Hellenist of his time, the diversity of his gifts got in the way of his achieving what Housman did in pure scholarship. As a scholar Murray did effect a revolution in the appreciation of Euripides, whom the nineteenth century had not appreciated, and Jowett actively disliked. Murray established the best text; but, more, his translations performed on the stage conquered London audiences (would they today?) and effectively introduced Euripides to the wide reading public. A Periclean democrat, he had a passion for bringing Greek literature and life alive again to people in general, and a proper conviction that it was for scholars to do it. But few could.

Murray won wider international renown by his work for the League of Nations – of which he was one of the original inspirers, with Lord Robert Cecil – for international peace and intellectual co-operation. He bore his part in rescuing scholars and bringing refugees from Germany to Britain. Though he hated cruelty and its organized extension in militarism, he was no pacifist: he thought 'some things were worse than war'. Edward Grey's sober, sad speech on Germany's invasion of Belgium in August 1914 convinced him that Britain had to fight not only for her own existence but for the liberties of Europe and civilized standards.

Tragically, the long struggle from 1914 to 1945, though it finally settled Germany's hash, exhausted Britain. She would never have been able to resist but for the recruits that came to her aid from all parts of the world – such men as came to Oxford, in Florey and Lindemann, Hugh Cairns and Gilbert Murray.

Sir Arthur Evans (1851–1941) was another Celt. He had the historic good fortune to uncover Knossos, and to bring to light a new world of culture in prehistoric Minoan civilization. Made keeper of the Ashmolean, which had fallen into neglect, he revivified it with his life-enhancing touch, and enriched it with his finds and benefactions. A rich man himself, in the days when private wealth could confer discriminating public benefits, he was a founder of the British School at Athens and of the British Academy. Up on Boar's Hill he created in Youlbury, his estate, an 'earthly paradise' for three generations of friends, especially young people. Happy to say, this tradition has been carried on by his successor, Arthur Goodhart, one of the noblest benefactors of the university in our time.

Out of the classical stable, since it was the leading arts school, came politicians, civil servants, churchmen, lawyers; philosophers, historians, archaeologists, linguistic experts and pioneers in new schools of modern languages, particularly English, which was to have such an expansion all over the world. We can only mention here those who had a marked influence beyond the walls. Among politicians there were, for example, Asquith, Rosebery, Curzon, Edward Grey, Morley. All of these had careers that were part of English history. Asquith was elected from a scholarship into a Fellowship at Balliol and, prime minister for eight critical years, managed to keep contact with the university, of which he should have been chancellor. This 'last of the Romans', however, said peaceably that some wouldn't vote for him because he was a Bachelor (he hadn't taken his M.A.), others because he wasn't a bachelor (i.e. was married to Margot). Rosebery left without taking a degree, but made not the less a cultivated book collector and admirable author. John Morley was a professional writer, author of many books, as well as a somewhat starched political figure, Liberal secretary of state for India without much feeling for or understanding of the subject.

Curzon had the understanding that Morley lacked – and more appetizing intellectual interests too. A Fellow of All Souls, he was also one of the brilliant set of 'The Souls' in London. In addition to his political services as viceroy, he deserves to be remembered in history for his preservation of wonderful Indian monuments of the past, as well as of such buildings as Bodiam and Tattersall Castles and Montacute at home. On his return from India, he was made chancellor at Oxford in 1907, and took up residence as such. This was as unwelcome as it was unprecedented, at least since the Middle Ages. But the odd thing was that he turned out a reformer, and thus succeeded in staving off government intervention. Off his own bat he drafted a long memorandum, *Principles and Methods of University Reform*. This supposed reactionary favoured a larger place

Left: Gilbert Murray, the foremost Hellenist of his time and 'a secular saint'.

Right: Warden Spooner of New College, the originator of 'spoonerisms' – 'sharp as a needle but kind of heart'.

for women and degrees for them. In 1910 a delegacy for women students, i.e. non-collegiate, was set up; others of Curzon's suggestions had to wait until the war was over.

Of eminent lawyers turned politicians Birkenhead (F. E. Smith) and Simon occupied much space in the public prints in their day; it may be doubted whether their services to the nation were commensurate with the notice they received. The former's record in regard to Ulster before 1914 was worse than irresponsible. Avowing himself 'to be eager for posthumous fame, he was inclined to rest his claim to remembrance on the part played by him as a law reformer'. He piloted through the Lords the large Law of Property Act (1922), the work on which had been done by others. His rival, Simon, had not even this to his credit: his long career with the so-called National Government was almost wholly deleterious, his record as one of the inner group – with Chamberlain, Halifax and Hoare – responsible for appeasement, disastrous. In justice one must say that Halifax's record as foreign secretary was worse than Simon's. In the end, with Baldwin in the background, these men ruined their country.

The churchmen had better records but, in modern secular society, very little real importance. From the death of Benson to the appointment of Michael Ramsay, the Church of England was run by five Oxford men, 1896–1961. The aged Frederick Temple went right back to the blithe days of Arnold's Rugby;

Randall Davidson carried on that tradition as a son-in-law of Tait – a simple good man, he was a dexterous ecclesiastical statesman. Cosmo Lang, a complex character, might have figured as a cardinal of the Curia; he had been a pupil of Jowett, a friend of university extension and the WEA, like the religious R. H. Tawney and the irreligious G. D. H. Cole. William Temple, who avowed himself a socialist, was a Balliol man too, a friend of these last; but he did not live long as archbishop. He was succeeded by Geoffrey Fisher, a headmaster who held his bench of bishops in tight rein, like a sixth form, and put the C. of E. in good financial order.

A churchman whose name is known over the world was Warden Spooner of New College, for he unawares contributed a word to the language. Spooner was an albino, sharp as a needle but of a kind heart. A curious *lapsus linguae* went with his make-up; a well-known example is his announcement of the hymn, 'Kinkering kongs their tikles tate'. This became known as a 'Spoonerism', and there were many of them, authentic and fabricated. Spooner himself said to my friend, Lionel Curtis: 'I never said any of those silly things; all that happened was that I was in the High and my hat blew off, and I found I was chasing a little dawg.'

We cannot go into the work of top civil servants so important in the state. Warren Fisher, a Hertford man, was for long a key figure at the treasury, holding the reins of power 1919–39. As such he was largely responsible for the economy drive, when what the country needed was Keynsian expansion; since the Second War, when economy and the rebuilding of resources were the basic necessities, we have been given uncontrolled expansion in the wrong circumstances – hence runaway inflation.

A more creative public servant was Michael Sadler (1861–1943). At Oxford he was the leader in the university extension movement, a dynamo of energy. By 1893 he had four hundred courses of lectures going all over England, with summer schools and conferences at Oxford. A missionary zeal for education was generated by these men. Recruited to the department of education, he carried forward the propaganda for a national system of secondary education so powerfully urged from Oxford; Morant was Sadler's assistant, and they converted Balfour, a Cambridge man, to it. It helped to lose him the next election.

Wonderful creative work for the new civic universities was done by these men in these years, going out from Oxford to become vice-chancellors: Sadler at Leeds, H. A. L. Fisher at Sheffield, Richard Lodge and Grant Robertson at Birmingham, W. M. Childs at Reading, John Murray at Exeter, Lord Eustace Percy – who had been an admirable minister of education – at Newcastle. Sadler headed a commission which revolutionized Indian education. When he came back as master of University College 1923–34, creative as ever, he founded the Oxford Preservation Trust (would it had been in existence fifty years earlier!) and the Friends of the Bodleian.

H. A. L. Fisher made his name as an historian: *par exception* he had gone to the Ecole des Chartes in Paris for training and was a sceptical disciple of Renan, rather than of the rebarbative Germans. He was drafted from Sheffield to be president of the board of education in 1916, and as such brought forward his Education Act to provide continuation schools, on a proper selective basis, for adolescents, instead of hugger-mugger comprehensiveness, in pursuit of the chimera of equality. Fisher, too, returned for the last phase of his career, and to write his large-minded *History of Europe*, from the point of view of a disillusioned liberal. 'Disinterested curiosity is the life-blood of civilization': Fisher was a very civilized man, and disinterested curiosity is at a low ebb today.

T. F. Tout, a pupil of Stubbs, went forth from Balliol to create not only the history school at Manchester, which won a name for itself, but the faculty of arts, i.e. to establish humane studies on Oxford standards, as W. P. Ker did for London and Selincourt for Birmingham. In the second half of his career, a prodigy of energy, Tout virtually created the study of medieval administration, with a roll-call of books and articles. At Balliol he had been friends with C. H. Firth, Richard Lodge, R. L. Poole, J. H. Round – all to make important contributions to historical research and writing. Grant Robertson achieved more as vice-chancellor at Birmingham: he brought about the establishment of the Barber Trust, the foundation of the Barber Institute, with its fine collection of pictures, and the creation of the Birmingham medical centre.

We must regard these public-spirited achievements as just a few outstanding examples of the kind of thing those late Victorians – they were missioners – accomplished before and after the first catastrophe.

The creation of schools of English language and literature was the order of the day. The historian Firth, who knew more about seventeenth-century England than anyone has ever known and continued Gardiner's work, took keen interest in creating schools of modern languages, especially of English. It would have been better if these last had a more historical approach, as Firth envisaged. W. P. Ker exemplified it in his life's work, building up an English school at University College, London, 1889–1922, and helping to mould humane studies from the senate throughout the university. Very cogently, with his vast knowledge of European literatures, he exemplified the historical approach in his books. *Epic and Romance* is a classic, throwing the light of history and sense into hoary old literary problems incapable of solution without them. The result is that all and every piece of Ker's work stand firmly: his books on medieval literature, English and European, on form and style in poetry, studies ranging from Iceland to Cadiz, when so much literary criticism is chaff blown with the wind.

Quiller-Couch ('Q.') did not have the historical approach, but he was widely read in classics and had the advantage of being a creative writer, with a touch of genius, as novelist and short story writer. He had a large public as humane critic and as the creator of the series of Oxford Books of Verse. He was recruited to the just-started school of English at Cambridge, 'which, in a manner of speaking,' he once said to me shyly, 'I created'. His idea was to bring over trained men from classics to set good standards; he was grieved when his recruit, Rupert Brooke, died in the war (as did Q.'s only son).

To shape the new English school at Oxford a Cambridge man was brought in: Walter Raleigh. At Liverpool he had succeeded A. C. Bradley, admirable philo-sophic critic, brother of the great philosopher, F. H. Bradley; and was succeeded by Oliver Elton, another Oxford classicist to carry on those standards. Raleigh, like Q., was not a precise scholar, and he did not much care for the academic study of literature, let alone pedantry. He brought a breath of fresh air into Oxford and was a wonder-working lecturer, as professor from 1904 to his premature death in 1922. An original and gifted man, his letters recapture the atmosphere, the anxieties and heart-ache of those years. On the outbreak of the war he wrote to Legouis, a French authority on English literature:

I am glad to be rid of the German incubus. It has done no good for many years to scholarship – indeed it has produced a kind of slave-scholarship, though there are still some happy exceptions ... We shall have to pay more than we can easily imagine. We shall get there all right, and the little children of today will live in a better world than we have known.

Alas for those hopes!

Raleigh well understood what was being fought. 'The nastiest thing about the war is not the brutality of the Germans, but their low deceit and brag. They are brave, yet they lie and boast like cowards, or rather, their vulgar government does.' He hoped, optimistically, 'that the day will come when the sentimentalism of brutality, which they call *Realpolitik*, will be wildly unpopular in Germany'. So far from this, they improved on their performance from 1933 to 1945, all the way from Hitler's legal accession to power to Rotterdam and Auschwitz. Raleigh's intuitive gift saw further than most people into the way things would go, and the upshot. 'They are going to be beaten far more completely than any one war can beat them. We shan't see more than a little of it.' At the worst moment, his intuition told him, 'They will be an ugly sight about 1920. Pitiful.' They were. But the upshot: 'I believe this may be the last act before the centre of gravity shifts East or West. Exit Europe.' This was to be, after the second attempt, the historic result of the betrayal of Europe by the strongest people occupying its strategic centre. Nobody could live with them.

But the price of resisting them was appalling. I often think of it as I go round the colleges looking at the war memorials: those of the First War my seniors, those of the Second, some of them, my pupils and friends. The holocaust of the First German War was much worse than the Second, for Britain was unprepared: there was no conscription till 1916, and all the finest young men volunteered for service. There followed the massacre of a generation – particularly of the officer classes: hundreds of names of the dead are inscribed on the walls of the bigger colleges. At Christ Church, New College, Balliol and Magdalen (as at Trinity and King's at Cambridge) it reads like a roll-call of names out of English history. It had been a good world for them: they died for it.

Here is Raleigh writing to Lady Desborough, after the deaths of her sons, Julian and Billy Grenfell. They had had a wonderful time up at Balliol, splendid young athletes, as gifted in mind as in body. They were among the early ones to be killed. 'The great things seem cold, but they are there all the time, and Julian and Billy believed in them, and had splendid lives. Anyhow, they have made life the little thing it is.' But is that true? And it is cold consolation for what the country lost with that generation, for they would have been its leaders, they were its elect spirits.

They can only be written about in poetry, of which there was a rich outpouring from them – from their education – with their blood. Raleigh himself quotes Julian Grenfell's 'Into Battle', the poem he had sent home to his mother from Flanders:

> Through joy and blindness he shall know,
>   Not caring much to know, that still
> Nor lead nor steel shall reach him, so
>   That it be not the Destined Will.
>
> The thundering line of battle stands,
>   And in the air death moans and sings;
> But Day shall clasp him with strong hands,
>   And Night shall fold him in soft wings.

Noel Hodgson was not much more than a boy at Christ Church when the war broke out, a more religious spirit than the Grenfells:

> By all the glories of the day
>   And the cool evening's benison,
> By the last sunset touch that lay
>   Upon the hills when day was done,
> By beauty lavishly outpoured
>   And blessings carelessly received,
>   By all the days that I have lived,
> Make me a soldier, Lord.

Oxford

By all of all man's hopes and fears,
 And all the wonders poets sing,
The laughter of unclouded years,
 And every sad and lovely thing;
By the romantic ages stored
 With high endeavour that was his,
 By all his mad catastrophes,
Make me a man, O Lord.

I, that on my familiar hill
 Saw with uncomprehending eyes
A hundred of thy sunsets spill
 Their fresh and sanguine sacrifice,
Ere the sun swings his noonday sword
 Must say goodbye to all of this –
 By all delights that I shall miss,
Help me to die, O Lord.

Many are the poems written at that time by Oxford men who were to die; some who wrote survived and came back after the war, like Robert Graves, Edmund Blunden, Robert Nichols, or Herbert Asquith, whose more brilliant brother Raymond, the prime minister's eldest son, was killed. Graves tells us that 'the first World War permanently changed my outlook on life'. Others there were inspired to write about Oxford and their friends, like Maurice Baring's 'In Memoriam' for Auberon Herbert, Lord Lucas. Flecker, from the Near East, remembered the university, as Edward Thomas had recalled the old county town outside the guide books.

Noon strikes on England, noon on Oxford town,
– Beauty she was statue-cold – there's blood upon her gown:
Noon of my dreams, O noon!
 Proud and godly kings had built her, long ago,
 With her towers and tombs and statues all arow,
With her fair and floral air and the love that lingers there,
 And the streets where the great men go.

Oxford inspired many poems onwards from Bridges' and Hopkins' on the felling of Binsey Poplars; there had been Belloc on Balliol and Mackail on Arnold Toynbee, Binyon's 'Bablock-hythe' and Q's 'Alma Mater':

Know you her secret none can utter?
 Hers of the Book, the tripled Crown? . . .

Gerard Manley Hopkins, the publication of whose Victorian poems, by Robert Bridges in the 1920s, added a new figure to English literature.

Now Binyon, Q's contemporary at Trinity, returned to 'Oxford in War Time':

> It is as if I looked on the still face
> Of a Mother, musing where she sits alone.
> She is with her sons, she is not in this place;
> She is gone out into far lands unknown ...

Then after recalling the places where they were, in France, in Flanders, in Macedonia, in Sinai and Palestine, in that other Mesopotamia fighting their way up the Tigris:

> She is with her sons, leaving a virtue
> Out of her sacred places ...

A most sensitive observer from abroad was here in those years, and has left his memories in literature. George Santayana's novel, *The Last Puritan*, has Oxford, still more Iffley, in its background; while his *Soliloquies in England* is one of the most perceptive books ever written on the subject.

The outbreak of war in the year 1914 found me by chance in England, and there I remained, chiefly at Oxford, until the day of the peace. During those years, in rambles to Iffley and Sandford, to Godstow and Wytham, to the hospitable eminence of Chilswell [he was a friend of Bridges], to Wood Eaton or Nuneham or Abingdon or Stanton Harcourt,

> Crossing the stripling Thames at Bablock-hythe,

these Soliloquies were composed. Often over Port Meadow the whirr of aeroplanes sent an iron tremor through these reveries; and the daily casualty list, the constant sight of the wounded, the cadets strangely replacing the undergraduates, made the foreground to these distances.

The big Examination Schools were a hospital in those years (as again in 1939–45). Through the wall a door was made into New College garden where the wounded might sit: now walled up, a secret place nobody knows. Santayana goes on: what filled his mind were

English images, and the passion was the love of England and, behind England, of Greece. What I love in Greece and England is contentment in finitude, fair outward ways, manly perfection and simplicity ... There is, or was [alas, we must now say, there *was*], a beautifully healthy England hidden from most foreigners: the England of the countryside and of the poets, domestic, sporting, gallant, boyish, of a sure and delicate heart. I could see clearly that this England was pre-eminently the home of decent happiness and a quiet pleasure in being oneself. I found here the same sort of manliness which I had learned to love in America, yet softer, and not at all obstreperous ... entirely absent also from the doctrinaire of the German school, in his dense vanity and officiousness, that nothing can put to shame.

With his Latin clarity of mind Santayana was 'surprised that there should be so many Hegelians in England, and in such places of influence'. He knew that 'Hegel was not looking for the truth' but, like the Germans, for power and domination. It was odd that the English should have fallen for it, Oxford and Balliol in particular: largely a reaction against the English school of empiricism and the bleak dominance of John Stuart Mill. This was the case with Bradley, the one philosopher of genius, whose classic works – notably *Ethical Studies* and *Appearance and Reality* – were written at Merton. Santayana wrote here his searching diagnosis of what is wrong in the German soul – since a people's philosophy mirrors its very soul – in *Egotism and German Philosophy*. 'Egotism – subjectivity in thought and wilfulness in morals – is the soul of German philosophy.' Writing in 1916 Santayana foresaw the hideous future this would have:

The thing bears all the marks of a new religion. The fact that the established religions of Germany are still forms of Christianity may obscure the explicit and heathen character of the new faith: it passes for the creed of a few extremists, when in reality it dominates the judgment and conduct of the nation. No religious tyranny could be more complete. It has its prophets in the great philosophers and historians of the last century; its high priests and pharisees in the government and the professors; its faithful flock in the disciplined mass of the nation; its heretics in the socialists; its dupes in the Catholics and the Liberals, to both of whom the national creed, if they understood it, would be an abomination. It has its martyrs now by the million, and its victims among unbelievers are even more numerous, for its victims, in some degree, are all men.

No wiser or more searching words ever came out of Oxford; they went totally unheeded, though they pierced to the root of the matter and foretold precisely what would come about with the Third Reich. Most people in Oxford and elsewhere were quite unaware of the words or the man of genius who had uttered them; they preferred the humbug of the third-rate – and paid the price.

Santayana pointed the poignant contrast.

> Instinctively the Englishman is no missionary, no conqueror. He carries his English weather in his heart wherever he goes, and it becomes a cool spot in the desert, and a steady and sane oracle amongst all the deliriums of mankind. Never since the heroic days of Greece has the world had such a sweet, just, boyish master. It will be a black day for the human race when scientific blackguards, conspirators, churls and fanatics manage to supplant him.

This is precisely what happened. The English never had 'mastery', but in those days a certain primacy. Has it been better for the world – or a better world – since they lost it?

For a brief space in the 1920s men hoped that, after such a lesson, things might go better. Men like Gilbert Murray gave devoted service to building a League of Nations, the effort towards a better international system to maintain peace. An able civil servant like Arthur Salter, of Salter's Steamers at Folly Bridge, had worked with Beveridge and Morant to bring into being social insurance and the Welfare State. Salter now gave his energies to the International Labour Office (his little Thames steamers played their gallant part in evacuating the army from Dunkirk in 1940 before the renewed onrush of the barbarian hordes).

Men who had survived the holocaust of 1914–18 came back to Oxford, and a wonderful lot they were: like their sons who came back after 1939–45 – men who had had heroic and terrible experiences all over the world, on Arctic convoys, on the submarined seas, in the air (many had been shot down over hideous Berlin, *fons et origo malorum*); in France and Flanders (again), in Italy, the Mediterranean, Africa; the jungle and the desert. We can cite only one example of world-wide renown. T. E. Lawrence had been at Jesus before the war, whence he was recruited by D. G. Hogarth and Leonard Woolley for the diggings at Carchemish. Both these were remarkable men, Woolley himself the discoverer of Ur who brought to light early Sumerian civilization. With these men and in these parts Lawrence developed his preference for desert-life which equipped him for his Arab campaign; that has become part of history and legend. In 1919 All Souls elected him to a Fellowship: here he wrote *The Seven Pillars of Wisdom*, the most remarkable book to come out of the war.

On Boar's Hill clustered the poets. Bridges had been joined up there by Masefield for neighbour. Masefield, though shy, was hospitable; Lamont, the American banker, built him a theatre in the garden, to which we would flock up for performances of his and other plays. Equally the war poets would descend for

235

performances at the primitive Playhouse, with its uncomfortable creaking chairs, or come to address our undergraduate literary societies: Robert Graves, Robert Nichols, Richard Hughes, among others.

Among us undergraduates, already beginning to write, were the novelists to be: L. P. Hartley, Evelyn Waugh, Graham Greene and Henry Green; among critics, Lord David Cecil, Cyril Connolly, Peter Quennell. These were very shortly followed by a very well-publicized group of poets: Auden, MacNeice, Day Lewis, Betjeman, Spender, Philip Larkin, whose proliferation did something to reduce the lead, in this century, which Cambridge curiously established in poets of earlier centuries. (It was a regrettable accident that that Oxfordshire man, John Milton, should have gone to the Puritan university: it confirmed his adolescent prejudices.

It is too early to estimate the work of my own generation of writers, and especially to disentangle the Oxford strain in it: to some of them it meant a great deal, others shied away from it or reacted against it. Though Graham Greene lived on in Miss Broughton's Holywell for a time (in which street Beazley lived and Berkeley died), he preferred in his work the seedier shores of Mexico or Cuba, Africa or Indo-China. But Evelyn Waugh devoted his one regular novel, *Brideshead Revisited*, to the life of the 'aesthetes' in the 1920s, with such fidelity that several of them are recognizable. David Cecil spent his working life as professor there, and owed everything to it – along with Hatfield; as I have owed everything to the twin inspiration of Oxford and Cornwall.

Among the poets Betjeman is full of Oxford. Everything appears, one way or another, in those ambivalent nostalgic verses: the 'pink may, double may, dead laburnum' of north Oxford, the 'reddened remorselessness' of Byzantine brick St Barnabas, the bells of St Giles's before he undergoes an anaesthetic at the Radcliffe, Oxford as it appears in an old-fashioned water-colour, the university town of Myfanwy (Mrs John Piper):

> *Her* Myfanwy? *My* Myfanwy.
>   Bicycle bells in a Boar's Hill Pine,
> Stedman Triple from All Saints' steeple,
>   Tom and his hundred and one at nine,
> Bells of Butterfield, caught in Keble,
>   Sally and backstroke answer '*Mine!*'

Or there is the poem in memory of a Pembroke don – lucky don to be so commemorated. Betjeman's half a dozen Oxford poems place him in the select company of Arnold and Bridges and Hopkins.

Of the familiar group – Auden, Spender, MacNeice – it is likely that the poetry of MacNeice will last longest, as more purely and completely poetry, less journalism and ephemeral topicality. Besides, he was an excellent classical scholar, his poetry thereby more accomplished, with his metrical mastery: an altogether more finished poet. Auden (Odin) was proud of his Viking descent and, taking the English school at Oxford (with a third), was influenced by the Icelandic poetry he at least read for it. He remained always grateful to his tutor, Nevill Coghill, who opened up this and other worlds to him: this he celebrated with a graceful poem later. Coghill himself was more than a tutor: he had a wonderful gift for producing plays, bringing to life such reluctant material as *Everyman* and *Samson Agonistes*, penetrating the London stage with his *Canterbury Tales* and *A Midsummer Night's Dream*, and revealing all the beauty of *The Tempest* in Worcester Garden, with Prospero's barge sailing away over the lake under the rising moon.

An Oxford taste, much advanced by C S. Lewis, Coghill and Auden, was for Tolkien's world of 'hobbits', which has since gone round the globe. It is a taste I have not acquired; but there is no doubt that the Professor created a whole imaginative world. Perhaps we may regard him as a twentieth-century parallel to Lewis Carroll.

And this time, too, has contributed one of the most significant of English composers of music in Walton. He was a choirboy at Christ Church, educated at the Cathedral Choir School. In a more cosmopolitan life than usual for an English musician, he has managed to keep some touch with Oxford, with Christ Church and the Anglican liturgy. For the coronation he wrote a resounding 'Te Deum'; and his elaborate setting of Auden's 'The Twelve' was first performed at their old college. This was followed by a 'Missa Brevis', and a 'Jubilate'. It is pleasant to think that, even with the modish and sophisticated spirit that created 'Façade' and 'Scapino', those early influences have not ceased to bear fruit, while it is possible that 'Belshazzar's Feast' may outlive all.

In the 1920s the ancient university was filled with new ardour, doing its best to catch up and be worthy of the men who had died. No more resistance to the claims of the women. A foolish dictum of Dr Pusey had been that the establishment of a women's hall was 'one of the greatest misfortunes that have happened even in our time in Oxford'. At once after the war women were admitted to full membership and degrees, in 1920; their historian, Vera Brittain, notes that at Cambridge, 'the only other university to which Oxford pays much attention', not until after the Second German War, in 1948.

Meanwhile, how brilliantly the Oxford women justified themselves in the history of the nation! Gertrude Bell was a perfect foil to, and as much of a phenomenon as, T. E. Lawrence. As good an Arabist as he was, and as intrepid, she had penetrated into parts of Arabia no European had been in. Her books were worthy of comparison with his, especially *The Desert and the Sown*; she was as brilliant a letter writer and, if he was largely responsible for freeing the Arabs from the Turkish incubus and founding an independent state for Feisal, she bore no less a part in the formation of Iraq. He was a tortured genius, a conjured spirit; she had a happier life, fortunate and fulfilled, an indubitably great woman.

Perhaps most noticeable have been the women novelists – Rose Macaulay in the lead, with a long and distinguished row of books to her credit. Dorothy Sayers had a wider public with her detective stories; she came back to Somerville at various times to write *Gaudy Night*, but she was a good playwright and Dante scholar too. One cannot do justice to the diverse talents of such novelists as Naomi Haldane, Winifred Holtby, Margaret Kennedy, H.F.M.Prescott and Margaret Lane. Helen Waddell combined exquisite scholarship with creative writing; so too Carola Oman, sound historical sense – the daughter of an eminent historian, Sir Charles Oman – with a creative gift as biographer and novelist. We trench here upon the field of academic scholarship, where Mildred Pope became the leading authority on French philology, Dorothy Hodgkin in crystallography, along with good historians like Maude Clarke, Lucy Sutherland and C.V. Wedgwood. Among literary scholars, Helen Darbishire's life's work on Words-worth stands out. She was also the principal of Somerville; and that even princi-pals of Victorian ladies' colleges could be human we may infer from Miss Wordsworth's verses addressed to Jowett:

> If all the good people were clever,
> And all clever people were good,
> The world would be nicer than ever
> We thought that it possibly could.
>
> But somehow, 'tis seldom or never
> The two hit it off as they should;
> The good are so harsh to the clever,
> The clever so rude to the good.

There can be little doubt that Miss Wordsworth was both clever *and* good.

The Royal Commission of 1919 found nothing much to reform, and confessed as much by setting up a statutory commission for the university to carry out what itself thought desirable. This was headed by Lord Chelmsford, an ex-viceroy of India, of the Montagu-Chelmsford Report, which set India on the path towards parliamentary self-government. This was in accordance with the ideas of a remarkable constitution-maker, a kind of Abbé Siéyès, Lionel Curtis. He had taken an important part in the creation of the Union of South Africa, and was to do in framing the treaty which created the Irish Free State. He might have said (if he had known French), like Napoleon: '*J'avais le goût de la fondation et non de la propriété*'; for he also created the Royal Institute of International Affairs and the Oxford Society. Halifax followed on in the path towards self-government in India, though with no marked success except for his hobnobbing with Gandhi. They shared a religious outlook; when asked if he had not found Gandhi very tiresome, he remarked, 'Some people found Our Lord very tiresome.' The remark did more to throw light upon himself than to solve the problem.

Sir Maurice Gwyer helped forward Indian education by rescuing the university of Delhi from obscurity, dirt and neglect, attempting to set standards for others to follow. Sir Penderel Moon performed an historic mission for India at the time of partition, in organizing the exchange of whole populations, Hindu and Moslem, that might have been exterminated along the racial frontier; and thereafter as Nehru's right-hand man in directing the economic development of India. A curious contribution was that of F. W. Bain, who taught most of his life in India, and wrote a dozen exotic stories suggested by Indian folk-lore, the best known *A Digit of the Moon*. Curzon, Bain, Chelmsford, Curtis, Halifax, Gwyer, Moon were all All Souls men. Cornelia Sorabji, of Somerville, was a pioneer of equality for women, and actively advanced the cause as a legal adviser; with her knowledge of the status of women in India, she was opposed to independence. With the formidable Mrs Gandhi as prime minister, another Somervillian, it might have reconciled her to it.

In the increasing diversification of studies the continuing influence of Oxford outside is to be seen notably in the social sciences, as of Cambridge in the physical sciences. History now had the largest number of students. A. F. Pollard, besides being the leading Tudor historian, was the effective builder of the school of history in the university of London; he founded, too, the Institute of Historical Research, with its periodical *History*, and the nation-wide Historical Association. The Manchester school remained in close contact with its parent, with whom it interchanged professors. F. M. Powicke returned thence to make Oxford, while he was Regius professor, the leading centre of study in medieval history in Europe – not so today.

The importance of Namier as an historian has been exaggerated; he was an exhaustive analyst over a small field, the 1760s, and a brilliant essayist, but not a constructor of historical works. He was an original mind, with a tragic and prophetic cast, who perfectly understood the futility and folly of appeasement while it was going on. He had, of course, the advantage of being Jewish and the original vantage-point of eastern Europe from which to view the behaviour of the Germans; and he had no illusions. It is, however, not realized that Namier's too much respected card-index technique was patented by the Webbs before him. His contemporary at Balliol, G. N. Clark, knew this, himself the successor of Firth in the seventeenth century and the creator of the new Oxford History of England. The biggest achievement in ancient history has been that of A. H. M. Jones, an All Souls man who took his vast knowledge over to Cambridge, where he wrote up his prolific researches. A more fastidious spirit from the Antipodes, Syme, remained here to exert more influence with an original book, like *The Roman Revolution*.

The most original mind in political theory was Graham Wallas, and the most searching book in the subject his *Human Nature in Politics*. At Oxford it was not held possible to appoint as professor one who had 'publicly expressed disbelief in revealed religion'; so he went to help to create, with the Webbs, the London School of Economics – that place, it used to be said in the thirties, 'where they don't believe in God, and don't think P. G. Wodehouse funny'. Here L. T. Hobhouse created the school of sociology in London university. J. A. Hobson was another heterodox mind, too much out of step with economic orthodoxy to be recognized in his day. He was, however, recognized by Keynes as his precursor in stressing the importance of under-consumption in the cyclical crises of capitalism. This should have had its influence in the 1930s, when it was appropriate; we are now, since the war, suffering from the opposite, an overdose of Keynsian economics, in inappropriate circumstances. Historians well know that human beings will hardly ever take the right line at the right time.

Who represented Oxford in literature in these years?

Primary place must be given to Bridges, still occasionally to be seen down in Oxford, with his splendid leonine head; up on Boar's Hill his long life did not end till 1930, the year after he had summed up his life's work and faith in *The Testament of Beauty*. Yeats was a friend of Bridges and was living here at the time when he wrote his fine poem, 'All Souls' Night':

> Midnight has come and the great Christ Church bell,
> And many a lesser bell, sound through the room;
> And it is All Souls' Night,
> And two long glasses brimmed with muscatel
> Bubble upon the table. A ghost may come . . .

How many ghosts indeed there were to come back to Oxford that All Souls' tide at the end of the war!

Up on the opposite hill at Elsfield, looking out over Otmoor, lived John Buchan, who also maintained close contact with the university. A Scot, he had chosen to come up not to Balliol but to Brasenose, out of admiration for Pater – who died, however, when only in his fifties. Buchan was a gifted and popular novelist; with a natural gift for language, he made also an admirable essayist and man of letters. Then, too, a good historical scholar, he wrote standard biographies, the best to be written on Scott and Montrose. Extraordinarily prolific, he wrote one or two classics in their kind, *The Thirty-Nine Steps*, for example. His autobiographical *Memory Hold-the-Door* beautifully depicts all that loved countryside round Oxford and recalls those hospitable days, now rendered impossible.

Hilaire Belloc had been very much an Oxford figure earlier. President of the Union where he was remembered and sometimes re-appeared in his best days before 1914. He had wanted to be a don – with his cult of Balliol – and never forgave All Souls for not electing him. (The successful candidate, H. W. C. Davis was a far better historian.) Belloc stayed on for a couple of years in Holywell (where lived another novelist, the redoubtable Rhoda Broughton, author of *Belinda*, and Belloc wrote a *Belinda* years later). To these years belong some of his best verses, the *Essays in Liberalism* by Six Oxford Men he brought together, and *Danton*, his most sympathetic biography. Oxford had a strong impact on his life, in forming his tastes and prejudices, and even by way of reaction – when old and famous, he refused an honorary Fellowship at the college he had so much loved when young: they were too late. A man of immense literary gifts, he threw away, by sheer intellectual perversity, more than would equip most writers for life.

Not so his Balliol junior, Aldous Huxley, who made all – and rather more than all – that his original endowments warranted, by sheer intelligence and application. He began as a poet at Oxford, with his 'Leda', and then went on to try every literary form, becoming particularly distinguished as an essayist. With his family background he had a considerable knowledge of science and was a good deal of an encyclopaedist. Though his novels made the literary headlines, he was not by nature a novelist, since he had little creative gift. But in his early *Crome Yellow* he left a recognizable, if caricatured, portrait of the literary circle round Lady Ottoline Morrell, at Garsington out on another hill beyond Oxford. The Morrells were a well-known brewing family, dispensing hospitality from seventeenth-century Blackhall in St Giles's and up at Headington Park (the mansion now Robert Maxwell's, the park a city pleasure-ground). Lady Ottoline made a bird of exotic plumage against the grey academic background, but, a marvellous talent-spotter, with a passion for the arts and a kind heart, she drew together a salon at Garsington which now has its place in the history of literature. Cambridge was much to the fore with Russell and Strachey; Oxford was represented by the Sitwells, Leonard Woolf, Huxley, Middleton Murry, Lord David Cecil, and Maurice Bowra. Her difficult *protégé*, D. H. Lawrence, was helped by the university press commissioning his book, *Movements in Modern European History*.

T. S. Eliot was an outlier of this group. He had come to Merton during the war, hoping to study philosophy under Bradley. It is doubtful if he saw much, or indeed anything, of that curmudgeonly old recluse who relished nobody's company and had expressly stated that he wanted no disciples. However, the young Harvard man persevered with his thesis on Bradley – and somewhat absurdly published what was left of it years afterward, when he had ceased to be able to understand it. Not but what Oxford stood for something in Eliot's make-up. He ultimately won through to something of Matthew Arnold's position as a pundit in criticism and letters; he knew Arnold's prose so well that he could recite whole passages from it, and the influence is discernible in his own chaste prose. Eliot had difficulty in making his way in England at first; but Geoffrey Faber of All Souls 'saved him for literature', when he founded his firm and gave Eliot 'a kind of fellowship' within it. Faber failed to make Eliot a Fellow of All Souls – a failure on the part of the college – but was a good writer himself, who wrote the best recent books on the Oxford Movement, *Oxford Apostles*, and on Jowett.

A name to become very well known during the Second War was another survivor from the First: C. S. Lewis. Indeed his *réclame* had something adventitious about it, for his works of popular theology, *The Problem of Pain* and *The Screwtape Letters* on the Problem of Evil, appealed very strongly when there were so much suffering and evident evil about. Lewis was a convert to religion, and was as dogmatic after as he had been before; these facts of human experience – due more to man's stupidity and folly than any 'original sin' – were intellectual problems only to those who held his views about omnipotent deity that yet inflicted so much evil upon his creation. Nevertheless Lewis had original talent as a writer, best seen in his children's stories. His scholarly work suffered from the perversity of the Ulsterman (a more agreeable specimen was Louis MacNeice, a poet of genius). Lewis disliked humanism, so he preferred sterile medieval logic-chopping, while his *Allegory of Love* was out of touch with the facts of medieval life. He despised the historical approach, having no historical sense. However, he was by far the most distinguished member of the English school here; they never offered him a chair, so he went to Cambridge. Though not happy in the proximity of a Leavis, he was able to put him in his place, with his *Experiment in Criticism*.

In these humane studies two men of genius stand out: Collingwood and Beazley. R. G. Collingwood (1889–1943) was more generally known, for he was equally distinguished as philosopher and as historian of Roman Britain. Indeed, he exemplified the Renaissance ideal of *l'uomo universale*, for he was also a talented musician, could compose and paint, was very deft with his hands and a good sailing man. His parents were poor, and a friend helped the boy to Rugby. He had originality, exceptional imagination, which put him right out of the range of the ordinary academic – and this he knew quite well. He added to it breadth of

Lady Ottoline Morrell – 'a bird of exotic plumage against the grey academic background'.

T. S. Eliot, who first came to Oxford to study Bradley's philosophy during the First World War.

learning in his two chosen fields. Philosophy came first and was the more important to him. He was the most original thinker of his time in Oxford; but Ryle says, 'I think he was as unhappy in the company of his philosophical colleagues as he was, I gather, happy in that of archaeologists and musicians. I surmise that he had been quite early lacerated by the Joseph-Pritchard treatment, but lacked the resilience to retaliate.' On the contrary: Collingwood simply did not think it worth while. Ryle did not know Collingwood; he continues with the opinion that Collingwood 'then, very unwisely, deemed all philosophical colleagues to be unworthy'. This does not get the situation quite right. Collingwood had, rightly, a fine conceit of himself; but, like Bradley, he considered most philosophical argument a waste of time. He preferred to think things out for himself and – a more subtle consideration psychologically – he instinctively realized that endless discussion with ordinary pedestrian minds merely wears away the energies, and the edge, of a more sensitive intelligence.

His own was precariously balanced, for he imposed a heavy strain upon it by his dual interests and distinction. He was the foremost historian of Roman Britain. His concern with history deeply influenced his philosophical outlook, though he was just that much less good as an historian for being a philosopher: too ready to put forward theses. We cannot estimate him as a philosopher. Like the unstable Russell, he completely reversed his philosophical position at the end from what it had been at the beginning, and virtually reduced philosophy to history. To what point these intellectual syntheses? Collingwood had enormous intellectual ambition; at the end he wanted to subordinate politics and even natural science to his scheme, which, from being religious at the beginning, with *Speculum Mentis*, became one of historical scepticism with *The Idea of History*. A broken mind, with the burdens he placed upon it, he was only fifty-four when he died.

J. D. Beazley (1885–1970) was marvellously fortunate in his life's work, recognized as the world's greatest scholar in his chosen field, and likely always to remain so; for in the course of a long life, he was in at that subject's beginnings, set out all its main lines of development by his own work, so that after him there remained only to fill in details or gaps, or occasionally to refine upon it. As an undergraduate the poet Flecker had been in love with him (he was beautiful), and they wrote verse to each other – the secret reason why Beazley destroyed all his and 'in later life he would never speak of his poetry'. Flecker died abroad, and after the war Beazley married his exotic wife, who helped him immensely in the subject to which he dedicated his passion.

This was the study of Greek vases and vase painting, to which he brought a combination of rarely paralleled scholarship with extreme aesthetic sensibility. Like Housman, he was a perfectionist. Thus 'Beazley revolutionized the whole study of Greek painting, and helped other scholars to an incalculable degree by his published writings.' (Housman frightened them off, so that Oxford had to recruit a German-Jewish refugee, Fraenkel, to its chair of Latin.) Beazley was able to identify and reconstruct the *oeuvre* of many hundreds of vase painters in the ancient world – a fabulous achievement. 'In the course of his work he built up a body of photographs, drawings, and notes on vases surpassing that of any institution in the world; and these passed at his death to the university. His complete library, with an unrivalled collection of offprints, he bequeathed.' Besides this, he gave his collection of more than eight hundred objects, 'ranging from vases and small bronzes of the first rank to sherds and smaller antiquities'. For thirty years his presence made Oxford 'the focus of the world for the study of Greek art'. His own writings and books, some of them in German – he was a master of many languages – are classics in their subject; in English his prose, concise, witty, naturally distinguished, was that of one who had been a poet in his youth. 'He was without doubt a genius, but a genius whose dominant motive was a sense of duty; he seemed always to be conscious of the need to make the fullest use of time, and of his talents, in the pursuit of truth.'

Of such are the elect who have raised man from the mud.

With the democratization of society after the war there was an opening of the ranks: not only increased numbers but an increase in the proportion of grammar-school boys to some forty per cent, compared with sixty per cent from public schools. After the Second German War the proportion was reversed, until with the general levelling up (and down) the vast majority of students everywhere are state-aided or -maintained. (Today some of them behave as if society owes them a debt for their existence.)

Expansion was the order of the day, and that of the motor industry transformed the city and its environs and greatly affected the university. '*Oxford – The Place Where Morris Cars Are Made*' announced the placard at the railway station; to which the university replied by describing itself as 'the Latin Quarter of Morris-Cowley'. Morris, later Lord Nuffield, came of Oxford stock on both sides, with the family farm at Headington. The boy's ambition had been medicine, his hobby bicycles. From this he began to build motor cycles, and with the development of motor cars found himself upon a moving escalator. From 1913 dates the original Morris Garages in Longwall – now an adjunct of the hardly less famous Blackwell's, the best bookshop, taken all round, in Britain.

By the 1930s Morris had achieved the leadership of the car industry. The millions he made could have been absorbed in the television sets, the shopping-bags and on 'the dogs', of his employees – and sunk without trace. Morris had better ideas and had at heart, not the waste consumption of the masses on trivial objects, but medicine and the healing of disease. He began with the extension of the Radcliffe Infirmary, he bought the Observatory and its grounds to add a lung to it; he rebuilt the Wingfield Orthopaedic Hospital at Headington. He founded new professorships, and after six years of planning endowed a school of medical research, with Hugh Cairns to head it. This Rhodes scholar from Australia became the first of brain surgeons, and before war was renewed by the Germans in 1939 had established a neuro-surgical service for the army just in time. He was responsible for mobile surgical units, the compulsory wearing of helmets that saved so many lives, the organization of a special hospital for head injuries at St Hugh's. Cairns saved many lives; his own he could not save: he died at the height of his powers.

In 1936 Nuffield established his medical school trust with two million pounds; he proceeded to found dominion research studentships and, when penicillin came along, research Fellowships in that subject. Altogether his benefactions reached nearly £30 millions, nor had he been backward in helping out the poorer colleges with donations. He wished to found a college for the study of engineering, but was over-persuaded by the sanguine (and socialist) master of Balliol, A.D. Lindsay, who favoured philosophy, politics and economics – already well enough provided for. When the war came there was an acute shortage of engineers: the intuition of the man of genius had been right after all. Whether there is much value to be attached to the *academic* study of politics, or the *academic* study of economics, for these are practical activities to be learned in the field of action, is open to question. On retiring from Balliol, Lindsay went to found a new university in accordance with his ideas at Keele – whether it has much of a contribution to make to the country still remains to be seen.

The really significant development has been in science, where Oxford was backward, especially compared with the unparalleled record of Cambridge in mathematics and the physical sciences. Between the wars, from 1922, there came into being large government aid to science at both; and Oxford was beginning to catch up. In 1916 the Dyson Perrins laboratory for organic chemistry was founded; shortly Oxford established the lead in chemistry, and was able to recruit to it the first organic chemist in the country, in Sir Robert Robinson. In physical and inorganic chemistry there were Soddy and, later, Hinshelwood. Soddy was an Oxford man who worked with Rutherford in Canada on radio-activity, the research which initiated the scientific revolution of our age: the disintegration theory that led to splitting the atom and starting nuclear physics.

Before these developments the colleges had borne the brunt of the teaching of chemistry – for example, Sidgwick at Lincoln, a notable teacher (Tizard was only one of his distinguished pupils) and propagandist for his subject. Tutors had to pursue it, as if surreptitiously, in holes and corners and college-basements – like Sir Walter Ralegh in his chicken-shed at the Tower. Sidgwick helped to change all this, with his influential standard books too: by half-way through his life 'Oxford was recognized as a leading school of chemistry throughout the world.'

Soddy was succeeded by the fantastically gifted Hinshelwood, who was a classical scholar as well as a chemist: in 1958–9 he was uniquely president of both the Royal Society and the Classical Association, and to his many languages he added Chinese. 'With the wide sweep of his mind, his exquisite gift for languages and his aesthetic interests, he bridged the gap in the minds of others between science and the humanities. He maintained that natural science was today the foremost of human studies.' This is a very Oxonian inflexion – I suspect he was right, and have endeavoured to put forward that perspective in this book.

On becoming professor, and with the possibilities opening up with the new university laboratories, Hinshelwood gave himself to organizing his department and, for all his reserve, built up a team of workers. His own fundamental research lay in 'the mysteries of chemical change and its dependence upon the energy and environment of the molecules'. But in 1936 he characteristically entered a new field of work, 'the dynamics of living processes as exemplified by the growth and characteristics of bacteria'. He was criticized by the third-rate for invading another field – much as a historian might be for intruding into the realm of literature. He devoted himself to investigating the adaptability of bacteria to environment, and showed that they could be trained to alter their habits by successive changes in environment.

In physics the Clarendon had fallen far behind the Cavendish – and under

Townsend, who had been a promising pupil of J. J. Thomson at Cambridge. In 1919 Lindemann was brought in, to bring the Clarendon abreast and by 1940, when the new laboratory was completed, he had accomplished it – a life's work in itself. Trained in Berlin, Lindemann did his own best scientific work from 1910 to 1924; during the First War he had won renown in aeronautics, by deducing the fundamental mechanics of *spinning* aircraft and successfully putting them into practice experimentally. He had intuitions characteristic of genius, as a physicist the power of reducing problems to their simplest form, with a very wide knowledge of the subject. He also had a good eye for recruiting the best men, Franz Simon for instance, and building a team. So he was probably right to opt, instead of pursuing his own research, for reconstructing the Clarendon, and making it 'comparable in importance with any physics department in the country'.

Other departments were being revivified or created anew: two of them by Cambridge men. A. G. Tansley brought new life into the department of botany, with its interesting past: during nearly thirty years here he made himself the first authority in plant ecology, writing a couple of Oxford classics, *Practical Plant Ecology* and *The British Isles and their Vegetation*. C. S. Orwin created the Institute of Agricultural Economics, from which he sent out students to staff many universities and himself urged forward the campaign for larger farm-units. Besides this he wrote a number of fascinating historical books, on the open field system, the reclamation of Exmoor, etc.

Oxford was now on the verge of making the noblest contribution in all her history to human welfare: this was the chemical stabilization of penicillin, the foundation of the whole science of antibiotics, the greatest boon for man in his long struggle with disease and pain. Alexander Fleming had discovered the healing power of the mould elaborated by a living organism, far more effective in treating wound infections, syphilis etc, than chemical acids. Fleming had a wide experience from the 1914 war, but had not been able to stabilize the preparation. To him 'competition was the breath of life' – rightly.

Florey took up the challenge; he had been a pupil of Sherrington and, a Rhodes scholar, was much impressed at Oxford by 'the personal interest shown in young men and their work, and the trouble that was taken to foster their abilities'. We must register this Australian tribute to the unique feature of the tutorial system, which makes an Oxford education more efficient, if more expensive, and leaves more of a stamp upon the mind than elsewhere. It is, or was, true that the tutors were apt to be sacrificed for the benefit of the undergraduates – I have known tutors who have taught as much as forty-eight hours a week. No one would think of doing so today – the average is nearer twelve hours (at Cambridge less).

Florey was an experimenter of exceptional skill, working for nearly thirty years as professor at the new Sir William Dunn school of pathology, a gift from Canada, while the Rhodes trustees had established a chair. Florey brought over a refugee from Hitler's Germany, Chain, with his laboratory workers. In 1940 the penicillin was produced and immediately wrought wonders; but the problem was to obtain enough for use. Here, with the war raging, the immense facilities of the American chemical industry were mobilized, and by 1944 every wounded man on the various fronts was being treated. During the last years of the war, 1943–5, the Nuffield Trust supported the good work. The research was opening up a new world in bacteriology; a team of seven authors from the school of pathology contributed to the standard work on *Antibiotics*, published by the university press in two volumes. What a breath-taking achievement it all was – reaching back to those seventeenth-century experiments of Mayow and Lower, and forward to what a future!

It is sad to have to record, as a matter of history, though we will go into no detail here, that a number of eminent Oxford men were high in the support of Chamberlain in the fatal policy of appeasement of Germany: Halifax, Hoare, Simon. To these we must add the deplorable support it consistently received from *The Times* – an appalling record – under Geoffrey Dawson and Barrington-Ward, muddled heads who did not know whom they were dealing with or what they were doing. It is only fair to record that there were as many Oxford men who were opposed to it: Amery, whose admirably consistent record was better than any; Brand, the banker and economist, never agreed with his Cliveden friends on this; Eden and Cranborne (later, Lord Salisbury), who knew Europe and Germany far better than Chamberlain or Halifax, Simon or Hoare – all ignorant of Europe – were consistently opposed; so were Macmillan and Duff Cooper. But these people, who were right, were kept out by the old men, left-overs from before the previous war. Attlee, who had fought in Gallipoli, was hamstrung by the pacifist delusions of the left; nor was he wholly right, as Hugh Dalton was, a Cambridge survivor of Rupert Brooke's circle.

It is an interesting fact that, though Cambridge retained its primacy in most physical sciences, and turned out a much larger quotient of scientists, the two who had a dominating part in the war effort were Tizard and Lindemann. We may regard them as statesmen of science; it is hardly too much to say that without the work of these two men Britain might not have survived the second onslaught. Certainly, without Tizard's work on radar, the Battle of Britain in the air would not have been won – and then what? Various people had got on to radar before the war, and in fact the Germans had radar which was, in some respects, technically superior. But, strangely, and providentially, there was little interplay between the scientists and the Luftwaffe. This was precisely what Tizard provided here: 'Air defence thinking was much more fundamental in Britain.'

The paralytic government of the 1930s, advised by the air ministry, held the defeatist view expressed by Baldwin, 'The bomber will always get through', an announcement in itself enough to encourage the aggressor. Tizard would never stand for this. A Magdalen man, trained under Sidgwick, he had had first-class practical experience in aeronautics in the First War, testing aircraft performance and doing basic research on fuels. It was said at the time that 'his natural place in the world was – Headquarters'. The essence of Tizard's campaign was that at all costs the scientists must work hand in hand with the air pilots. By 1936 we were 'trying desperately to make up for lost time, to improvise means of doing what we ought to have done five or ten years earlier'. The ineffable government of the 1930s excluded armament and bombing from the directors of scientific research, with the result that British bombs were inadequate in 1939. But Tizard, who was full of original ideas, with a practical knowledge of aeronautics, and was a good team-worker, succeeded in bringing his *operational* defence system of radar, a network all round the country, into being, just in time. The bombers did *not* get through without warning.

After this signal service Tizard came back to Magdalen as president; after a brief tenure of some three years an historian friend of mine managed to get him out.

Lindemann's services to the country were hardly less valuable, and better rewarded. In 1932 he hitched himself to the star of Churchill, then under eclipse, heeded by no one. Churchill had no confidence in the air ministry, which had given such defeatist advice to Baldwin, and turned to Lindemann to supply him with better facts and figures. He found out that the air ministry had greatly over-estimated German air strength and its reserves, and thus there was no reason for counsels of despair and consequent defeatism. Moreover, he found that departments were exaggerating the demands likely to be made on them, with waste and inefficiency as a result. Lindemann had marked gifts of intuition: he was certain that British bombing was inaccurate, found it was so by a series of tests, insisted on more effective bombs and more precise navigational aids. Later he was pressing for better instruments for sighting submarines as previously they had been wholly inadequate. He was having new ideas all the time – naturally, not all equally viable; but his mind was a wonderful instrument for summarizing facts and figures, statistically – and for Churchill, graphically – over the whole range of the war effort.

What the country owes to him is immeasurable; without either Tizard or Lindemann it might have gone down. Nor was Lindemann wrong in his prognostications as to our economic prospects and what our policy should be after the war. He was a great deal more right than the optimistic illusions of the professional economists – people like Keynes and Beveridge – with their encourage-

Above left: Lord Nuffield, earlier William Morris, founder of the motor car industry at Oxford. Born there, he became the greatest benefactor to the university in this century.

During the last war Oxford contributed two outstanding scientists 'without whom the nation might not have survived'. *Above right:* Sir Henry Tizard, creator of an *'operational* defence system of radar'. *Opposite:* Professor Lindemann, Churchill's scientific adviser.

ment of illimitable consumption instead of placing the emphasis on production and the building up of capital resources. If Lindemann's warnings had been heeded, the country would not be enduring the perpetual economic crisis that emphasizes its decline in the world.

We should put a third man beside these two in winning the war, the finest civil servant of our time: Edward Bridges. The son of Robert and his mother, a Waterhouse, Edward was brought up in the atmosphere of the arts themselves, not of 'art appreciation'; as the old poet wrote before one of his books, 'The reader is invited to bathe rather than to fish in these waters.' Wounded in the First War – like his 'mate' at All Souls, E. F. Jacob – Bridges was brought back to the treasury, where he served much of his life. For seven historic years, 1938–45, he was secretary to the cabinet; while Ismay ran the military side, Bridges saw to the working of the general office machine. This was the nerve centre of the war effort, manned day and night, preparing the deliberations of the war cabinet, recording its decisions, responsible for their execution through the departments. Bridges and Ismay were fixed points in the machine, seeing to it that the decisions were taken, and oiling the wheels. In 1943 Bridges virtually created a separate

cabinet for home and civilian affairs, freeing the prime minister and the war cabinet for the war. The strain was terrific but, paradoxically – and contrary to what some suppose – the British government machine worked far more smoothly and efficiently than the German.

Some very successful recruits were made to it from academic life: we can only give one, the most outstanding example, Oliver Franks. When the war and a further period of service as ambassador to the United States were over, he presided over an internal commission to survey the university's new needs and requirements. The immense expansion of the Bodleian had led to a big new building on the old site by 1939; now the devolution into faculty libraries was heralded by a large law library in 1964, while others were expanded. Everything has been expanding in a too expansive, and expensive, society. A French magnate, Antonin Besse, to express his admiration for the Oxford graduates he had encountered in a commercial lifetime in the Near East, founded a new college, St Antony's, with a useful bias towards foreign affairs. New graduate colleges have been set up, notably Wolfson, the utility of which can hardly be questioned since it is for scientists, and the buildings, since they are by Powell and Moya, distinguished, on a fine site on the upper Cherwell, and out of the way.

The 'infilling' of the ancient city within its walls can only be deplored: it is bound to be a detraction since it disturbs the balance between grey walls and green spaces, the charm of the place, and brings more traffic and people into streets bursting at the seams, to ruin its peace. The tasteless Worthington did a lot to deface Oxford in the ruinous thirties – one can recognize his handiwork anywhere; Giles Scott and Herbert Baker did no better. Since the war there have been some good buildings to offset the bad: the Blue Boar quadrangle at Christ Church, a distinguished little building in the interior of Brasenose – both again Powell and Moya; a gay new building by a good academic architect at University; some fair work at the women's colleges, a distinguished modern building at Keble. But Magdalen put up a building which would do not much credit to a warehouse on one of the finest sites in the world, across the river from Magdalen Tower. While St Edmund Hall proceeded to disgrace the roofscape of the High, and itself, with a monstrous building looming disproportionately down upon the old quadrangle, whose diminutive scale was part of its charm.

But the age has lost all sense of proportion, since it has itself lost the human scale.

In a period of decline a certain scholasticism overtakes subjects, as at the end of the Middle Ages. One may take, for example, the so-much-advertised Oxford school of philosophy. J. L. Austin was a remarkable man – I knew him – and his analysis of linguistic usage, especially speech habits, of use. But what are we to think of the absurdly exaggerated cult of Wittgenstein, when the prophet himself had doubts of the possibility or value of the subject? In so far as this school has reduced the over-riding claims of philosophy to lay down the law for other disciplines – so intolerable in one's youth – it is welcome; and that much may be said for it.

The struggle of 1939–45 formed in one sense an apogee of Britain's history, and put a period to her secular role. A mere expansion of numbers is nothing to be proud of; history judges peoples by their achievements, and exceptional achievements are always the work of exceptional men, men of genius or talent, the elect. Quality is what ultimately counts; this is what Oxford always stood for, and will either stand by – or fall – in what future there may be for us.

Index

Index

OXONIVM *nobile Angliæ oppidum, Septentrionalem* I *ripam elegantißimo atque salubri situ illus̄ trat.*

Depingeb. Georg. Hoef: nagle.